The Art of Cyber Warfare

Peter Kestner

The Art of Cyber Warfare

Strategic and Tactical Approaches for Attack and Defense in the Digital Age

Springer

Peter Kestner
Hohenzell, Germany

ISBN 978-3-658-43878-4   ISBN 978-3-658-43879-1   (eBook)
https://doi.org/10.1007/978-3-658-43879-1

Translation from the German language edition: "Die Kunst des Cyberkrieges" by
Peter Kestner, © Der/die Herausgeber bzw. der/die Autor(en), exklusiv lizenziert
an Springer Fachmedien Wiesbaden GmbH, ein Teil von Springer Nature 2023.
Published by Springer Fachmedien Wiesbaden. All Rights Reserved.

This book is a translation of the original German edition "Die Kunst des
Cyberkrieges" by Peter Kestner, published by Springer Fachmedien Wiesbaden
GmbH in 2023. The translation was done with the help of an artificial intelligence
machine translation tool. A subsequent human revision was done primarily in terms
of content, so that the book will read stylistically differently from a conventional
translation. Springer Nature works continuously to further the development of tools
for the production of books and on the related technologies to support the authors.

This Springer imprint is published by the registered company Springer Fachmedien
Wiesbaden GmbH, part of Springer Nature.
The registered company address is: Abraham-Lincoln-Str. 46, 65189 Wiesbaden,
Germany

Paper in this product is recyclable.

For my parents, my wife, and our children.

May they never like this book
must consult.

Introduction: *1984* and the Lessons of the Past

"History does not repeat itself, but it rhymes."
Aphorism of unknown origin

Especially in today's "digital" age, quotes like that of the philosopher George Santayana seem dusty. He said: "Those who cannot remember the past are condemned to repeat it." We presume—like every generation before us—to possess more knowledge. At the latest since the breakthrough of new technological revolutions such as the Internet or the smartphone, many are certain: The events of today's time have never been like this before and cannot be compared with the past. Our understanding of history is closely linked to a progressive thinking that only knows one direction: forward. Technical devices like the first iPhone, which are barely more than 15 years old, already seem to us today like relics from a distant past, which it hardly seems worth remembering.

Yet when we look at our methods and tactics that shape our daily behavior, one could quickly start to ponder.

A closer look shows that we do not act so differently from our ancestors. Just as thousands of years ago, the reasons are still the same that lead us on a psychological level to initiate or fend off conflicts. And the development and mastery of technology has been one of the central motives for gaining and exercising power from the very beginning. But this also means that, regardless of the changed conditions of time, place, means and resources, but not of the physical laws, we can learn from earlier actions and their reactions.

From this perspective, we must question certain beliefs and convictions today. Are we really entering uncharted territory with the internet and new technologies, for which we have neither maps nor compass? With this book, I want to show that we have actually only transferred old methods into our era, but have forgotten to translate their reasons and effects and the lessons resulting from them. Engaging with history and human nature would help us understand certain drivers as well as triggers and outcomes of actions, and perhaps even predict them. Because, as thousands of years ago, the reasons for human negative actions remain the same: wealth, fame, power, and honor or pleasure. Whether we call it money, political influence, patriotism, or whatever today—the fact is that these drivers have always psychologically tempted us and our ancestors to start conflicts. However, by understanding and analyzing them precisely, we could learn to intelligently control the current and future outcomes of conflicts, such as the cyber war of the future. Accordingly prepared, we should already today encounter cryptography, steganography, unique identification, Trojans, malicious code, or fake news. Knowing their origins and effects helps us not only understand the underlying drivers and outcomes of actions, but even predict and, in the best case, ward them off. If we do not do this, even the darkest visions of the future could become reality, such as the one George Orwell describes in *1984*.

1984—Between Past, Present, and Future

The significance that the past can have for the present and the future can be illustrated by one of the most famous novels of the last century: George Orwell's *1984*. What led George Orwell to write this book in 1948 was the desire to understand what was happening around him. On one hand, there was the recent totalitarian rule in Nazi Germany, and on the other hand, there was the beginning of the Cold War between the West on one side and the USSR on the other. And even though Orwell himself was much concerned with the surveillance state as it had emerged in the Soviet Union at the time, his work goes far beyond that. The story about the novel's hero, Winston Smith, tells of the domination of man by technology and language. An element that must have seemed new and unimaginable to contemporaries at the time is that of permanent and total technological surveillance. The "big brother" observes and controls the population at all times.

But how should one imagine the life of a person in the novel world of *1984*? Everywhere in public and private spaces, the so-called "telescreens" and microphones are installed, through which Big Brother can keep an eye on everything at all times. Areas of life that cannot be seen with technical means are monitored by spies. The state has introduced a new language concept called "Newspeak", with which thinking itself is to be revolutionized. With "doublethink", even logic is suspended—What could possibly go wrong!?—The word freedom has been banned and the language has been reduced to such an extent that certain thoughts are no longer conceivable. It is mandatory to keep the television on around the clock. Thinking for one-self is not desired. Moreover, the person from *1984* hardly has time for this, as they are constantly involved in rou-tines and rituals such as the communal hate ritual, where everyone swears against a common enemy. Most people do not know what a different life could look like, because the government has rewritten history and destroyed books. Because whoever erases the memory of what once was, takes away people's ability to compare the past with how it is today. And thus, they also take away the possibility of thinking about what one can learn from history, how to behave better, or how to change the present. Forgetting or in this case rather: suppressing the past is a tool for con-trolling the population in the world of *1984*. This also means that dealing with history represents something powerful. Because the lessons from history enable people to distance themselves, to think about themselves and life, to make reflected decisions, and to determine how the future should be shaped. Or, as it is said in *1984*:

> "Who controls the past controls the future: who controls the present controls the past."

In addition to this central insight about the value of the past and history, *1984* offers many more visionary insights that are interesting for the context of this book. Of course, George Orwell did not have a crystal ball with which he could look into the future. Nevertheless, much can be learned from his book about future developments and some frightening parallels to our present world can be rec-ognized. Because anyone who reads 1984 today, possibly does so at a moment when several cameras are pointed at them. One from the tablet on which they are reading the book, one from the phone lying next to them on the table, and one from the television hanging on the wall.

And while in *1984* spies listened in on all conversations that were held in private through microphones, today voice assistants like Alexa or Siri listen attentively. The regulation of language also confronts us, for example, in the field of economics, where there are no problems, only challenges, or on Twitter, where every complex event must be condensed into a 280-character message. And the debate about so-called "Cancel Culture", "Social Justice Warriors" and fake news once again show that language can become a battlefield today. Political parties or leaders who convince their followers of an "alternative" truth that does not correspond to reality, are becoming more and more common in our country, but can be observed daily in other parts of the world such as China, Russia or the USA. The talk of the post-factual age and alternative facts should also give us pause.

Even though the world depicted in Orwell's *1984* could hardly be more bleak, the book also provides a reason for hope. Or at least there are a few breadcrumbs scattered throughout the book that one can follow. Because one must indeed ask, what is the greatest enemy that Big Brother wants to fight: It is the free, independent thinking of each individual. We should never give up this valuable asset lightly, and if the bleak end of the novel shows one thing, then it is this: A great deal of energy and effort must be expended to break the free will and independent thinking.

However, before I write more about the ideas of this book, its intentions and objectives, I would like to write a few lines about myself.

About the Author of this Book or: "Who Cares Who's Speaking?"

First of all, I am not an author. I am a computer scientist. Therefore, writing is not really one of my specialties. In my studies, I only learned to think and express myself in code. The intention to write a book, however, has grown over many years. Slowly, but steadily. I am someone who has been dealing with the topic of cybersecurity for over 25 years, and I still do—although it was not always called that. In the past, what I do was simply called computer security. But no matter what it was or is called, there was one experience that kept repeating itself over the years. During this time, I kept encountering people, stories, and situations that triggered the same reaction in me: We've seen all this before, exactly like this or at least very similar! But by that I don't mean so much that I kept encountering certain technical errors. It had more to do with my other passion, which kept pushing itself into my consciousness in my professional activity. Even though my professional background is in computer science, so I know a thing or two about computers, security, and our networked world, I have always maintained a great fascination for history and exciting historical events alongside it. Both have much more to do with each other than most people might realize, and that's exactly why I want to connect both areas in this book.

This book is essentially based on a simple question: "What can we learn from the past for our present and our future?" And while this section carries the heading "About the author of this book", it doesn't really matter who I am and what I have done so far in my life for this book as a whole. With the author Samuel Beckett, one could almost say: "Who cares who is speaking?" I don't want to convince anyone of anything, I don't want to sell a cyber security course, and I don't want to present a 12-point plan that promises absolute security if you simply follow all the points. For one thing, I don't want to do that because I know that there has never been and will never be absolute security. Mistakes often happen precisely when one feels too secure. On the other hand, I don't want to present a recipe because that would be the exact opposite of what I want to achieve with this book. Because such plans or advice have only a short half-life in the IT world and would relieve each individual of their own thinking. Therefore, no one should simply trust what I say or write here. One of my most important concerns that I pursue with this book is to get people to think and to think independently. If I succeed in this even a little, then more is gained than with any guidebook on cybersecurity.

Since my own passion for our past and exciting stories has helped me, I want to do exactly that: discuss exciting historical events. After all, history is full of experiences, successes, missteps, and instructive examples of cunning, deception, and manipulation—in other words: it is an ideal material to learn from, to avoid repeating the same mistakes over and over again.

About this Book

At first glance, it seems to make little sense to ask: What can we learn from history about future warfare in cyberspace? After all, there has never been anything like "cyber warfare"—so why should we be able to learn something about the war of the future by looking back into the past? Although I personally believe that we can learn a great deal from history, I am also convinced that it does not simply repeat itself. Rather, it is like the saying: "History does not repeat itself. But it rhymes." Therefore, we should try to understand our prehistory, learn from where we come from, and incorporate what we have learned into our considerations to understand why we behave the way we do. Because even though the weapons and techniques have changed over the centuries, the tactics and strategies often remained the same. And the results were frighteningly often the same. Hardly any other work from contemporary history demonstrates this constancy more clearly than *The Art of War* by Sun Tzu. Only Carl von Clausewitz's treatise *On War* holds a similar rank to Sun Tzu's work. Together, these two works make up the most important treatises ever written on military strategies and tactics. These two texts have greatly influenced great characters and rulers throughout history and were often prescribed as mandatory reading for their subordinate commanders and sometimes even for every single soldier. At most military schools, these two books are still studied in depth today, and the lessons drawn from them are incorporated into today's attack and defense strategies. The analysis of these works and the transfer of their contents into today's age is therefore at the beginning of the book. In doing so, I am not the first to have noticed that the procedures described in these works can be applied successfully not only militarily, but also politically and economically. Despite their age, both works have repeatedly proven on all three of these levels that their practicability, if intelligently transferred, is not outdated. Historically, this can be explained by the fact that there were times when commanders and soldiers switched to politics or business after wars and entered into the operational leadership of a country or founded companies. Since most of them, if any, had only a military education and no experience in the business or commercial world, they brought their patterns of behavior into this new world. They started ventures like attacks, led them like a military unit, or positioned themselves politically with tactical preparations for a higher goal. *The Art of War* thus also became a guide for success outside the battlefield. Many respected economists see Sun Tzu as a kind of business guru, as the military tactics described in his work are still valid on today's economic and trading floor, coupled with the old life philosophy and spiritual orientation of the authors. For this reason, many of Sun Tzu's procedures and key terms can be found in today's business management manuals as exact copies.

If we now take a step further into the networked world of the Internet and cyberspace, one will quickly find historical artifacts there as well. The "Trojan Horse" is probably known to fewer people today from history lessons than from reports on hacker attacks or—in the worst case—from personal experience. But this example in particular makes it clear how instructive dealing with history can be for everyday life in the digital age. Anyone who remembers the episode from Greek mythology knows that it was a seemingly harmless gift, but it was actually a disguise. For inside the hollow belly of the wooden horse was a handful of soldiers who thus gained access to the interior of the city of Troy. At night, they left their hiding place unnoticed and opened the city gates to allow the waiting army to enter. The hacker tactic named after the Trojan Horse works on a similar principle. The malware also usually enters the system disguised as a harmless email attachment, where it can then open access to it unnoticed. The language itself still vaguely reminds us that gifts can be poisoned. Because in English, gift actually still means "gift". The origin of both the German word "Gift" and the English "gifts" is Old High German, in which the gift or the gift was ambiguous for a long time and could also mean "harmful substance" or "deadly gift". In German today, only the word "Mitgift" still has the original meaning as a gift. So, in the future, anyone who receives a gift should perhaps also view it with some suspicion.

In addition to classics like the Trojan Horse, there are numerous other historical events that hold many helpful lessons. There are even so many that one could probably fill entire book series with them. Naturally, I therefore had to make a small selection for this book, but I am sure that the chosen examples and the analysis of historical procedures are instructive. Because that's what it's all about at its core: learning and independent thinking.

The only solution is: Learning

After the many years that I have now been working in the field of cybersecurity, and the thousands of pages that I have read about the past, as well as reading the books of the best strategists in history, I know one thing above all: There is no comprehensive solution that addresses all problems. The world will continue to evolve. And therefore, the threats and dangers will always present themselves somewhat differently. For this reason, the ability to learn from the lessons of the past for the future is the best defense strategy in the cyber age. Because even the most expensive hardware is useless if someone does not use their brain. The strategy must therefore be to constantly expand one's own knowledge, to acquire basic knowledge, to learn from history, and to understand tactics such as "camouflage and deception". Those who do this can gradually look beyond their own horizons, make better decisions, and develop a sensitivity for situations and potential dangers.

This means: It won't work without thinking for oneself. Therefore, I hope that I have succeeded in selecting from the vast treasure of history exactly those examples that stimulate my readers to think and learn. Because the greatest security there is in the cyber age is a treasure trove of stories, know-how, and knowledge that one always carries with oneself and constantly expands. Such a foundation of knowledge can help to go through the world with open eyes, if one constantly remembers what has been heard and read and lets the learned flow into new situations. In this sense, I now wish my readers an inspiring read, much joy in reading, learning, and understanding the episodes from history presented here, and the courage to draw their own conclusions from them.

Contents

Part I

Lessons from the Past

In the first part of the book, I want to look back into the past and work out the lessons that are useful for cyber warfare and a better understanding of our modern world. At the beginning, I deal with one of the oldest recorded strategy texts ever: *The Art of War* by Sun Tzu. From early Chinese history, we move on to Greek and Roman antiquity. There we find the beginnings of cryptography and steganography—both methods and the competition between encryption and decryption continue to this day and hold a story that is more exciting than many a crime thriller. Finally, in this section, I want to deal with the Middle Ages and trace the lines of connection between that time and ours.

1

The Art of Cyber Warfare and the 13 Lessons of Sun Tzu

> *"In peace, prepare for war,*
> *in war, prepare for peace."*
> Sun Tzu, The Art of War

The title of this book—*The Art of Cyber War*—obviously refers to the title of another, very famous book that I already mentioned in the introduction: *The Art of War* by Sun Tzu, who is also called Sunzi, Sun Tse, or Sun Wu. However, Sun Tzu's work provided more than just the inspiration for the title. The engagement with this work was important for the creation of this book as a whole. Moreover, the general significance of *The Art of War* can hardly be overstated. First of all, it is considered the oldest and one of the most important works on military strategy. So it is one of the central sources for dealing with strategic thinking. History is rich in evidence of the role it played in wars and conflicts over the centuries. Even after the

© The Author(s), under exclusive license to Springer Fachmedien
Wiesbaden GmbH, part of Springer Nature 2024
P. Kestner, *The Art of Cyber Warfare*,
https://doi.org/10.1007/978-3-658-43879-1_1

death of Sun Tzu, the first myths about the book emerged: Those who had read it were considered unbeatable. In the field of martial arts, Sun Tzu's work is also considered an indispensable classic. Last but not least, *The Art of War* is a prime example of how relevant thinking from past times and the history of that time are for our present day. However, reading and transferring Sun Tzu's thoughts to the modern world is not entirely straightforward. Anyone who has taken the trouble to pick up Sun Tzu's work will quickly have noticed how cumbersome many statements sound. Why is that?

Sun Tzu's Writing Style and the Transfer of His Work to the Present Day

The first and most obvious reason for the difficulties in transferring is the sheer age of the treatise: *The Art of War*, consisting of nearly 6000 Chinese characters, was written about 2500 years ago. Even some works that are only 50 or 150 years old need to be interpreted to correctly grasp the meaning of their statements. The next reason why Sun Tzu's work needs explanation is his writing style. Sun Tzu generally avoids long chains of argument and justification. He presents his views more in the form of postulates, maxims, rule sentences, and aphorisms. This is not unusual in itself and quite corresponds to the typical Chinese style of the time—but it does require interpretation. Rhetorical devices such as juxtaposing thesis and antithesis also demand independent thinking from the reader. In addition, it is very likely that what we know today as "the book" *The Art of War* comes from two or even more different authors. Archaeological finds suggest this assumption and an analysis of the style supports this thesis. Especially the last chapters are characterized by much longer and more expansive text passages. Even the division of the text into chapters did not come from Sun Tzu or the other authors, but was only made retrospectively, long after the text was written. To understand what *The Art of War* is actually about, it is worth taking a step further and keeping the original in mind. 2500 years ago, book printing had not yet been invented. In China, bamboo sticks or tablets were used, which were written on and then tied together to record and pass on thoughts. The bamboo tablets on which writing was done were dried over fire and were about 2.5 centimeters wide and 30 centimeters long. They were tied together at the top and bottom with a string, creating a continuous band. Extensive works quickly became very heavy and carts were needed to transport them. The bamboo book as a medium is therefore an important reason why one had to be brief. In this context, it is also helpful to briefly recall the conditions of Chinese culture. Copying the thoughts of others was not considered plagiarism as it is today, but quite the opposite, a privilege. The fact that the text of Sun Tzu also contains the wisdom of others and that there was not one author as we might imagine today is therefore likely. In addition, there was no uniform writing system in China during the first 500 years of the text's transmission and tradition. This was only established in the time of the Qin and Han dynasties, about 2200 to 2000 years ago. Whether parts of the thoughts found in *The Art of War* are much older and part of an orally transmitted tradition can only be speculated.

And finally, there is another hurdle that the text had to overcome in order to exist in the form we know it today. *The Art of War* has a long history of translation. The first version that circulated in Europe was by a French missionary. Father Jean Joseph Marie Amiot translated the text into French in 1782. This is the version that Napoleon knew and to which he attributed many of his military successes. At that time, the work was not yet called "The Art of War," but "The Thirteen Articles." This translation is not a literal transfer from Chinese to French, but a meaningful interpretation, written with the aim of being easier to understand. That is, the first interpretation of the work took place already during the translation. The second version of the text known in Europe is the English translation. This was done by Captain Everard Ferguson Calthrop, a member of the military, not a translator. His 1905 translation was much closer to the original, but is considered mediocre, which is why other translators set to work just a few years later. In the USA, the Hollywood film *Wall Street* by Oliver Stone in 1987 sparked a wave of Sun Tzu literature and management courses based on it. In the film, the main character, successful stockbroker Gordon Gekko, referred to Sun Tzu's theses. But without going into further detail about the history of translation and impact, this brief overview is intended to show two things: The phase of reception of *The Art of War* in the Western world is relatively short and complicated. Or in other words: There is still much we can learn from Sun Tzu.

What is the Art of War?

Before I delve deeper into *The Art of War*, I would like to first ask, what is this: the art of war? What does war have to do with art? War and art are two terms that at first glance seem difficult to reconcile. Because while we associate war primarily with terror and the death of people, we associate art primarily with beauty and the sublime. By art here, I mean the skill with which the means and methods are applied. So it describes a craft, and a craft is something that can be learned. When it comes to classifying the work of Sun Tzu and its categorization, however, another term must be introduced: Because when we talk about "the art of war", we are in the field of science. *The Art of War* is therefore, in the broadest sense, a scientific treatise that deals with the methods and procedures, or strategies and tactics, of warfare. The deeper reason why the work of Sun Tzu is still relevant today is probably that conflicts between people have structurally similar patterns for many millennia and often have the same causes, both in the past and today. Greed, envy, jealousy, and the longing for power are simply timeless.

The scientific, or one could also say: the systematic study of the art of war also has historical reasons. Sun Tzu, a general by profession, probably lived between 544 and 496 BC, a phase in the history of China known as the "Warring States Period". It was a time of great economic, technological, political, and social changes. With the introduction of new tools in agriculture and crafts, a layer of wealthy farmers and merchants, a kind of first bourgeoisie, and a nobility emerged. This changed people's demands and a changed property law led to the redistribution of lands. As always, growing prosperity also came with power struggles and distribution battles. And so, seven kingdoms—smaller states that emerged from principalities—fought for supremacy: Zhao, Qi, Qin, Chu, Han, Wei, and Yan. According to legend, Sun Tzu was hired by the king of a smaller kingdom named Wu as the leader of his army during the battle between Wu and neighboring Chu. It was in this battle between the two states that Sun Tzu probably developed his theories on the art of warfare.

Whether Sun Tzu really existed is indeed often doubted. Although his life dates are included in the historical work

Shiji by Sima Qian, the first historian of China and at the same time the founder of Chinese historiography. However, there are hardly any other sources that prove his existence. Perhaps it's a bit like the case of the author of that book—because with the *Art of War*, neither the content of the work nor its impact matters much who Sun Tzu really was. What does exist, however, are numerous legends and reports about Sun Tzu and his deeds. One of the most famous and often quoted stories is about how he became a commander in the army of Wu. The King Held (514 to 496 BC) of Wu had heard of Sun Tzu's writings and wanted to test him. So he invited him to an audience and asked him to demonstrate the content of his treatise in practice. However, Sun Tzu was not to teach soldiers, but some of the court ladies in the art of war. Sun Tzu was not deterred by this and approached the task with full seriousness. He equipped the court ladies with armor and weapons, divided them into departments, and gave them the command to perform an exercise. For the court ladies, however, all this was just a big joke and they just giggled instead of carrying out the instructions. To make sure they understood him correctly, Sun Tzu repeated his commands once more. But again, the ladies just giggled. Then Sun Tzu had two of the court ladies step forward and gave the order to behead them. When the king heard this, he tried to prevent the beheading. However, Sun Tzu did not back down from his order and the two ladies were killed. From this moment on, all court ladies carried out Sun Tzu's commands with full seriousness and without further giggling.

What do we learn from this story? Well, above all one thing: Sun Tzu—if he existed—was not to be trifled with. At the same time, this episode from Sun Tzu's life also tells us a lot about him as a person, his thinking, and his work. Because it shows how serious he was about his cause.

When it comes to military success, executing orders, and carrying out actions, there is no room for jokes or silliness. Discipline was a key for Sun Tzu so that the army could fulfill the military tasks. Or in other words: to act tactically in order to achieve strategic goals—which brings us to two other key terms for understanding Sun Tzu.

Strategy and Tactics

Before we delve into strategies and tactics from the past and present, we should first understand these terms in detail. Contrary to the relevant literature, these terms are often misused (especially on the internet). Here you can find guides like "The 10 Strategies for Better Presentations" or "The Best Strategies to Gain More Followers". People also talk about "strategy changes" to achieve x, y, or z, but these statements purely refer to tactical behavior. This is often confusing. Although both terms intertwine, they can be sharply separated.

A strategy can be compared to the plan for building a house. A house has a clear architecture, based on floor plans, and a defined exterior and interior. The architect determines a style of construction and plans a certain time for completion. In this example, the tactic can be seen as the material (bricks, shingles, beams, etc.). These small components, the building material needed, are assembled according to a predefined plan, resulting in the finished house. In short, the strategy is the big picture, the goal to be achieved. Tactics, on the other hand, are the necessary individual steps that enable the strategic goal to be achieved. Carl von Clausewitz, who will be discussed in more detail later, summarized the difference between strategy and tactics as follows: "Tactics is the doctrine of the use of armed forces in combat. Strategy is the doctrine of the use of individual battles for the purpose of war". In short: Strategy is the *What* and tactics are the *How*. Sun Tzu defines both terms more simply by calling his strategy the victory and the methods used his tactics.

The *Art of War* by Sun Tzu

Now it is finally time to turn to the legendary work of Sun Tzu himself. Generally speaking, *The Art of War* addresses various aspects of war preparation and warfare, as well as their conditions. The contents of the currently known version are divided into 13 chapters, as already mentioned. Given the sometimes very different translations, it is not surprising that the headings vary depending on the translation, as the following overview clearly shows.

1. Planning and Preparation/Fundamental Assessments
2. On the Art of War/Going to War
3. Strategic Attack/Offensive Strategies
4. Disposition of Military Strength/Tactics/Treatise on Deployment/Formations
5. Energy/Force/On Strength/Influence and Authority
6. Weaknesses and Strengths/Truth and Untruth/ Maneuvering
7. Battle for the Initiative/The Battle
8. Nine Variations of Tactics/The Nine Adjustments/The Nine Variable Factors
9. The Army on the March/Taking Battle Position/ Marching
10. Terrain/Terrain Formations/Land
11. Nine Variations of Territories/Nine Terrain Formations/ The Nine Types of Terrain
12. Attack(s) by/with Fire/On the Art of Attack by Fire
13. The Use of Spies/Deployment of Secret Agents

Which formulation is the best, I do not want to decide and is ultimately hardly decisive for a deeper understanding. For me, when reading *The Art of War*, the current perspective was particularly important. For example, when Sun Tzu talks about the higher or lower position, or the terrain on which one positions oneself, I always asked myself: What is our terrain today? How can one gain a lofty or elevated position in it? These questions are being asked anew today. Because the virtual world is without borders and it is possible to launch attacks distributed across different time zones and all over the globe. That was the exciting thing for me when I read *The Art of War* for the first time. I had the feeling that within the complex text history there is another form of translation, by transferring Sun Tzu's thoughts into the world of the digital age. His thoughts on the weather play no role in the cyberspace in a too literal sense. After all, I can attack the Sahel zone from Finland, regardless of whether it is snowing here and the sun is shining there—although of course one can tactically use the weather on site, both in the past and today.

Even if some of his theses are adopted unfiltered and applied in military or economic areas, a look at one of the most famous sentences from *The Art of War* shows why the work is only understandable with commentary today. "The greatest achievement is to break the enemy's resistance without a fight." What exactly does this mean? To be productive in today's economy, this sentence could be translated as follows: If the characteristics of two products are comparable, there will be a price war between two competitors. This can either lead to falling margins or ultimately require a withdrawal. To avoid this fight, factors such as higher quality, faster delivery routes, or a good company image must be worked on. This would be much more advantageous than fighting each other in the low-price segment.

From a military perspective, the tactic of weakening the enemy before the actual battle—such as through misinformation, the old method of "camouflage and deception" or the demoralization of the opponent—is also much more advantageous than facing mass against mass with an uncertain outcome. The quote "If you know the enemy and yourself, you need not fear the outcome of a hundred battles. [...] If you know neither the enemy nor yourself, you will succumb in every battle" means nothing more than that a strengths-weaknesses analysis is needed to be successful in military, business, and hacking. Sun Tzu's tactical principle of being first teaches us that it is more advantageous to occupy a battlefield first and await the enemy with a well-thought-out action. Numerous start-ups try to take advantage of this competitive strategy by setting a technological standard and planning their market launch in such a way that they do not have to compete with any comparable product. This competitive advantage can achieve higher market shares and higher prices. Today, the faster often wins over the slower, not the bigger over the smaller as in the past.

In preparing this book, I also noticed that Sun Tzu is often used as a quote giver or referred to because his name and his work are meaningful. However, rarely is there an attempt to delve deeply into the text, to analyze what is there, and to understand what it means for our time today. That's why I want to find out exactly that in the following, and examine chapter by chapter what reading *The Art of War* can mean for us. Since learning is in the foreground, I would like to speak here of 13 lessons.

Lesson 1: Planning and Preparation

"Peace is only the pause between two wars."
Jaroslav Rudiš

This insight is known to every military and therefore it is essential to know and evaluate one's own current situation at all times. But this is also of high importance in the business world. There too, one must protect oneself from attacks by the competition. "The big ones eat the small ones and the fast ones the slow ones" is a standard statement that often applies if you have not analyzed the market, competitors, and attackers in time and evaluated your own position in it. The time before the actual conflict is crucial according to Sun Tzu: "A general who calculates everything down to the smallest detail before the battle will win, and he has a lot to consider. However, those who consider little before the battle will lose. Those who consider everything will win, those who consider little will be defeated, and woe to those who have considered nothing! Based on these preparations and views, I can already recognize the winner."

In addition, Sun Tzu mentions five essential factors that are crucial for evaluating and defeating the enemy or competitor:

- the morale or discipline,
- the weather,
- the terrain,
- the command,
- the doctrine.

Let's go through these points in order to understand what exactly is meant by them. Morale, or more modernly expressed discipline, is important when it comes to having a well-planned, graded organization. Anarchy in an army or a company turns it into pure chaos. But it's about more: Everyone must not only do their job, but they must also do it well. For this, it is important to have a scale of commands and it is forbidden to bypass or circumvent this scale. Only in this way can it be ensured that the daily execution of operations or the organization of logistics is carried out with consistency. If everyone were to make their decisions without being prepared, without having had training, without adhering to the established guidelines, this would lead to the destruction of the army or the bankruptcy of the company.

Next, we talk about the weather. When it comes to military conflicts, it is not the same whether it is winter or summer, day or night, rainy weather or sunshine. Attack and defense work very differently. Whoever knows the weather in advance will be able to make decisions that significantly influence the final result. For example, during the Second World War, British General Montgomery threw himself into the Battle of Alamein against Rommel's troops during a full moon in October 1942. He applied the strategy of night attack, but also used the natural light of the moon. Today, such circumstances can still be exploited in other areas. The different time and climate zones can play a role, for example, when planning and carrying out a cyber attack. If I know that an entire region is currently enduring a sandstorm, I choose the timing of my attack so that the defensive reaction is as minimal as possible. Specifically, in this situation, it was calculated that the sandstorm would keep the local people so busy that they would be less focused on defending against the attack. Differences in cultural conditions can also be used much better in this way in the age of the internet. An example of this is the attack on the Saudi oil company

Saudi Aramco in 2012, for which experts from all over the world were flown in late in the evening to defend against it. The reason for this was as simple as it was effective: The attack was perfectly timed and took place exactly on one of the most important holidays during the Ramadan festival, Lailat al-Qadr, specifically after work. Because on this day, the moment is remembered when, according to tradition, part of the Koran was revealed to the Prophet Mohamed. In the evening, people pray together, read the Koran, or visit the mosque. This circumstance led to the fact that most employees were already off work when the cyber attack started. While armies used to meet on the field and could use the local conditions to their advantage or disadvantage, the question today is more: What is the absolutely worst time for the opponent? If my target for attack were in Cologne, for example, one would probably attack during Carnival. The probability that the system admins are intoxicated and celebrating in the streets and would not be able to react as quickly in an emergency is very high. Considerations like these can and should definitely be taken into account in the area of crisis management. Sun Tzu advises: "Attack him (the enemy) when he is unprepared and does not expect you." Therefore, especially in this area: Keep your eyes open when choosing a profession. Forensic scientists, for example, often have to work on weekends or go out just when others are finishing work. This is no coincidence, but has to do with the tactics of the attackers. Because with a bit of luck, the phone is switched off at the weekend for those who could fend off the attack. In any case, a longer reaction time than usual can be expected.

The situation is very similar with the terrain. In the military field, it is essential to know the geography of the place that is to be attacked or defended. This means that it must be assessed whether it is mountainous or steep, whether the sea is nearby or not, whether it is protected or whether it is a flat plateau. All this information must be evaluated to know what significance they have for attack and defense. Anyone who knows nothing about the terrain to be attacked or where the defense is to be placed will hardly be able to win the battle. One of the most striking examples of the importance of terrain are undoubtedly medieval castles. If you look at these more closely, you will find that most castles were planned as defensive fortresses and were usually built on a mountain or hill. From above, you can see well from which direction enemies are attacking. In addition, the walls and other defensive installations naturally offered increased protection. Therefore, the most common form of attack at that time was the siege. A direct attack was often impossible. However, a besieged castle could not be easily left by anyone and often the inhabitants surrendered due to diseases or simply from hunger. The terrain also played a role in military conflicts in recent decades. During the Vietnam War, the Vietnamese army relied on jungle warfare, where the defensive terrain served as an additional attack weapon. This is evident from the fact that the Americans were virtually at war with the trees themselves. They dropped napalm—a fire weapon that contains a viscous mass of the main components of gasoline—on the Vietnamese rainforests, where the enemy was hiding, using large bombers. A fight with usual weapons or devices like tanks was almost useless in jungle warfare. During the Vietnam War, the US Army had to deal with the terrain until the end. The entire supply had to be regulated via the airspace. For this purpose, forest areas were cleared to create clearings where the helicopters could land. The North Vietnamese fighters, on the other hand, took advantage of the advantage that the jungle offered them. They hid in the thicket, so they were not visible. Later, the US Army therefore relied on patrols that roamed through the forest until they encountered enemy troops. After that, they informed the air force via radio and gave the coordinates. However, they then had to leave the place as quickly as possible in order not to become victims of the air attack themselves. This time also benefited their opponents, who could also withdraw. Just as the terrain in the Vietnam War became an actor, this can happen today in the cyber world. Although the geographical terrain does not necessarily play a role here, but rather the "technical" one. Is the target of an attack, for example, a data center that is monitored around the clock, or an unlocked server room in the basement that hangs on an overloaded line? Each computer network also has its own topology, which makes a significant difference for attack and defense. Is it a fully meshed, a ring-shaped or a star-shaped network or one that has a tree structure? The exact topology determines the fail-safety and its performance as well as the security in the event of cyber attacks.

The importance of command or order to Sun Tzu was made more than clear by the episode about the military education of the court ladies, which was already discussed above. Sun Tzu knew: The army or the staff that best follows instructions and regulations has the greatest chances of success. It is therefore important that those responsible are ready for action. This also means making and executing the right decisions. Of course, certain qualities are necessary for this, such as wisdom, sincerity, benevolence, courage, and discipline. Without these qualities, Steve Jobs would never have been able to make his company Apple one of the largest, most innovative, and important companies in the world. Finally, doctrine or "indoctrination" refers to the training of soldiers or employees. If you are able to convey your own ideas to them and convince them of these, they will follow you blindly wherever you want to take them. And this conviction of ideas will increase their performance, whether on the battlefield or at the workplace, even beyond the measure of their ability to act. Sun Tzu was sure: Whoever considers all these factors will certainly achieve victory.

But that's not all. What else do you need to prepare for battle optimally? Sun Tzu advises an astonishing but time-tested tactic: deception. "War is deception. Those who are capable show incapacity, those who are active show inactivity. Those who are near demonstrate to the enemy that they are still far away, and those who are far away show proximity. Lure the enemy by granting him an advantage, feign confusion and withdraw from him. When he feels safe, be prepared, when he is stronger, avoid him. If he has a hot temper, provoke him. Pretend to be weak so that he feels superior. If the enemy is inactive, give him no rest, scatter his army when it is united. Attack him when he is unprepared and does not expect you. The victory over such an opponent must not be announced in advance." The art of war is therefore based on deception. Strong attackers should appear weak to create trust in the enemy. Those who only have a weak defense should try to appear strong to instill fear in the enemy.

The Battle of Tannenberg during the First World War is an excellent example of this. It led to the almost complete annihilation of the second Russian army. This battle was characterized by the rapid mobilization of German troops on the railway, which enabled a single German army to form a front against two larger Russian armies. The Battle of Tannenberg shows that it is worthwhile to attack the enemy when he is out of operation and shows his weaknesses. If the enemy is not waiting for you, he will be weak, it is your chance to defeat him. If, on the other hand, you see that the opponent is strong and organized, try to maneuver to disorganize him. Destabilizing him will bring his misery to the surface.

When it comes to attacks in cyberspace, the weighing of chances of victory and defeat is even almost more important than in other areas. Because a targeted attack on critical infrastructures such as the power grid often requires many months and sometimes even years of preparation, as was clearly demonstrated by the cyber attacks on the German Bundestag in 2015 or the Foreign Office in 2018. The art is to penetrate and destroy or disrupt several levels/systems simultaneously with a targeted, meticulously planned and coordinated attack (English: APT = "Advanced Persistent Threat").

A realistic assessment is necessary on both sides—both on the attacker's and the attacked's. Especially in the past two decades, the dangers that can arise from cyber attacks and the consequences of a domino effect have been underestimated. It is therefore all the more important to recognize the importance of cyberspace and the tactical implications associated with it. Even if attacks cannot always be prevented or defended against, it is sometimes enough to become aware of them early on. This was recently demonstrated by the case in which a hacker attacked a waterworks in the USA: the waterworks in Oldsmar, Florida. The hacker gained access to the dosing system for treatment chemicals and increased the concentration of sodium hydroxide, also known as caustic soda, by a hundredfold. This solid substance reacts with water and other liquids (such as those of the mucous membranes), causes severe skin burns and can lead to blindness if it gets into the eye. By chance, an employee immediately noticed the increased values and was able to prevent worse.

Lesson 2: On the Art of War, or: When Initiating Actions

"The goal of war is victory, not prolonged duration."
Sun Tzu, *The Art of War*

Sun Tzu states: "When it becomes known that a war is being conducted hastily, it does not necessarily mean wisdom, but if the war lasts a long time, there is no advantage for the state. Whoever is not fully aware of the damage a war can cause is also not able to use the war to his advantage." This means that as soon as a competition or conflict has begun, the goal must be to achieve victory as quickly as possible. Essentially, the war in Ukraine would already be the best example of this. However, we will talk about this war later, as it is relevant to the context of this book in another respect. Just this much: The Russian war of aggression against Ukraine is a prime example of complete disregard for the teachings of Sun Tzu. For he teaches us: If a dispute, an attack, or a market competition is maintained for a long time, this only results in the continuous consumption of resources. Another striking example of this is provided by the Second World War. In 1942, Hitler sent his troops as an offensive to the Russian front to defeat Stalin's army. In the first attempt, he quickly and easily conquered the Donets Basin. Moscow was supposed to fall in the same year. However, his generals, who were more prepared and also more experienced in military strategy than he was, advised him otherwise: to regroup the troops, resupply them, rest, and wait another year. What the commanders recommended to their leader would have been the wisest decision. But Hitler, convinced of himself, ignored this advice and sent his troops back into battle, or rather, into a disaster. The Russian army did its job, but it had the best ally one could wish for in this situation: winter, which brings us back to the topic of "weather" from the previous chapter. The effects were, as mentioned, disastrous: Almost 2.5 million Germans died on the Eastern Front. Mostly from cold and hunger. No wise general has ever kept his troops at the front for a long time. The mental wear and tear, the wear and tear of weapons, and the consumption of resources, which is usually the most costly, as long-distance conflicts require very high transport costs, often lead to the failure of the operation.

Therefore, attacks should be as quick and effective as possible. In this way, the soldiers can rest and refuel soon. If you have achieved a quick victory, stockpile the resources that the enemy has lost, and you do not have to send and reduce your own. In addition, the removal of enemy resources serves as motivation for one's own soldiers—commonly known as looting.

Sun Tzu even goes further: "The soldiers are to be enraged so that they destroy the enemy. Whoever captures an enemy and takes his supplies should be rewarded. If ten or more wagons were captured in the wagon fight, the one who first laid hands on the wagons is to be rewarded." What he means by this is essentially internal competition as motivation! Indeed, motivation is crucial for the troops or also the employees of a company to stick together and stay strong. Rewards, for example, are suitable for this. Obviously, the size of an entire army being rewarded would also ruin the one who would try to reward all members of the army. So one must proceed intelligently. One possibility is to offer a reward to a certain number of outstanding soldiers after a victory. This also motivates the rest of the troops to be next in line to be rewarded. This strategy is perhaps the most widespread strategy in companies today and is known as a "bonus". If, for example, a sales company only offers its employees a fixed salary, it may be that the employees end up receiving only half as much as they should. Whether an individual sells more or less is basically irrelevant, because he always receives the same salary. More and more employees will therefore not be happy after a while. However, if they are offered a reward at the end of the month, either according to target specifications or according to a percentage of the sales profit, the salespeople will be enormously motivated, because they know that the more they sell, the more they earn. And the company's profit will also be much higher in the end.

On the other hand, Sun Tzu emphasizes that one should be benevolent when it comes to punishing one's opponent. He therefore advises treating prisoners well, because then there is a chance that they will defect and even fight for the other side. This increases the power of one's own army and also provides a strategic advantage, because one gains information about the enemy that would otherwise have been much more difficult to obtain. At the same time, however, this may also create future spies, saboteurs, and brakes. The Romans, therefore, not only simply conquered other countries and regions, but also always colonized them at the same time. They offered their soldiers rewards in the form of land, for example, to settle down and thrive. In this way, they mixed with the locals of the conquered zone and also granted them certain competencies and capacities for self-administration. These were the so-called provinces, and by acquiring citizenship, Rome continuously gained military potential and resources of all kinds. This is a well-known and extremely successful strategy that can also be transferred very well to the economy. Even today, recruiting talent is vital for companies. In the future, this will become even more important because there will be fewer and fewer workers or skilled workers due to low birth rates and a new healthier attitude towards "work-life balance" among the younger generation. Rewards and poaching talent from (inferior) competitors will increasingly determine economic—but also military—success in the future.

How relevant such considerations are for the cyber war of the future is demonstrated by a look at North Korea. Because what do you need more for attack and defense in cyberspace than suitable, motivated talents? And while North Korea may lack many things, one thing must be conceded to this small and otherwise very poor country: It has an enormously powerful cyber army. The attacks of this army are considered extremely sophisticated and very successful. According to a UN report, North Korea has already earned several billion through this. Where do the cyber soldiers come from in a country where the slightly more than 25 million inhabitants can only access the country's own intranet with a few official pages? On the one hand, there is a suspicion that they are paid mercenaries operating from outside the country. But even within North Korea, there is a sophisticated program designed to identify the most talented students, train them as hackers, and ultimately transfer them into government service. To this end, those with the best grades in mathematics are taken out of the regular classes and added to a career path that leads them to the best schools and universities, such as the Technical University or the University of Automation in Pyongyang, but also in countries like China, Russia, and India. In this way, North Korea employs around 7,000 hackers, many of whom work in Office 121, the espionage and reconnaissance department of the North Korean secret service. There, they learn the art of cyber warfare not from books, but directly in practice. They are likely responsible for numerous attacks on banks around the globe, involvement in the attack on Sony Pictures in 2014, and probably the WannaCry malware, which since 2017 has encrypted data on several hundred thousand computers, demanded users to pay a ransom, and caused damage of 4 billion dollars. However, this whole story should be taken with a grain of caution, as many pieces of information come from unconfirmed sources and reports from North Korea must always be viewed against the backdrop of propaganda.

Lesson 3: Attack with Strategy, or: On the Proposals of Victory and Defeat

"He who defeats the enemy without battle truly understands warfare."

This quote from Sun Tzu seems to me to be particularly visionary—and it is the quote that most often leads to misunderstandings. Because as I will show, he is not really talking about pacifism here, as it is often misunderstood.

But let's start from the beginning. A battle is always somewhat of an admission of defeat, as all other means and ways are exhausted at this point. There is a basic principle in this section that could be formulated as follows: Keep your enemy intact, rather than destroying him. This means that there are more ways to win battles than to completely destroy the opponent with violence. Anyone who chooses violence as a means should always remember that the opponent will respond with counter-violence and one will inevitably suffer losses. However, if you conduct a thorough analysis of the enemy beforehand, know his strengths and weaknesses, you can manage to topple him with other means. Therefore, one should try to explore the opponent's weaknesses in detail in order to build one's own defense on them. Sun Tzu advises to give up one's own morale and take prisoners to further weaken the enemy. If you do this for a while without shedding a drop of blood, you will eventually get to the generals. It's not about winning more battles, but about demoralizing the enemy and bringing him to surrender. That is the secret of great leaders. The best example of how to win without violence is that of Gandhi in India. He was the architect of India's independence (1947). The most inspiring thing for me about his figure is not the goal he pursued, but rather the means by which he achieved it. Three decades of perseverance were necessary to achieve the goal with the form of peaceful activism, based on non-violence and the strength of convictions: the abolition of castes, social justice, the transformation of economic structures, and harmony between religions. As a man of extreme rigor and modesty, Gandhi is one of the great characters who questioned and changed the political and ideological establishment of the world in the 20th century with their thoughts and actions, and became a reference point for all kinds of mobilizations against injustice. In a country where politics was synonymous with corruption, Gandhi brought ethics into public life by word and example. He lived in poverty without relief, never granted privileges to his relatives, and always rejected political power before and after India's liberation. This characteristic has made the apostle of non-violence a unique case among revolutionaries of all times, and one of the most admired (if not revered) modern spiritual leaders.

What specific strategies and measures are there to defeat the enemy without battle? One of the most important measures is planning. One must prepare one's own army for the specific goal being pursued, and do so diligently until one can be sure that it is fully trained and an action plan with clear instructions is in place. One should also look for alternatives for all eventualities that can occur before and during the execution of the action. Nothing should be left to chance. All necessary resources must be calculated in advance and be available. Logistics are just as important as the battle plan. It is important to develop the plan with a cool head and not to be carried away by emotions. These are often the cause of mistakes. Sun Tzu names five factors that are important for victory:

- Only those who know exactly whether they can fight or not will win.
- Whoever knows how to use many or few soldiers will win.
- When the ordinary soldier and the officer are filled with the same spirit, victory is certain.
- Whoever is prepared for everything and waits until the enemy is unprepared will win.
- A capable general will win if the prince does not stand in his way and interfere.

The great goal is victory, without harming the enemy, this is the essence of *The Art of War*. Without a complete victory, there is no victory. And this happens when the enemy finally surrenders. This destroys the enemy's plans, dissolves his pacts and alliances, interrupts his supply routes or paths, and ultimately defeats the enemy without having to fight. Sun Tzu makes it clear that this is an ideal. There are certainly cases where it is worth fighting and situations where one must flee. He explains this using ratios: "The strategy to be applied is as follows: If the ratio is ten to one, the enemy is surrounded on all sides, at a ratio of five to one he is attacked, and at two to one divide the army, and you can attack the enemy in battle from two sides. If you are outnumbered, the enemy is to be observed, and if you are not equal to him, you should flee from him. A small group of soldiers can resist the enemy, but will ultimately be captured by a larger enemy force." Frederick the Great was certainly not an innovator who established new military methods. But his tactical and strategic knowledge was unsurpassed in his time. As a proponent of relentless attack, he always enforced his four principles, the legacy, as we have seen, of Sun Tzu: rigid discipline, logistics, offensive action, and practical sense. In the Seven Years' War (1756–1763), he managed to defeat enemies who were far more powerful than Austria, such as France. A good general must know when to fight and when to retreat in time. He must know how to distribute the number of units. Sometimes more are necessary, sometimes none at all. When it comes to fighting, he looks for the right moment, which he recognizes because he has thought through all possibilities and studied history. Then it is only a matter of waiting for the right time and knowing the enemy's weaknesses. Sun Tzu concludes the chapter by saying: "If you know others and know yourself, you will not be in danger in a hundred battles; if you do not know others, but know yourself, you will lose one battle and win another; if you know neither others nor yourself, you will be in danger in every battle." We see: Sun Tzu is not about avoiding the fight or the battle at all costs. It is about putting oneself in a position that guarantees victory. The battle is not always the ideal means for this.

Today's activities in cyberspace must also be viewed from this perspective. As Russia's war of aggression against Ukraine shows, hybrid warfare is already the norm today. The attack on communication systems and the targeted crippling of the government side was part of the first wave of attacks. But this also means: States, organizations, and other actors are actively dealing with the methods to use cyberspace for war purposes. If we apply Sun Tzu's thesis of attack with strategy to today's scenario, this means knowing and developing one's own capabilities in order to be able to assess how one can and should act at the decisive moment.

Lesson 4: Tactics

"In war, there are five tactics to be observed:

- *the measurement of the terrain*
- *the assessment of the population's capacity*
- *the number of soldiers*
- *the comparison between the armies*
- *the calculation of victory and defeat."*

As already mentioned in the previous chapter, it becomes clear that *The Art of War* proceeds according to strict mathematical principles or equations. "The elements of the art of war are: measurement of distances, estimates of quantities, calculations, comparisons, and the chances of victory." When the terrain of a country is measured, this results in the capacity, that is, the population (and also their resources), from which the number of soldiers can be calculated, which is to be compared with that of the enemy. If these factors are taken into account, according to Sun Tzu, a victory is predictable. Knowledge of one's own position of strength is therefore a crucial ingredient of the art of war.

So what does "measurement" mean specifically in our time, when we have computer-aided calculations? Anyone who wants to recognize a terrain must find out what conditions they are getting into. That means: If you want to work as a lawyer, find out if there are already many law firms in your city. If there are many law firms, then find out what specializations they have and so on. When it comes to evaluation, it means evaluating the available options. It is mentioned in the consideration that this is about a perspective in the literal and figurative sense. The measurement of a terrain therefore has a direct reference to the strategist's view. Once we have the measurement and the evaluation, a good general must calculate the advantages and disadvantages, the resources to be used, the number of troops needed, the time of preparation for the battle before acting. Then comes the comparison. The first three steps inevitably lead to comparison. Here too, new knowledge is brought to light. One must compare the origin of the conflict, where is one army going and where is the other coming from? What are the moral and ethical inclinations of the fighters in battle? What are their intentions and what motives lead them to it? One should also compare the capacity of their weapons with one's own and their strength in relation to one's own. What are their weaknesses in relation to yours? What degree of motivation does the enemy army have compared to your own? Finally, it is necessary to ask what conclusions can be drawn from the comparison and what advantages and disadvantages can be derived from it. If all these steps and calculations have been carried out with care, the strategic plan can only lead to victory, precisely because one goes into battle with knowledge of one's own strength. "Good strategists easily win battles that are easy to win. They do not win battles by chance. They are stronger and they know it and they use this power intelligently."

In cyberspace, it is crucial to know the different actors as precisely as possible. It makes a big difference whether an attack is carried out only by so-called "script kiddies", i.e., children or teenagers who try to hack companies or networks for fun, or whether an attack comes from a hacker group from North Korea. It is also important to distinguish and know the types of attacks precisely. An APT ("Advanced Persistent Thread", in German:

"Advanced, ongoing threat") is an attack where the attackers make a great effort to penetrate a network. Anyone who is exposed to such an attack must mobilize all forces to fend it off. Knowledge of the motivation and the possibilities available to the opponent is of crucial importance.

Lesson 5: Power

> *"A rock or tree trunk is harmless at rest, but dangerous once it starts moving. Angular can be stopped, but round continues to move incessantly. Good fighters are therefore like a rockslide, which rolls down the mountain slope unstoppable. That is power."*

Power is accumulated or perceived energy. Therefore, power is very changeable. Those who master this relationship with great skill are able to defeat an enemy by creating a favorable perception for themselves and thus achieve victory without having to use their power. An episode from Chinese history dating from 341 BC, the already mentioned time of the Warring States, illustrates this. At that time, the two states Qi and Wei were at war. Tian Qi and Sun Bin—the son of Sun Tzu and also the author of a work on the art of war—faced General Pang Zhuan, Sun Bin's personal mortal enemy. According to legend, Sun Bin said: "The state of Qi is sadly famous for its cowardice, and therefore our opponent despises us. Let's use this circumstance to our advantage." So he devised a ruse. When the enemy army had crossed the border of Wei, he ordered a hundred thousand fires to be lit on the first night, fifty thousand on the second, and only twenty thousand on the following night. This was to create the impression that the army was retreating. Pang Zhuan therefore took up the pursuit. Sun Bin lured his pursuers to a narrow pass in this way, where he had a tree peeled and the following words carved into the wood: "Under this tree, Pang Zhuan will die." When night fell, Sun Bin set up a strong detachment of archers near this ambush and ordered them to shoot immediately if they saw a light. When Pang Zhuan later came to this place, he saw the tree and lit a light to read what was written on the tree. His body was immediately pierced by countless arrows and his entire army thrown into confusion.

This art of deception is what Sun Tzu is all about in the game of forces: "Mastering chaos is possible in many ways. Hiding bravery behind cowardice is a sign of inner strength, hiding strength behind weakness is the outward appearance to deceive the enemy." An example of a company that has almost perfected this power play is Apple. Many are familiar with the annual ritual of launching a new product or improving one of the existing products that has already surprised the market. Apple wants to drive its competitors ahead with this tactic and demonstrate strength. This positioning is a basic principle of marketing, which puts it at the forefront of other companies in the industry. To some extent, this is of course also a deception, which a direct comparison of product features can easily reveal. But Apple has perfected the illusion of demonstrating strength. To achieve this, it is necessary and absolutely essential to design a strategic plan that allows companies like Apple to secure this positioning again and again. Apple's tactic is often surprise. Because every time a new product is introduced, the company organizes a spectacular event that turns the product into a star. The surprising effect thus comes to the fore. Part of Apple's strategy is also to interact with its customers in such a way that they feel like part of the Apple family when buying the product and an important and special part of it. And finally, the company tries to find new ways to meet needs that not even the customers knew they had. Apple controls the surprise factor along with the speed of its own actions and attacks with carefully studied business and marketing strategies when it comes to bringing a new product to market and turning customers into fans. With clear goals and well-structured methods, the company carries out these strategies, which has made it the most well-known and important technology company in its industry and the most valuable company in the world. One of the success strategies that Apple uses for this is the mastery of competition by demonstrating its own strength—or as Sun Tzu describes it: "Whoever knows how to keep the enemy moving, uses the outward appearance so that the enemy follows this deception."

Lesson 6: Weaknesses and Strengths

"The highest art of the warrior is to be invisible and formless, so that even the enemy spy deep in one's own ranks can spy out nothing and the wisest can suspect nothing."

In this section of the *Art of War*, Sun Tzu deepens and expands his explanations of tactics and strategies that lead to victory over the enemy. And from today's perspective, it becomes particularly interesting. Because it also deals with strategies that work when the numerical ratios between the parties facing each other suggest a position of weakness. But there are also strategies to achieve victory from a position of weakness. Sun Tzu gives some very practical tips: "When the enemy is rested, be able to tire him. If he is well fed, starve him. If he is resting, make him move. Appear at places he must hurry to." Elsewhere he writes: "Attack the enemy's places that are unprotected, and you will succeed. Your own protection must be strong, even where no attack is expected. A good attacker does not know where to defend, and a good defender does not know where to attack." Hackers nowadays use exactly such considerations of attack and defense and the apparent imbalance of strength and weakness. They sometimes attack companies that are superior to them in every respect. From the number of employees, to the available resources, the infrastructure, and so on. Hackers therefore often choose the path of least resistance when attacking a company. They look for the weakest point in the defense to attack there. Like companies, hackers act economically. That is, they strive for an optimal ratio of cost, benefit, and effort. Why should an attacker try for weeks to bypass a firewall when he only has to write a single convincing phishing email, in which he has to ask individual users for their login name and the corresponding password? Sun Tzu also advises to avoid the direct and hopeless fight, because it is pointless in view of the ratio of strength and weakness: "According to my calculation, the soldiers of Yüeh are numerically superior, but this does not decide victory or defeat. Victory can still be achieved! If the enemy is numerically superior, a fight must be avoided." Of course, one must not forget that such tactics are also used for deception maneuvers. Du Mu, a Chinese poet who lived during the Tang Dynasty, reports in one of his works of a ruse of war. One of China's most famous military strategists, Zhuge Liang, devised this in 149 BC when he had occupied Yangping. Just before the attack of the opposing army, he suddenly had his banners pulled in, the drumming stopped, and the city gates opened. Behind the gate were only a few men seen sweeping and watering the ground. This unexpected action did not miss its desired effect. The opposing general suspected an ambush. So he gathered his army and retreated.

This means that clever strategists let their opponents come to them, but by no means let themselves be lured out of their fortress. When the opponents come to challenge someone, one should not fight them at all costs. Rather, it is worth initiating a strategic change to confuse and unsettle them.

As an example of how to masterfully handle the differences of strength and weakness, the battles of Quatre Bras and Ligny can be cited, two of the three battles of the Waterloo cycle, in which General Napoleon was finally defeated. Both battles took place simultaneously and were only a few kilometers apart. But from the beginning: On June 15, 1815, General Napoleon left his exile on Elba and attacked the Belgian border north of Charleroi with 128,000 units of his troops. It was a surprise attack, as the enemy general, the Englishman Wellington, had not considered an attack on Belgium. Wellington was thus trapped and forced to move his troops to help those who were trying to contain Marshall Ney at the Quatre Bras junction on the morning of June 16. Ney, for his part, committed gross negligence by no longer occupying this indispensable strategic position. He compounded his mistake by not starting the battle in the morning and then using his 4,000-strong cavalry to go against the English infantry. However, the total catastrophe came when Ney repeated this mistake three days later in Waterloo: the attack against an intact infantry formation without his own support.

Also on June 16, the majority of hostilities took place in Ligny between Napoleon's main army of 71,000 units and Blücher's 84,000 Prussians. The allied Austrians had made the grave mistake of not having measured the terrain beforehand. And so they eventually scattered in a marshy terrain, although Napoleon's movements were not much better. He delayed the battle until the afternoon, as this gave him the opportunity to win without fighting, since the enemy troops had revealed their weaknesses, and launched a furious attack to destroy and defeat the Prussian lines. For nearly two hours, the fierce fighting continued, almost never with distance weapons, but in close quarters, with bayonets and shots at close range. The Prussian losses reached 19,000 and although Blücher left the field, Napoleon also lost 14,000 lives, having missed the original advantage. He then sent Marshal Grouchy to chase the rest of the Prussian army with 30,000 soldiers. But the Marshal did not have the determination to conscientiously execute his general's orders and carry out such a light pursuit. However, he could afford not to return home, but to go west, where Wellington was waiting for him. Sun Tzu says that formations are like water: "The course of water is determined by the earth formation, victory over the enemy is achieved by controlling him. War adapts to situations and conditions, just as water has no specific form. Whoever can adapt to the enemy is able to seize victory and has understood the spirit of war. The five elements [according to Sun Tzu] always exist side by side and the four seasons alternate in rhythm. There are short and long days, and the moon waxes and wanes." Thus, an army also has no constant formation, just as water has no constant form. Therefore, the ability to adapt to the enemy and to constantly change in order to achieve victory is referred to as a stroke of genius.

Hardly any area is better suited to obfuscate one's own traces, hide identities, play the game of confusion and deception, than the digital space. It is hardly possible to clearly identify attackers, as they can lay false trails. At the same time, actors can use cyberspace to appear larger than they actually are. Clicks or followers can be bought or manipulated, so that a weak opponent can appear strong. Such tactics could be observed in numerous elections, where supposed outsiders could very quickly experience a large influx of approval. The case of Cambridge Analytica, a British data analysis company that gained notoriety during the 2016 US election and has since filed for bankruptcy, bears a disgraceful testimony to this. It became known that the company was involved in more than 40 candidacies and numerous elections around the world. The company claimed to have data that enabled them to specifically influence voters. Whether it is to specifically unsettle opponents or to make one's own side appear larger and better than it really is—the tactical game with strengths and weaknesses still decides victory and defeat today.

Lesson 7: Struggle for the Initiative, or: The Strategies of the Direct and Indirect

"Victory belongs to those who can make use of the crooked and the straight. This is how battles are fought."

In this chapter, Sun Tzu essentially deals with the question: When is the right time for action? The answer to this question depends heavily on the size of the army that needs to be mobilized. The challenge of mobilization is one of the greatest. Sun Tzu describes the solutions for this as the strategies of the Direct and Indirect. An example he gives is: "The most difficult thing is to make the most direct path out of a winding route and to turn misfortune into advantage. Therefore, march an indirect path and divide the enemy by offering him bait. Thus, one could start the march after the enemy and still be at the destination before him. Someone who is able to proceed in this way understands the strategy of the Direct and the Indirect." Although here the tactic should be meant rather than the strategy.

To illustrate the choice of the right moment, an anecdote from Li Chuan, a Chinese author and chronicler, is often referred to. He reports about Cao Gui, a protégé of Prince Zhuang of Lu. When his state was attacked and the prince wanted to rush into battle immediately after the first beating of the enemy drums, Cao Gui stopped him. He advised him to let the drums beat two more times and only then give the order to attack. When they fought together, the attackers were devastatingly defeated. After the battle, the prince wanted to know from Cao Gui why he had advised him to delay the attack. His answer was: "In battle, a brave spirit is everything. The first drumbeat awakens this spirit, but by the second it is already fading, and after the third it is completely gone. I attacked when their spirit had left them and ours was at its peak. That's why we won. The value of an entire army—a powerful association of a million men—depends on one man alone: This is the influence of the spirit."

The fact that not only a delay of the attack can be the right answer to the question of the best moment is proven by an episode that took place almost 2000 years later. The idea of blitzkrieg originated in World War II. Adolf Hitler wanted to conquer Europe as quickly, effectively, and powerfully as possible at the beginning of the war. Therefore, a military strategy was developed together with his commanding generals, which was characterized by the simultaneous use of several military columns at several fronts. They pursued the immediate goal of causing more irreversible and deeper damage not only in enemy territories but also in the countries they wanted to invade, in order to conquer them immediately in this way. For this reason, ground troops, warships, military aircraft, tanks, and other vehicles were mobilized simultaneously during the blitz-krieg. The strategy also included advancing in the form of spearheads into the various areas to devastate them in a spectacular way. For this approach to be truly effective, the movements had to be fast and synchronized. Hence the name blitzkrieg, which acts decisively and efficiently to give the enemy no time to react. With this tactical plan, the German army marched into Poland and conquered the country, which eventually became one of the main goals of the Reich. The key to Hitler's victory in Poland lies in the coordinated approach mentioned above. Germany also had the most advanced and efficient weapons devel-opment at the time, making it the first military world power—even before England and France, the two main enemies of Germany at the time. The strategy of blitzkrieg was so innovative that the German word was adopted into English, where it still describes this tactic today.

Interestingly, Sun Tzu's text is written so openly that this tactic of blitzkrieg is in line with what is described in *The Art of War* as follows: "A clever tactician avoids battle when the enemy's fighting spirit is still pronounced, he attacks when it is sluggish and worn out. This is the right way to deal with the fighting spirit." The time of day—the attack on Poland famously started in the early morning hours—was chosen as Sun Tzu would certainly have recommended. Because: "During the early morning, the morale of the troops will be strong." And: "Therefore, he who is experi-enced in war avoids the enemy when his morale is strong, and attacks him when he is weak". At the same time, it becomes clear that *The Art of War* is also a child of its time. When one reads today what difficulties in maneuvering Sun Tzu describes as a challenge, it becomes clear that with the advancement of technology certain situations are easier to master. A mobilization on the scale necessary for blitz-krieg was certainly hardly imaginable 2000 years ago.

Lesson 8: The Nine Variable Factors

Rarely is Sun Tzu as explicit and clear as in this section, so that it sometimes almost sounds a bit like a guidebook. For example, when he mentions the nine variable factors that are crucial for the art of war:

"In low-lying terrain, no camp should be set up.

In contiguous territories, one should ally with one's allies.

In desolate territory, one should not linger too long.

In enclosed terrain, one must conserve resources.

In dead territory, fight.

There are roads that should not be followed and troops that should not be attacked.

There are cities that should not be besieged.

There is terrain that one should not attempt to occupy.

There are situations in which the prince's commands should not be obeyed.

A general who has extensive experience in the advantages of the nine variable factors knows how to set up an army."

Even when it comes to selecting personnel for the army, more specifically the leaders, Sun Tzu has some extremely helpful tips in store:

"There are five characteristics that are dangerous in the nature of a general.

1. If he is reckless, he can be killed.
2. If he clings too much to life, he can easily be captured.
3. If he is hot-tempered, he can be ridiculed.
4. If he is too honor-driven, he can be slandered.
5. If he is compassionate, he can be harassed.

These five character traits are serious mistakes for a general and disastrous for military operations. The destruction of the army and the death of the general are the inevitable consequences of these deficiencies. They must be thoroughly considered."

That is, it is important to recognize the terrain in which the possible conflict will take place, and to appropriately choose the place where the troops go into camp. This terrain must be under optimal conditions for us. They must be well communicated in order to mobilize units if necessary, access must be easy, and basic resources such as water must be available. Both in attack and in defense, the general must adapt to the terrain, the climate, all adversities that arise, calculate the advantages and disadvantages of defense and attack well, and evaluate the profitability of the efforts. Often such decisions are not easy. Because it is difficult to expose oneself to certain losses for the sake of victory. But it is these decisions, to minimize the damage as much as possible, that make the difference between a great strategist and a mediocre one.

Great leaders are characterized by taking responsibility, they are firm in their decisions and they can adapt to any situation—like water. They are not carried away by their feelings, but by objective and plausible criteria. The measurement of the environment, rationality in decisions, and seizing opportunities determine victory and defeat.

A clear example of an incompetent general who led his army into a total disaster is provided by James Wilkinson during the War of Independence of the United States against England. As a general of the army, he was a spy for his enemy, Spain, against his own country. His codename for Spain was *Agent 13*—what could go wrong with this number!?—and he is said to have made good economic gains with his espionage activities. Before that, he was responsible for the logistics of the U.S. Army. Some later testimonies suggest, however, that he had withdrawn as chief of staff because he was also diverting funds into his own pocket in this function.

In addition, his strategic preparation as a military commander speaks for itself. During the invasion of Canada in 1812, his four thousand strong troop was defeated by less than two hundred Canadian soldiers. So if he was demonstrably unsuitable on and off the battlefield, the only way to remain a general was his ability to be a corrupt, traitorous, and professional intriguer. He went through court-martials, congressional investigations, and investigative commissions, but always came out on top. Of him, historian Robert Leckie said: He was a general who never won a battle and never lost a court-martial.

Lesson 9: The Army on the March

"If the enemy is near and remains quiet, then he is not afraid because he is in a strategically good position. If the enemy is far away and provokes a fight, then he wants your troops to advance because his position is advantageous."

What can we learn from observing the behavior of others? The answer is clear: a lot. The art of empathizing with others—be it the attacker into his target as well as vice versa the victims into their aggressors—is a central aspect when it comes to actual combat. These considerations always played a role when, for example, castles were besieged in the Middle Ages. The question was not, contrary to first intuition, how can I penetrate a fortress. The key is rather to put oneself in the shoes of those who are in the fortress and ask what their needs are. Because even if you are holed up in a castle, you need water to drink and food to eat. This means that the supply routes or the internal resources, such as wells or animals etc., are the central weaknesses that need to be controlled. In addition to such basic considerations, this chapter is mainly about finding out what the best position for the attackers is. As we have just learned, these clues are just as important for those who want to defend against an attack. For Sun Tzu, these are mainly geographical features that need to be taken into account in attack and defense. He advises: "The camp should be pitched on elevated ground, facing the sun", "Always fight downhill" or "Never attack uphill." Military maneuvers or even hacker attacks are always the result of plans and tactics that aim to win in the most favorable way. Strategies and plans determine the mobility and effectiveness of the troops and the individual's approach. One of the great strategists in history, Alexander the Great, provides the best example of what the principles of an effective tactic for victory can look like. Alexander the Great (356–323 BC), the king of Macedonia, was admired for his strategic wisdom. The Macedonians ruled all of Greece when he began his reign at the age of 20. They had unmatched military principles and strategic bases. However, victory also requires a firm goal and a plan on how to achieve it. All military units—from middle commanders to soldiers in service—must know exactly what role they play. Alexander's goal was nothing more and nothing less than to become the ruler of the then known world. To do this, he had to "only" defeat his enemies with more power. At his time, these were the Persians, commanded by their king Darius. Alexander therefore shared his battle plan and strategy with his generals, so that everyone knew what measures he had to take.

Napoleon Bonaparte once said that no battle has ever been won in the defensive. To win, it is necessary to innovate with carefully researched tactics for each troop mobilization and to create new, more effective and devastating weapons. Alexander also knew that he could only defeat the Persians in direct combat. And indeed: The generals defeat their opponent by grouping the majority of their forces at a precise location, at the right time, and with predefined movements. They only attacked after they had studied how they could best attack their enemy and after they had found his weaknesses. Alexander did it by creating a gap in the Persian lines.

The efficient generals are usually the winners of all their battles and so the opponent was defeated. Their approach requires always being flexible, weighing the pros and cons of every moment, evaluating every terrain they move on, and planning accordingly. One must be ready to move forward, backward, and sideways like on a chessboard—whether for attacking or defending, for advancing or retreating. Sun Tzu emphasizes that movements in the group, with constant support for each other, are fundamental. Alexander always had full confidence in his troops because he himself had trained them to be the most disciplined soldiers in the world. It is important to indoctrinate teamwork, in which the soldiers consider the army as part of themselves, so that the overarching goal becomes theirs. Alexander also used the element of surprise to weaken enemy troops. Because it is necessary to unsettle the enemies with one's own movements, with feints or new weapons that have never been seen before. It takes a lot to lead a troop well or to lead a team. The following sentences, attributed to Alexander the Great, reveal his wisdom in leading his army:

"There is nothing impossible for the one who tries."

"The fate of everything depends on the realization of each individual."

"I am not afraid of an army of lions led by a sheep; I am afraid of an army of sheep led by a lion."

"For me, I have left the best: hope."

"In the end, when everything is over, only what you have done counts."

"When we give someone our time, we are actually giving a part of our life that we will never recover."

"Effort and risk are the price of glory, but it is a valuable thing to live and die bravely and leave eternal glory."

"If I wait, I will lose boldness and youth."

"When the enemy's envoys speak modest words, while the enemy increases his war preparations, it means that he is advancing. When high-flying words are spoken and one ostentatiously advances, it is a sign that the enemy will retreat."

However, winning a battle is far from everything: Once the victory is won, one must know how to maintain it. It is important to continue one's own movement to take advantage of the gained advantage. The enemy will try to recover and will sooner or later switch from defensive to offensive actions to regain lost terrain, so we must consistently follow the plan set up. A painful experience that all attackers had to make who tried to conquer Afghanistan with military means in the past hundred years: Because it is one thing to take a territory, and another to hold it for a longer period.

Lesson 10: Terrain

"We can distinguish six types of terrain: accessible terrain, hindering terrain, balancing terrain, narrow passes, steep heights, positions far from the enemy."

As we have already seen in the previous chapters, considerations of the terrain, the concrete local conditions, are important to Sun Tzu. A contemporary reader should always read an extension in their mind, instead of rocks and valleys one should consider what a digital rock or digital valley could be. So what could such objects look like digitally? One could imagine a certain market situation, a sphere of influence, or a networking into other areas. "A certain terrain can be quite helpful in a battle. The supreme commander must be able to assess the enemy in order to win, he must include dangers and risks, distance and proximity in his considerations. If he knows all the risks and then attacks, victory is certain. If he does not take all this into account, defeat is certain. If the supreme principle in war is victory, fight, even if the ruler orders not to fight. If the goal is not victory, and the ruler orders to fight, then do not attack."

For this reason, field study is an essential starting factor that should be carried out before developing the strategy. Depending on the difficulties you encounter, you will base your movements, your wear and tear on troops and resources, and the needs you need to take care of accordingly. A similar approach is taken by many attackers today in so-called social engineering. Translated: The high art of manipulating people. This is a practice that is also used for attack purposes. Basically, it is about exploiting the characteristics and weaknesses of people to use them for an attack on a system. Similar to a field study, it is also necessary to get as accurate an insight as possible into the local conditions in advance—starting with the processes in companies to all possible information about the employees. Whoever knows as much as possible about the internal connections and the people in the company can exploit these structures and their possible weaknesses.

Sun Tzu advises: "If the battlefield is easily accessible, try to get there before your enemies and choose the best position to establish yourself, start an attack and position the defense, the right ways to transport supplies and move troops. It is important to have this advantage over his rival." In hacking, sometimes the same approach is taken: you attack or log in, prepare the system for later and leave a backdoor through which you then have access at that time. If the system or the terrain or other local conditions are difficult to access, the advantage is basically lost. Then you have to look for solutions for difficult terrain. Here too, knowledge about the enemy decides: You have to know whether he is ready to fight or not, whether his soldiers or employees are more motivated than your own, how they are trained, and so on. Whoever has this information will be able to find an alternative solution for victory. However, if you come to the conclusion that you are still at a clear disadvantage, Sun Tzu reminds you that retreat can be the best strategic decision.

The most famous strategic offensive, considering the terrain and the art of deception in history, is probably that of the landing of the allied troops in Normandy in June 1944 during the Second World War. "Operation Overlord," as the Allies called the landing offensive in Normandy, a sea and air attack from the French north coast, which was in the hands of the German troops until then. June 5 was the date chosen by the Allied army for the largest amphibious attack in history. However, the weather conditions forced the attack to be delayed by one day. The decision for this tactical change is exactly what Sun Tzu talks about in *The Art of War*. The environment—and that includes the weather—are crucial for the success of an operation. And so, on June 6, 1944, now known as D-Day, about 156,000 American troops landed on the French coast—the rest is history, as they say.

However, the plan for this attack began a year earlier, during the Trident Conference, where U.S. General Eisenhower and British Commander B. Montgomery took over the entire organization and preparation of the landing that was to lead the allied troops through the English

Channel to France. Hitler, who knew the Allies' plan, commissioned Field Marshal E. Rommel to defend the beaches of Normandy. The preparation by both sides was crucial for the outcome of the battle.

The Germans built the so-called Atlantic Wall. This consisted of obstacles and ambush traps, both on land and at sea, to make it difficult for the armed forces to access the beach, mines and barbed wire as well as bunkers and machine gun nests for defense, and a series of trenches and anti-tank pits. The Allies, for their part, based their strategy on deceiving the German High Command. They sent false radio conversations and disinformation about an alleged landing in the area of Calais, which they let fall into the hands of the German spies. This was crucial for the Allies' victory. This tactic of deception and confusion of the enemy had already been used by the British army with General Montgomery during the desert war. The absence of Rommel on the battlefield and the success of the false information given to the Germans about the landing in Calais destabilized the German troops and led to a disadvantageous situation for them. Hitler also refused in his endeavor to conquer Russia to move a part of the troops destined for the Eastern Front to Normandy. All this, together with the effective bombing of the allied planes, led to the allied troops taking Normandy at the end of "D-Day" and from there continuing their advance to recapture the European territory occupied by the Nazis. The beginning of the end of the Second World War was underway.

When applied to cyberspace, one inevitably has to think of network attacks via DDoS (Distributed-Denial-of-Service) in such scenarios, in order to test or distract the security center. In this case, a system is virtually overrun with requests, causing it to become overloaded and ultimately fail. This form of attack originally arose for reasons of vandalism or as an expression of protest. Today, these attacks are deliberately used to overload system-relevant networks in the course of an attack, or to harm economic competitors.

Lesson 11: The Nine Types of Terrain

"The terrain formations can favorably influence a war. Territory to disperse, light terrain, battleground, open terrain, strategically advantageous terrain, difficult terrain, dangerous terrain, enclosed terrain, deadly terrain must be considered."

Once again, *The Art of War* deals with terrain in this chapter. More precisely, with the nine different types of terrain that Sun Tzu says need to be considered. It is no coincidence that this information is given such high importance. Sun Tzu even compares the knowledge that can be acquired about it to the ability to form an alliance with other princes: "Without knowing the strategies of the other princes, no alliance can be formed. Without knowing mountains and forests, dangerous abysses and impassable salt marshes, an army cannot be set in motion. Without local guides, one cannot take advantage of the terrain. Whoever is careless in even one point cannot be a general of a despot."

Since the types of terrain can have such a decisive influence, we go through them one by one to see what they mean. When local interests oppose each other in a territory, as is the case in civil wars, this is called "the terrain of dispersion". This type of terrain was used by Fidel Castro's troops in Cuba to overthrow dictator Fulgencio Batista. After the defeat in Alegría del Pío, the insurgents dispersed easily and fled to the Sierra Maestra, from where they regrouped and began to reorganize—this time with successful results, namely the Cuban Revolution. When you invade the territory of another country, but do not do so deeply, it is called "light terrain". All wars of conquest usually start with a neighboring country. The troops can be moved there faster and are still relatively close to the army base, so they can advance or return more efficiently. The area that brings a great advantage when taken, and advantageous for the enemy if he defeats it, is referred to as "key terrain". As mentioned earlier in a previous example, Normandy proved to be an important terrain for the future of World War II. An inevitable battlefield is any defensive enclave or tactical step. An area that is equally accessible to you and others is referred to as a "terrain of communication". The area surrounded by three rival territories and first offering all people free access to this area is referred to as "intersecting terrain". It is the one where the most important communication routes converge by being connected to each other. Therefore, it is important to be the first to occupy such areas, because people usually then stand on its side. When you penetrate deeply into a foreign territory and leave many cities behind, this terrain is described as difficult. It is a terrain from which it is difficult to return. If it involves forested mountains, steep gorges, or other difficult transitions, it is referred to as "unfavorable terrain". The jungle in Vietnam, for example, was considered unfavorable terrain for American troops. Ultimately, this categorization proved true, as they failed to take advantage of a much larger army to simply win the war. When access to an area is narrow and the exit winding, so that only a small enemy unit can attack you, even if their troops are more numerous, this is called an "enclosed terrain". Only those who are able to adapt well can traverse this area. This description inevitably brings to mind the Battle of Thermopylae. Back then, around 480 BC, at the beginning of the Second Persian War, on one side was the overwhelmingly large army of Xerxes, the King of Persia, and on the other side was the much smaller force of the Hellenic League led by Leonidas. The information about the Persian army comes from the historian Herodotus, according to whom the fleet counted over 500,000 units, the infantry over 1,700,000 men, and the cavalry was 80,000 horses strong. In contrast, there were only the famous 300 Spartan hoplites, 1000 Tegeans and Mantineans, 120 men from Orchomenos, 1000 from the rest of Arcadia, 400 from Corinth, 200 from Phleius, 80 from Mycenae, 700 from Boeotia and Thespiae, 1000 from Phocis and 400 Thebans. Long list, short meaning: the Hellenic alliance was hopelessly outnumbered. But even though the alliance ultimately lost, the losses they inflicted on Xerxes' army were enormous. The nature of the terrain alone ensured that only a small number of fighters faced each other. The numerical superiority was of little use to the Persians. Only when the Persians found a small bypass path were they able to break the defense of the Hellenic alliance.

Finally, there is the area where one can only survive by fighting quickly, this is called "deadly terrain". The Battle of the Somme during the First World War undoubtedly became a deadly terrain for the British Army. The speed of action is then the essential factor, as well as the exploitation of the opponent's mistakes, unexpected maneuvers, and the attack when the opponent does not expect it. This is also the case, for example, when small hacker groups take action against nationwide security measures, such as in the area of critical infrastructures. "Terrain" in the digital realm encompasses everything—air, land, water, and space—without borders and topographical challenges. However, the terrain in cyberspace sometimes has very different effects. A satellite may be a target for a soldier that feels infinitely far away. For a hacker with a laptop in New

Zealand on the opposite side of the earth, however, this can be a nearby, quickly reachable target. The terrain and related scales, which affect properties such as speed, must therefore be rethought and reevaluated in the digital age.

According to Sun Tzu, in the end, it is up to the general or the leader to proceed calmly, reservedly, fairly, and methodically. He warns: "The loss of any of these necessary qualities leads to an unstoppable defeat."

Lesson 12: On the Art of Attacking with Fire

"There are five kinds of attack with fire: In the first, people are burned, in the second, supplies are burned, in the third, equipment is burned, in the fourth, warehouses and storage facilities are burned, and in the fifth, supply routes are burned."

Especially the last point—the attack with fire on supply routes—immediately evokes associations with the danger mentioned earlier, which emanates from cyber attacks on critical infrastructures. Only today, no fire would be used, but a digital wildfire would be triggered. In the context of the new, hybrid warfare, such considerations will become standard in the future. When it comes to warfare in general, at a certain point the question always arises about the means chosen to fight a conflict. According to Sun Tzu, weapons as instruments are always a bad sign and war itself is a dangerous affair. The strategy is what counts for him, and if there is a better way to victory, direct confrontations should be avoided. In this way, catastrophic defeats can also be prevented. Therefore, it should always be carefully considered whether it is worth mobilizing an army for insignificant reasons: weapons should only be used when there is no other means. Where a senseless use of weapons leads, where the opponent must be outdone again and again, is shown by the dropping of the atomic bomb over Hiroshima and Nagasaki. Since the nuclear armament during the Cold War, the logic here is: whoever presses the button first, dies second.

So what is the point of using fire, which Sun Tzu expressly praises? He writes: "He who uses fire for an attack is wise, he who uses water for an attack is strong. With the help of water, the enemy's path can be cut off, but with water one cannot seize him and rob him." So it's about attacks on infrastructure. This puts us right in the middle of scenarios that concern our age. One of the recurring fears in connection with cyber threats are attacks on critical infrastructures such as the power grid. Here, hackers could set a "digital fire" and ensure that an opponent is hit hard without an actual combat action taking place. This is exactly what Marc Elsberg describes so impressively in his novel *Blackout*. This is about the dramatic effects of a Europe-wide power outage. The affected areas suffer more from the consequences of anarchy and looting than from military attacks. As with other operations, the tactic and the underlying strategic goal are crucial in this case. Because even the use of fire must have a basis and requires certain means. "There are suitable times for setting fires, especially in dry and windy weather." The use of fire must be done with care. It is essential to follow the changes caused by the fire in fire attacks. Because if the fire is fanned by the wind, one should be careful not to get in its way. Fires can be uncontrollable and should be used with this awareness. The pair of opposites of control and uncontrollability are the two key terms for attacks with fire. It's a bit like teaching children how to handle fire: if you play with fire, you can burn your fingers. Apart from such external circumstances, fire is for Sun Tzu another means in the arsenal that can generally be used to cause confusion in the enemy and thus attack him. However, it is necessary to acquire knowledge on how to use fire as a means. Even more: "It is not enough to know how to attack others with fire, it is necessary to know how to prevent others from attacking you." This advice can be directly translated into the digital age. Because viruses, malware or DDoS attacks, where countless calls to websites lead to their crash, can also be used as fire, i.e., as a means to cause confusion in the enemy. Viruses in particular behave like a digital fire: they can initially be spread in a controlled manner, but can also cause more damage uncontrollably and spread across networks. Therefore, the means to prevent such attacks, including the *Fire* wall, which is not named by chance, are all the more important today and in the future. One could say that it serves to isolate systems and thus act as fire protection.

Sun Tzu also recommends in this chapter to keep one's own emotions out of warfare: "A general must not use the battle to express his contempt for the enemy. Advance if there is profit in sight, stay where you are if there is nothing to gain. Anger can turn into joy and contempt into happiness." A government should therefore not mobilize an army out of anger or provoke a war for base motives. Because "anger can turn into joy and joy can turn into anger, but a destroyed people cannot be reborn, and death cannot turn into life." It is interesting that Sun Tzu speaks about the topic of anger and dealing with emotions in this chapter, which is about fire. The use of fire is often associated with revenge, deception, and the destruction of evidence. In a figurative sense, one can also speak of anger today as a wildfire that has spread in social media and in many Western societies. It is also no coincidence that there is repeated speculation that many of the activities that fuel anger can be traced back to the machinations of enemy powers. Russia is repeatedly suspected of being the puppet master and financier in the background when it comes to spreading fake news and defaming political opponents on social networks. One can only hope that those responsible have internalized the lessons of Sun Tzu and know what can happen when they play with fire and anger.

Lesson 13: On the Use of Spies

"They [spies] are a ruler's treasure."

The last lesson is certainly one of the most controversial from the perspective of many contemporaries. Because espionage does not have a particularly high value in our value system. At the same time, there is a certain fascination for this topic in our culture. Just think of the famous secret agent 007. If we take away all the action and the world-saving pathos, then James Bond is basically nothing more than an employee of an intelligence service. For Sun Tzu, the matter is clear: secret agents and espionage are among the most valuable institutions there are: "To raise one hundred thousand men and march them over a thousand miles costs a thousand coins a day, which empties the pockets of the common people and drains the resources of the state treasury. It causes unrest at home and abroad, people roam on roads and streets, and seven hundred thousand families are kept from work. The armies often face each other in their positions for years, with the prospect of one day achieving the decisive victory. Whoever regrets having to pay a hundred coins to the spy and therefore does not know the enemy and his behavior, behaves extremely inhumanly."

Sun Tzu distinguishes five types of spies: the local, the internal, the defected, the doomed, and the surviving spies. When spies are at work, ideally no one knows about their activity and their connections. Spies are primarily agents of knowledge. Their main purpose is to gather information about the enemy's situation. To this day, espionage is a powerful weapon with which rivals can be eliminated. Take industrial espionage as an example of another way to defeat the enemy without fighting. Industrial espionage is the mostly illegal investigation of a competing company to gain an advantage in the introduction of new products and to push the other off the market. The goal of such investigations is to steal every secret or piece of information that is of great value for the development of an attack strategy. Spies in the economic / industrial environment can be people who have been infiltrated into the organization to spy on it, or someone with contacts inside. But more and more often today, they are also hackers who manage to gain access to or infiltrate the computer systems of competitors in order to steal information. What "normal" espionage in the field of economy is, is shown by the industrial espionage scandal of the Volkswagen Group. In 1993, seven Opel executives, including their production manager, suddenly left the company and simultaneously switched to Volkswagen, the direct competitor. General Motors, Opel's parent company, soon accused Volkswagen of industrial espionage and claimed that its trade secrets were being used in this way to gain an advantage. The charge led to a four-year legal dispute, at the end of which Volkswagen agreed to pay General Motors $100 million and place an order for more than a billion dollars in auto parts.

Creating blueprints, stealing construction plans and internal memos, eavesdropping on video conferences, reading emails and other forms of communication—this is the playground of digital espionage. Today, due to digital networking, you no longer have to send people on site and you no longer have to physically shadow anyone—thanks to mobile phone tracking, many people do this themselves today. One could therefore say that espionage in the digital age has definitely become different and in many cases much easier.

Conclusion: The Essence of the *Art of War*

I would like to encourage everyone to tackle *The Art of War* themselves. It is one of the oldest works in the world and should attract attention for this reason alone. Rarely will one find a book that has shaped world history as much as this one. If one still attempts a doomed attempt and wants to create a summary of Sun Tzu's strategies and tactics, one might mention six essential points that lead to success both militarily and economically—everyone will have their own interpretation, but this is mine:

1. One should fight for a good cause
   Only a leader who goes to war or competition for a good cause is able to motivate his troops and can demand loyalty.
2. Good leadership means providing orientation
   If you want to ensure that your own team or troop follows you, you must always act wisely and courageously, but also strictly and benevolently in your own actions.
3. Pay attention to the environment or surroundings
   When planning, environmental conditions must be analyzed and taken into account in detail. Changes in this can ruin even the best plan.

4. The terrain determines the tactics.

Good leadership also means that the leader deals with the terrain in detail and aligns any tactics with it, so that his own troops are not destroyed by a surprise attack.

5. Organization and discipline decide.

Your own troop or team must always be well organized and disciplined to prevent chaos and win the confrontation.

6. Use of espionage as a means of knowledge acquisition

According to Sun Tzu, it is impossible to obtain reliable information and insights about the enemy without espionage. The acquisition of secret information about the enemy, their position, the number of troops, the prediction of movements, etc. are of fundamental importance for the final consequences of the battle.

Of course, it is up to everyone to follow or not follow these pieces of advice that were handed down in Sun Tzu's work. Ideally, everyone draws their own conclusions from it. However, Sun Tzu says in essence: Whoever forgets or ignores the prerequisites just mentioned risks having their own army defeated or their own company going bankrupt. However, anyone who observes all the strategic advice listed in *The Art of War* will secure victory or the success of a company.

2

Codes and Secret Messages: From the Ancient Origins of Steganography and Cryptography and their Relevance to Today

"Secret operations are decisive in war."

Sun Tzu, The Art of War

The Art of War concludes with the chapter on espionage and the use of secret agents. About them, Sun Tzu also says: "They are a ruler's treasure." Even though this chapter from *The Art of War* is often not the focus of reception, it deals with one of the most important topics when it comes to warfare and strategic action in general. Because the ability to acquire knowledge unnoticed and to communicate with one's allies without being discovered oneself is indeed of the highest strategic importance and is often over-looked—which has a good reason, as will become clear at the end of this chapter …

Around the time Sun Tzu was writing his thoughts on espionage, around 490 B.C., something happened 7000 km away that the world still remembers today and that significantly influenced the course of history. The Persian

© The Author(s), under exclusive license to Springer Fachmedien Wiesbaden GmbH, part of Springer Nature 2024
P. Kestner, *The Art of Cyber Warfare*,
https://doi.org/10.1007/978-3-658-43879-1_2

force had just reached the Bay of Marathon by sea, about 40 km from Athens. Ancient Greece was then a more or less loose confederation of states, in which conflicts repeatedly arose. Athens was then a rising city-state, where a few years earlier nothing less than the first democracy in world history had emerged. A development that not everyone liked at the time, because it represented a radical counter-model to the then common form of rule: the sole rule, also called tyranny. Darius I, the Great King of Persia, wanted to make the Greek peninsula part of his empire and therefore decided to attack Athens. The Persians landed near Marathon, hoping that this would initially go unnoticed in Athens and they could bring all their troops ashore and use their military superiority. After the Athenians had learned of the Persians' landing, the need was indeed great and the question arose as to which tactic they could use to overcome the Persian superiority. It quickly became clear that the Athenians needed support, and so they chose the fastest means of communication at the time to ask one of their allies for help: a professional runner, also called a day runner. Thus, the messenger Pheidippides was sent with a message to Sparta, 246 km away. Pheidippides covered this "Spartathlon" in two days and was sent back to Marathon with the news that the Spartans would support Athens in the war against Persia. When he arrived back in Marathon two days later, the Athenians had achieved the impossible and already won the victory over the Persian army. Therefore, Pheidippides was immediately sent with the message of this victory to Athens. Legend has it that Pheidippides died of exhaustion after having also covered this marathon. Despite this tragic end of the first marathon run, this sport enjoys great popularity today.

What exactly happened around the battle between Athens and Persia is still not known to historiography today. The events are depicted too differently in the surviving sources. There are many inconsistencies that make one wonder why they were recorded in this way by historians like Herodotus. For example, whether the Athenians actually managed to defeat the Persian army alone (or without the help of several allies) is hard to say. In other words, there were good reasons to create the legend that Athens had managed to defeat the Persian superiority more or less on its own. The question alone of whether the marathon runner Pheidippides actually existed is considered unresolved today. He is very likely an invention of the historians. Which shows that even then the first casualty of any war is the truth.

Since we can't say with one hundred percent certainty what exactly happened back then, let's venture a few thought experiments. First and foremost in relation to the messenger Pheidippides. This type of communication carried a huge risk. Let's just imagine for a moment what could have happened to the runner and his messages, going from the unlikely to the likely. Even as a professional runner, he could have had an accident on the long distance he covered, for example breaking a leg. Exhaustion death could also have occurred before the moment he delivered his last message. Calculable risks with a rather low probability, but within the realm of possibility. The fact that the Persians could have expected Athens to send a runner is more likely in comparison. They could have intercepted him and replaced him with a runner instructed by them with false messages. Alternatively, they could have captured Pheidippides and tortured him to find out what his mission was, and then forced him to deliver a different message. His death would also have been a possibility to disrupt or interrupt communication between Athens and Sparta. Not to mention the fact that the episode around Pheidippides is ultimately just a footnote in world history—from today's perspective, it is hard to imagine how the course of history would have developed if Athens had not been victorious. Perhaps the entire history of democracy would not have existed. How different our world would look today—and all because of the fate of a runner. This thought experiment shows the importance and far-reaching implications of secure communication. We will also see how closely this complex of topics is linked to the two techniques of camouflage and deception. These are two topics that also play a role in Sun Tzu—but secure communication does not appear in *The Art of War* in this way. Therefore, the historical development of steganography and cryptography, which are of essential importance for the digital age, will be traced here using the most important stages.

Hidden Messages: The Invention of Steganography

Let's therefore look at historical events from a slightly different perspective. Purely from a communicative point of view, the run from Marathon to Sparta, or from Sparta to Athens, was nothing more than the unencrypted transmission of a message. So let's ask ourselves on this occasion what possibilities there would have been at that time to improve this communication situation. A common alternative technique that could have been used already existed in ancient Greece at that time. We are talking about steganography. The first part of the word, 'Stegano', is derived from the ancient Greek word στεγανός (steganós) for 'hidden' and the second part, 'Grafie', from γράφειν (gráphein) for 'writing'. So literally translated: hidden writing, or: writing that is hidden. Steganography is essentially a collection of techniques used to transmit hidden messages. One way this was done was as follows: A person, more precisely a slave, was taken and his head was shaved. Then the message to be transmitted was tattooed onto the scalp. Once the hair had grown back, the message was no longer visible, and the slave could deliver the hidden message. At that time, it is hard to imagine anything more harmless or less conspicuous than a row of slaves walking around in the area, dressed only in a loincloth. And even if they were apprehended and examined, no one would be able to discover the messages. However, once the prepared slave had arrived at the correct recipient, he knew what to do. The hair was simply shaved off again and the message was revealed.

The weaknesses of this technique are obvious. A slave can only be used once to transmit a message. Since a slave's life was worth nothing and they were available in large numbers, this was not an insurmountable problem. But of course, this circumstance did represent a certain limitation. Another problem is the factor of speed. If it was a matter of transmitting an urgent message, this technique was also not particularly suitable, because one had to wait until the hair had grown back. The volume of the message that could be transmitted was also limited by the area of the shaved head. Nevertheless, at that time it was a widely used and effective way to transmit hidden messages.

Certain forms of steganography exist to this day, and they are also frequently used in the digital transmission of secret messages. For example, digital images can be used to hide messages in them. Instead of tattooing messages onto the skin, the messages are imprinted at pixel level into the image data. This is also referred to as so-called "digital watermarks". These can be hidden in image data as well as in video and audio files or text documents. Anyone who knows where to look for them will also be able to bring these hidden messages back to light. Especially in the field of espionage, when it comes to smuggling information out of the country unnoticed, agents like to use such means. No one would think that a large amount of holiday photos on a traveller's hard drive could be something suspicious.

Around 500 BC, however, there were other techniques for transmitting secret messages. One of them is still very popular with children today and could be on the verge of an astonishing revival: the invisible magic ink.

In addition to many civilizational achievements, ancient Rome is also known for the countless conspiracies, murders, intrigues and comparable fraudulent activities. When it came to forging secret plans or informing someone about a planned action, they liked to use this technique from the field of steganography. All you needed was a lemon and a piece of paper, or parchment. Instead of using normal ink, the secret messages were simply written with lemon juice—the juice of onions, vinegar, milk or urine can also be used in this way. Once the juice has dried, nothing remains but a piece of blank paper. The writing remains hidden until the sheet is held over a candle, fire or other heat source. Nowadays, an iron also works. Only the heat makes the secret ink visible. Throughout history, many more invisible inks have been developed that could be made visible with the help of acid or UV light. Even though it is not a widely used method of transmitting messages today, there have been reports in recent years that intelligence agencies such as the Chinese are working on a new type of secret ink that can be made visible and invisible again with special chemical processes, but does not react to heat or UV light. An astonishing development, but one that makes sense. Especially in the digital age, such methods that are considered long forgotten or outdated can become interesting again. Because while all concentration is focused on the new, digital transmission paths, the old ones are forgotten and could be used unnoticed for this very reason. Simply because of the sheer amount of data, this focus has shifted. Today, information is practically hidden in the mass that is transmitted in gigabytes per second. In the case of the newly developed ink, however, a pack of paper tissues could become the carrier of secret messages and appear as inconspicuous as a few slaves on their way to the king two and a half thousand years ago.

The Holy Grail of Steganography

The ultimate goal of steganography is to transmit a message completely unnoticed. This desire has continually driven human ingenuity in the search for methods to transmit secret messages. In the Renaissance era, the polymath Giambattista della Porta (1535–1615) invented two different techniques for hiding information in eggs. He described the first method in his work "Magiae naturalis sive de miraculis rerum naturalium," published in 1558. It has since been proven that this method was indeed used by female spies at the time. The fact that it was unusual for women to be politically active at the time contributed to their disguise. However, the fact that they used something as inconspicuous and everyday as eggs for espionage purposes was downright ingenious. To hide messages in the eggs, they first had to be soaked in vinegar for several hours. This softens the shell and allows it to be carefully opened with a knife to insert a flat-folded paper into the egg's interior. The egg is then placed in cold water for a while, which hardens the shell again. Afterwards, it looks like an ordinary egg. If you put it in a basket next to many other eggs, it does not differ in any way from the others.

To ensure that the written message remains legible and is not smeared by the liquid egg white, the paper must be written with a special ink. Della Porta recommends iron gall ink, which has been in use since the 3rd century BC and is preferably used in conjunction with feathers. Della Porta describes the second technique in his work "De furtivis literarum notis" from 1563. This is much simpler and was therefore much more widespread at the time. The secret message is written directly on the shell of a boiled egg with a special ink made from a mixture of alum and vinegar. Afterwards, the still visible traces on the outside can be removed, leaving apparently nothing more than a boiled egg. However, when this is peeled, the egg reveals its secret, i.e., the message on the egg white.

Two aspects characterize "bio-steganography," making it so significant and virtually the holy grail of secret message transmission. Firstly, the fact that every egg looks like the other, regardless of whether it carries a secret message or not. The second special feature has to do with the integrity of the shell when the recipient receives the message egg. Because he can know without a doubt that the secret message was not intercepted and/or falsified. A similar function is performed digitally by the hash value or hash function. A unique numerical value is assigned to a specific file or information. The contents from a data set are first assigned to a key and then to a smaller hash value. While the key values can be different sizes, like the words "steganography," "art," and "spoon style," the hash values usually consist of a predetermined sequence of numbers like "01," "02," or "03." An algorithm, the so-called hash algorithm or hash function, determines exactly how the information is hashed (English "to hash" means "to chop up"). The hash value serves like a kind of fingerprint to either ensure the authenticity of a file or the identity of a sender. The hash values have another very practical function: they facilitate searching because they represent a representation of the contents. At the same time, the hash values do not allow any conclusions about the actual contents.

To this day, everyday objects are a popular means for agents to transport information and documents unnoticed from A to B. Just think of Edward Snowden, who made the NSA's surveillance activities public through data leaks in 2013. Snowden used a trick very similar to the manipulated eggs. In his memoirs, he tells how he smuggled the intelligence information past the security guards inside Rubik's Cubes. A few weeks before, he had given all his colleagues a Rubik's Cube, which were then seen everywhere and were among the most normal things the guards at the sluice saw every day. Snowden stored the stolen data on small micro-SD cards, which easily fit under the color stickers of the Rubik's Cubes. However, one cube looked just like the other from the outside. So Snowden managed to uncover one of the biggest surveillance scandals of our time with a centuries-old trick.

Throughout history, there have been many more ingenious inventions for transmitting messages in secret—double bottoms or hidden compartments in envelopes or packages, hollow heels in shoes, or microfilms. However, the methods for hiding messages have a serious problem: once it is known how the messages are hidden, the trick no longer works. Therefore, the history of secret communication techniques cannot be told without cryptography.

The Ancient Beginnings of Cryptography

The methods described so far belong to the series of methods that are assigned to steganography. As shown, being discovered is the greatest danger and also the most glaring weakness of this form of secret message transmission. But what if it was not a problem if the message was discovered because no one could read it? What if the shaved head read 'or the intercepted message in invisible ink only revealed: "Sieve soup only at the new moon for two weeks". With cryptic messages like these, we come to the story of another method with which sensitive messages are still securely transmitted today: cryptography. Cryptography also aims to hide something (the Greek word *kryptos* means "hidden"). In contrast to steganography, where the existence of the message itself is hidden, cryptography is about hiding the meaning of the message itself. While steganography is simply and plainly aimed at an effect, namely that outsiders should not even notice that two communication partners are communicating with each other, it does not matter in cryptography as long as someone listens or reads, as long as this person does not succeed in decrypting the actual message. The most exciting story and perhaps the most famous example outside the expert scene that can be told in this context is certainly that of the encryption machine called *Enigma,* which was used by the Nazis during World War II. To understand the encryption principle of the Enigma and to be able to classify the far-reaching significance of the history of decryption, we first look at the beginnings of cryptography. The history of encryption basically begins with the invention of writing. Even with the oldest writing cultures we know, the first attempts can be traced to hide meanings in texts or to decipher hidden meanings. Embedded in the religious-mystical context, for example, in the Kabbalistic tradition, we find the "Atbash method", which was used to try to read out hidden meanings from the sacred texts. The letters of the Hebrew alphabet were exchanged with each other according to a fixed system: the first with the last, the second with the penultimate, and so on. Hence the name of the method. The first letter is called "Aleph", the last "Taw", the second "Beth" and the penultimate "Shin". This game with the swapped letters was supposed to bring hidden meanings in the words to light. At the same time, this provided a method to hide the meaning in any text.

How this can be applied in practice can be illustrated if we briefly return to Pheidippides, the first marathon runner. Earlier, we used this figure as an opportunity to think about how he could have improved his communication situation. In addition to simply hiding his messages with the techniques of steganography, he could also have transmitted an encrypted message. The advantage: Even if he had been intercepted, no one but the recipient could have done anything with the message. Yes, not even he himself would have understood what the meaning of the message was that he was carrying.

In order to be able to classify the various cryptographic methods, it must first be established that there are basically two different ways to encrypt written messages: transposition and substitution. Let's first turn to transposition. In this form of encryption, the characters in a word or within a sentence are swapped according to a certain principle, so that the result in the end looks like a scrambled alphabet soup. Take the simple word *and,* then it can also be combined as follows: *dnu,dun,nud,ndu* and *udn.* The more characters or letters in the plaintext, the greater the number of permutations. To decrypt messages encrypted in this way, the sender and recipient must agree in advance on the procedure with which the plaintext is encrypted. A systematic transposition procedure is obtained, for example, by always swapping two consecutive letters with each other. The word *Transposition* then becomes *Rtnapssotioin*. There are no limits to creativity and the possibilities for variation are so great that in the end a result is on paper in which all the letters of the plaintext—i.e. the original message—are still present, but are nevertheless unreadable. Another method of transposition can be found in ancient Greece.

A few decades after Pheidippides had run to Sparta to ask the alliance partner for help in the war against the Persians, Athens and Sparta were at war with each other. The so-called Peloponnesian War, which lasted from 431 BC to 404 BC and ended with the victory of the Spartans, is also interesting for the history of cryptography. Because finds and reports by the Greek historian Plutarch show that the Spartans developed an encryption technique during this time and successfully used it in this war. This invention is considered the oldest military encryption procedure. Sender and recipient only needed a wooden stick, each with the same diameter, called a Skytale (from Greek *skytálē* for "stick" or "rod"). The message to be transmitted was written on a long leather strap or parchment. Whoever got it in their hands found only letters strung together that made no sense. However, anyone in possession of the corresponding stick could wrap the leather strap around it in a spiral, causing the letters to be arranged sensibly and the plaintext to gradually become readable.

Without technical assistance, such as we have today through modern computers, messages encrypted using transposition are very difficult to crack—although it is not impossible, as will be explained later. Especially at that time, they therefore represented a high degree of security.

During the Peloponnesian War, this very technique was used to transmit sensitive information. For example, when Persia was preparing an attack on Sparta and this was discovered by spies, they hastily sent five messengers with this message to Sparta to warn of the impending attack. The messengers even used another trick from the field of steganography and tied the leather straps with the writing facing inward as a belt around their stomach, so that it was not recognizable from the outside what they were carrying. According to legend, only one of the five messengers arrived and handed his belt to the Spartan general Lysander. After Lysander wrapped this around his skytale and thus learned of the impending attack, he was able to immediately initiate countermeasures, with which the Spartans actually managed to fend off Persia's attack.

The Caesar Shift

Let's now turn to the other category of cryptography: substitution. Literally translated, these are methods in which something is "replaced". Instead of rearranging the letters of the plaintext, completely different letters appear in the encrypted text. A simple way to achieve this would be to move one letter further in the alphabet. Instead of *und* (and), a text encrypted according to the principle of substitution would then read: *voe*. To demonstrate and understand how powerful this method of cryptography is, we must first jump back into history. More precisely, we stay in ancient Rome and dive into the world of the Gauls and Romans. One of the first substituting encryption techniques comes from none other than the Roman statesman and general Gaius Julius Caesar. Caesar was passionately interested in secret scripts and the encryption of messages and used them frequently. His motivation was clear: neither unauthorized third parties within the empire nor the enemy, in this case the Gauls, should be able to make sense of the messages. The so-called "Caesar cipher", "Caesar shift" or "Caesar encryption" was named after him, which the later Roman emperor used to communicate in encrypted messages with his generals. The Caesar shift is a comparatively simple encryption method in which all letters from the alphabet with which the plaintext is written (the so-called "plaintext alphabet") are replaced with letters from a new alphabet in which the secret text is written ("secret text alphabet"). Caesar, for example, used an alphabet in which all letters were shifted three places to the right. To illustrate this, both alphabets are first shown one above the other:

Plaintext Alphabet   a b c d e f g h i j k l m n o p q r s t
                        u v w x y z
Secret Text Alphabet   d e f g h i j k l m n o p q r s t u v w
                        x y z a b c

From *und* (and) becomes *xqg;* or from *Angriff am Morgen* (Attack in the morning) becomes *Dqkumii dp Prukhq*. Anyone who did not know the logic by which the letters of the plaintext were replaced had no way of reading the secret text. And even though it is possible to encrypt and decrypt messages without the use of technical devices, devices were developed over the centuries in which the Caesar shift was used that simplified the writing and reading of secret messages. The so-called cipher disk, which consisted of two rotatable disks, each with an alphabet engraved on it, greatly simplified the process.

Even though the Caesar shift was used successfully for a long time to encrypt messages, it is not a particularly secure cryptographic method. Once you have understood the mechanism, a maximum of 25 attempts are enough to crack the code. The Caesar shift is therefore no longer considered secure today. A computer would take less than a second to solve such a task.

But over time, this encryption method could be cracked with relatively simple means. Not only in modern times were newer and much more complex methods developed to encrypt texts. As mentioned, the Caesar shift can only create 25 secret text alphabets. It looks quite different when, instead of a linear shift, a secret text alphabet is generated by the random recombination of all letters.

Plaintext Alphabet: a b c d e f g h i j k l m n o p q r s t u v w x y z

Secret Text Alphabet: k c x e i o y z a n t l b m u d r w v f j p g h q s

An incredible number of 400,000,000,000,000,000,000,0 00,000,000 combinations of the letters of the alphabet are possible in this way. Only those in possession of the secret text alphabet are able to read texts encrypted with it. Caesar himself used secret text alphabets during the Gallic War, in which all letters of the plain text alphabet were replaced with those of another, namely the Greek one. Such encryption methods, as Caesar invented and used, like in this case the replacement of the letters of the plain text alphabet with the letters of another alphabet, are also called "algorithm". The "key", which is necessary for encrypting and decrypting messages, consists in the exact determination of how many places in the alphabet are shifted. When end-to-end encryption is mentioned today, for example in chat apps, this is exactly what is meant. Each participant has the key that can decrypt the messages that are sent. Anyone who would intercept them in the meantime could only read gibberish.

The tragic recent war between Russia and Ukraine shows how important encrypted messages are in the field of military communication. Again and again, reports are heard that Russian communication takes place over unencrypted channels and can simply be intercepted. Nowadays, it is even more difficult because a position determination can be carried out, which clearly exposes the sender. Such messages are therefore always to be viewed with reservation, as every war is always also an information war. The true backgrounds and facts are usually only revealed in the course of processing after a few years and sometimes even decades. Therefore, it is easier to use examples from further back in history, as these have already been analyzed several times. Current events are usually characterized by false information, deceptions, tricks, and also propaganda—so they should be enjoyed with great caution. Whether and what is true about reports should always be questioned. At the same time, the unencrypted communication could also be a deception maneuver, intended to deliberately transmit false information to the opposing side. Nevertheless, such statements from eyewitnesses are increasing, according to which the intercepted messages were actually used to locate the Russian attackers and specifically attack them. This example shows why successful generals like Caesar relied on encrypted message transmission. But history can teach us much more.

The Oriental Beginnings of Cryptoanalysis

The history of encryption could not be told without the history of decryption. Encryption and decryption are an eternal race. Sometimes one side is ahead and then the other. New methods and techniques are constantly being developed on both sides to gain an advantage again. Therefore, encryption or decryption according to "today's most modern technology" is only safe until this standard is cracked by the next technology and the other side is again improving. Let's therefore return briefly to the origin of encryption. Because Caesar's encryption marks nothing more and nothing less than just the starting point of a long development that lasted over many centuries and is still ongoing. A simple, deeply human motive drove the continuation of this story: the will to win or ultimately to survive. Because that's what Caesar's preference for encrypted messages was all about. The information advantage decides at least in war about victory and defeat or about life and death.

For a while, it seemed as if a fully randomized secret text alphabet had been found as a way to encrypt messages with a seemingly uncrackable system. However, encrypted messages have a very decisive disadvantage compared to messages hidden with steganographic methods: It is immediately obvious that they are encrypted texts. And long before there were high-performance computers that could be used to decrypt ciphers, clever minds set about decrypting secret scripts. And just at the moment when it was believed that a secure method had been found, a number of scholars from the Orient achieved the seemingly impossible. To understand how this happened—and how encrypted messages are cracked to this day—we need to take a trip to the heyday of Islamic-Arabic culture. The fact that cryptoanalysis was invented here is anything but a coincidence. Because during the caliphate of the Abbasids, which emerged around Baghdad around 750 AD and lasted until about 1250, the arts and culture, science and research, and religion flourished equally. Even though it is often and gladly forgotten, but the effects of this golden age of Arabic culture can still be traced in Western culture and history today. We owe many achievements and traditions in the field of medicine to this phase of Oriental history. The fact that we use the Arabic number system in mathematics, for example, and not the Roman one, has its historical reason here. Terms like algebra and the associated methods come from this time and the Arabic language. Also in many other areas, the traces lead here: We know the writings of Aristotle, for example, only because Arabic translators preserved and passed on his thoughts.

Texts were not only copied and stored in libraries, but also studied and scientifically analyzed. The emergence of cryptanalysis required the combination of several disciplines: mathematics, theology, and linguistics, that is, the scientific examination of texts, especially religious texts such as the Quran. The holy scripture of Islam is known to be based on the divine revelation received by the Prophet Mohammed. However, the suras and verses that make up the Quran are not arranged chronologically or by specific content, but are sorted by length, with the longest sura at the beginning. Scholars were interested in what God's statements were first communicated to the Prophet Mohammed. To find this out, they analyzed every word, indeed, every smallest sign and every letter as precisely as possible. They compared the text of the Quran with other statements and sayings that are handed down from Mohammed, and with other texts of different ages. They noticed, for example, that certain words appear more frequently in certain texts than others; that some terms were only invented or used at a later time; and they noticed that not all letters of the Arabic language are used equally frequently. With these clues, they tried to historicize the Quran (analysis of the temporal and content-related emergence) and to better understand the word of God. On the other hand, this created linguistic knowledge that enabled scholars to do completely different things. Among other things, they were able to assign certain styles to individual authors by analyzing personal linguistic preferences. At the same time, they laid the foundation for the decoding of encrypted texts. One of the oldest treatises on cryptanalysis comes from the theologian and philosopher Abu al-Kindi from the ninth century. In his *Treatise on the Deciphering of Cryptographic Messages*, one can find the basis of the so-called "statistical frequency analysis":

> "One way to decipher an encrypted message, provided we know its language, is to find another plaintext in the same language that is long enough to fill one or two pages, and then count how often each letter occurs. We call the most frequent letter the "first", the second most frequent the "second", the next the "third", and so on, until we have counted all the letters in the plaintext sample. Then we look at the secret text we want to decrypt, and also arrange its symbols. We find the most common symbol and give it the shape of the "first" letter of the plaintext sample, the second most common symbol becomes the "second" letter, the third most common the "third" letter, and so on, until we have assigned all the symbols of the cryptogram we want to decrypt in this way."

For statistical frequency analysis, we therefore need a sufficient amount of text—a circumstance that will later be of great importance in connection with the Enigma—we need to know in which language the plaintext is written, and we need a suitable reference text, through which we can determine how often certain letters occur. In the case of German, for example, the letter "e" is the most common, followed by "n", "i", and then "s". With this simple and elegant method, it was no longer necessary to try out 400 000 000 000 000 000 000 000 000 secret text alphabets until one had randomly found the right one. It was enough to analyze the frequency of the letters until one had deciphered a few of the encrypted words.

While the Islamic world was experiencing its golden age, the European continent was sinking into the Middle Ages. One does not have to look far for innovations in the field of cryptography and cryptanalysis. It was not until the Renaissance that interest in the topic of encryption revived. For at this time, numerous principalities and noble families were competing for power. The result was not only a lively exchange at the diplomatic level, but—as so often—power struggles, intrigues, and plots. It was therefore advisable to encrypt the messages that were carried from court to court or to other city-states. Of some significance in this context is the development of the cipher disk by Leon Battista Alberti, an Italian polymath who lived from 1404–1472. This is two metal disks, each with an alphabet or other symbols, which can be moved against each other. Depending on the position of the two disks, a combination of plaintext and secret text alphabet results. Alberti's invention made the encryption of messages much more practical, though not necessarily better.

Since this time, an increasing interest in cryptography can be observed. Just as the church also employed such people, cryptographic employees in the civil service soon became standard. However, as soon as cryptanalysis had found its way from the Arab world to Europe, the cryptographic arms race began. Alberti's invention merely marks the starting point of technical encryption and decryption, which was soon supplemented by methodological innovations. For in addition to the simple mechanics of the disks, only previously unusual signs and symbols on the side of the secret text alphabet were used as a novelty. But this development did not really counter the methods of statistical frequency analysis. This only changed when a few simple tricks were used to deceive the statisticians. For this purpose, random characters were simply inserted into the encrypted text, of which the recipient knew that they had no meaning. Someone who had intercepted the encrypted message and tried to decrypt it using frequency analysis had no idea which characters had meaning and which did not. It was also simple and effective to simply misspell words. This also made it more difficult for code breakers and decoders, because this also changed the frequencies.

In the coming centuries, cryptographers and cryptoanalysts engaged in battles worthy of a movie: The Vatican was undoubtedly the center of power at that time. It is no wonder, then, that interest in cryptography and cryptoanalysis was particularly high here. The Vatican quickly became a stronghold of cryptography and employed numerous cryptographers—foremost among them Giovanni Battista Argenti and Matteo Argenti, who were responsible for the development of secret codes in the papal service from 1585-1591 and 1591–1606 respectively. Their expertise during this time was unparalleled, and computer scientists, linguists, and historians are still working to decipher the immense volume of encrypted messages that began to pile up in the Vatican's secret archive (now known as the Vatican Apostolic Archive) since the 16th century. Above all, the papal correspondence and the so-called Nunciature dispatches (i.e., the "official news") were encrypted with the ciphers devised by the Albertis. To get an idea of what the documents in the Vatican's secret archives look like, here is the beginning of a letter that has already been deciphered:

72 40 16 26 22 50 40 26 44 40 92 36 40 26 22 14 26 36 62 12 46 22 44 40 72 30 18 44 52 40 50 28 72 36 62 32 82 92 14 72 22 72 32 22 62 42 82 34 22 30 72 16 34 92 20 26 22 18 26 66 28 30 92 44 40 26 30 72 22 26 72 24 92 42 26 52 20 28 44 72 52 44 36 64 40…

Such sequences of numbers sometimes extended over many pages. The Pope's cryptographers used several tricks to make deciphering the texts more difficult. For one, not all numbers represent plaintext characters. Some are simply there for filling purposes and to distort the statistics. On the other hand, common words like "and" or "the" were encrypted with several different numbers. And last but not least, a particular innovation makes cracking the codes a seemingly unsolvable task to this day.

Cipher vs. Code: The Secret Messages of the Popes

Even though much has changed over the centuries, one thing has always remained the same: The secrets of the popes are to be preserved particularly thoroughly. The introduction of codes was a bit more elaborate, but all the more effective. So far, we have been talking about encryption methods in which the plaintext is replaced with characters from a secret text alphabet. Apart from the trick just mentioned, where additional, meaningless characters are scattered into the text, the plaintext always has as many characters as the secret text. All these encryption systems are also called ciphers. However, texts can not only be encrypted by ciphering them, but also by coding them. Similar to the case of the two terms tactics and strategy, there is also a fundamental difference between code and cipher. Today, the terms cipher and code are often used synonymously—more precisely, the word code has replaced the cipher in many cases. The term cipher seems to have gone out of fashion in today's language and the more modern code has simply taken its place. After all, we also talk about "coding" when programming and about access code or passcode. Cryptoanalysts and hackers are sometimes colloquially referred to as code crackers.

However, when a word is coded in the original sense of the word meaning, it is replaced by something else: a code. The secret code therefore does not necessarily have the same number of characters as the plaintext in the end. The sender and receiver can, for example, agree that "A" stands for the word "taxi", "33" for "drive", "v1" for "Munich" and so on. The sentence "Drive the taxi to Munich" would be "33 with the A to v1" in secret code. If this sentence were encrypted, not only would statistical methods no longer lead to any meaningful result—even if the text were decrypted, one would not understand what it meant. Only someone in possession of a dictionary in which all coded terms are listed could decipher the actual meaning. The strengths and weaknesses of using codes are obvious. Only someone in possession of code tables or books in which all codes are listed would be able to fully understand the secret contents. Books or notes always carry the risk that they can be stolen, that they can be lost, burned or become unreadable for other reasons. At the same time, the method also has advantages because the number of characters used between plaintext and secret text changes through the use of codes. This makes it considerably more difficult to decrypt the secret texts through statistical frequency analysis.

Even when applied to the present day, it is worth considering the advantages and disadvantages of using codes. The risks associated with the use of books, tables or notebooks are the same as in earlier times. If only two people want to exchange ideas on a topic that is not too complex, they can also discuss codes with each other and simply remember them. However, human memory has its own pitfalls, so memory is not the best alternative. At the same time, the larger the network that wants to communicate using this method, the greater the risk of misunderstandings and other disruptions, or the secret codes leaking out through other channels. If this happens even once, all codes are useless and would have to be replaced with new ones. If the communication partners are spatially separated, this can take a considerable amount of time until a new secret communication channel is established. With paper-based data carriers like books, the amount of codes stored there quickly affects the volume and weight. And even the digital storage of code books does not solve all problems. Digital code books can be hacked and compromised or lost in other ways. Therefore, it is not surprising if this method is rarely or at least very rarely used today. The use of code books has been declining since the 16th century.

In connection with the decryption of the Enigma encryption, it will become clear once again why the use of code books has not become widely established. How important sufficient encryption is and what happens when one is too sure that no one is reading the secret messages is hardly as impressively demonstrated as by the fate of Mary Stuart.

Politicians Beware: The Drama of Mary Stuart's Encrypted Letters

One thing the historical development described so far has made clear: The need for truly secure encryption .continued to increase. State secrets, military actions, but also plots and sometimes state-bearing intrigues were transmitted and carried out using encrypted messages. The tragic story of Mary Stuart also illustrates how encrypted messages can be a matter of life and death.

For all those who can't remember their school lessons or Friedrich Schiller's play *Mary Stuart*, here's a brief flashback to her fate: Without exaggeration, it can be said that Mary was a dazzling figure. No wonder that several plays about her drama-filled life were created. Not only was she said to have stunning beauty, but she was also considered to be multi-talented and extremely intelligent. A few weeks after her birth, she lost her father, James V, the King of Scotland, and was crowned Queen of Scotland as Mary I in 1542 while still an infant. The struggle for power was always at the center of Mary's life. As a "child queen," she was taken to France, where she grew up alongside the heir apparent, Francis II, and was to become the Queen of France after their marriage. In this way, France and Scotland were to be united, which in turn was supposed to help Scotland in the power struggle with England. However, she was Queen of France for only about a year, as Francis died early at the age of 16, so she returned to Scotland as a widow in 1561. In the many years she had lived in France, not only had she changed, but Scotland had as well. While she clung to Catholicism more than ever, Protestantism was predominant in Scotland. At that time, there were mainly two ways to wage power struggles: war or strategic marriages. Personal emotions were often in conflict with power-political considerations. This conflict became world-famous in Shakespeare's *Romeo and Juliet*. Against this background, the numerous attempts to match Mary with one of the other surrounding royal houses or descendants from other noble families must be evaluated. All the more surprising was the hasty marriage between her and her cousin Henry Stuart, Lord Darnley, whom she apparently fell head over heels in love with. Mary quickly realized that Lord Darnley was an extremely brutal, jealous, and power-hungry character who was primarily interested in expanding his own sphere of influence. As soon as Darnley had Mary's private secretary murdered in front of her eyes because he feared they might be having an affair, Mary knew she had to get rid of Darnley. Although it is obvious, it is still not definitively clarified whether Mary was actively involved in a plot that subsequently unfolded. Because a number of Scottish nobles also wanted to get rid of Darnley and hatched a plan for an attack. Darnley narrowly escaped the bomb attack but was strangled by the conspirators while fleeing.

Mary's next marriage also failed spectacularly and completely turned the Scottish nobles against her. She ended up in prison and was forced to abdicate the throne to her son, who was born from her marriage to Lord Darnley. After a year in captivity, she escaped from prison, gathered an army of 6000 men behind her, and tried one last time to reclaim her throne. This attempt also failed miserably. Her only hope seemed to be her cousin, Elizabeth I, to whom she made her way. A fatal step. Elizabeth saw her primarily as one thing: a competitor. Mary was a descendant of the Tudor dynasty and therefore had a legitimate claim to the English throne. As a Catholic, she was also the secret favorite of the supporters of the Catholic Church in England, who anyway saw Elizabeth I as an illegitimate ruler because she was excommunicated by the Pope. Upon arriving in England, Mary ended up in prison again. Her involvement in the murder of Lord Darnley was given as a pretext, although it was clear that this was not the real reason.

As if all this were not enough, the truly tragic story only begins here. Because in captivity, Mary Stuart now tried everything in her power to get in contact with the outside world and regain her lost power. She writes letters to her son, who is now on the Scottish throne, but they never reach him. All her other letters, which she addressed to various recipients, were intercepted. Years passed. To be precise, Mary was in captivity for 18 years when she reached her lowest point and a state of absolute despair. Then the time seemed to have come for the tide to turn for her. Because interest in the famous prison inmate was also stirring in the outside world. A conspiracy, centered around Anthony Babington (1561–1586), also known as the Babington Plot, began to form with the aim of freeing Mary Stuart from prison, murdering Elizabeth, organizing a rebellion, and ultimately installing Mary as the rightful heir to the English throne. However, this plan was not to be implemented without Mary Stuart's consent. Therefore, they looked for a way to get in contact with her. But as she was heavily guarded as public enemy number one and cut off from the outside world, this was anything but easy. It must have seemed like a small miracle when one of the conspirators, Gilbert Gifford, arrived with a letter from Mary Stuart, in which she wrote that she had learned of Babington's plans and would like to exchange ideas with him. Thus, a secret communication channel was established between them. Knowing how sensitive the content they were exchanging was, they devised a secret code to encrypt their letters. The encryption method chosen by Mary Stuart and the conspirators around Babington is called a nomenclator. This is a system that consists of a combination of different encryption techniques. Mary Stuart's nomenclator consisted of a monoalphabetic secret script, but three letters were missing, a series of 35 coded terms (simple words like: "with", "is" and "there"), four meaningless characters that were only used for filling purposes, and a character that signaled double letters within a word. To anticipate: It was a remarkably weak encryption system that would not have posed a great challenge even for the first cryptoanalysts. A statistical probability analysis was sufficient to crack the secret text alphabet, and the code words were quickly guessed from the context.

What Maria and Babington did not know: The messenger who delivered their secret messages was a double agent. Although Gifford was officially also part of the conspirators around Babington, he was simultaneously working for Francis Walsingham, the Minister for State Security of Elizabeth I, who was known for his particularly cunning and thorough approach. Before Gifford brought the messages to Mary Stuart, they were decrypted by a cryptanalyst hired specifically for this purpose, copied, seemingly resealed with fake stamps, and forwarded to Mary Stuart. In this way, they collected incriminating information over many weeks. But instead of exposing the plot directly, the royal security officers continued to read along and waited to see what evidence they could extract from the correspondence. Because their goal was not only to uncover the conspiracy itself, but also to be able to prove in black and white Mary Stuart's complicity in the coup plans. She provided exactly this proof when she wrote in her letter of July 17 that she wanted to be freed from prison before the assassination of Elizabeth I. The danger was too great that she would be killed by the loyal guards while still in captivity.

In itself, this would have been enough to accuse Mary of high treason and sentence her to death. But even this was not enough for Walsingham. He wanted to find out the names of all the conspirators and therefore resorted to a trick. One of Walsingham's forgers used the nomenclator known to them and added a paragraph to Mary's letter at the end, in which Babington was asked for the names of all the conspirators. Allegedly, to be able to give him specific advice. In this way, it was possible to identify all the conspirators, prevent the assassination and the uprising, and charge Mary Stuart in court as an accomplice. Even though she denied any complicity, the judges came to the conclusion that she was part of the conspiracy and recommended the death penalty. Elizabeth I signed the verdict and on February 8, 1587, it was carried out and Mary Stuart was publicly beheaded.

The cardinal mistake that Mary Stuart made and had to pay for with her life: She felt too safe. She was absolutely convinced that no one could decipher her secret code. Let alone that someone was reading her messages and even adding text passages in her name. Today, such an instance is called a "man in the middle". The tragic story of Mary Stuart also impressively demonstrates how dangerous too weak encryption can be. Because opponents who can decrypt it can exploit it and use it as a weapon against oneself. Today, this would be even easier than 450 years ago. Because Walsingham still had to painstakingly forge Mary Stuart's handwriting. To intercept an email that is too weakly encrypted and add a few text passages to it, no great effort is needed today.

And even though questions of succession no longer play a decisive role in politics today and fortunately murders and other atrocities are no longer the order of the day, intrigues, conspiracies and plots are still part of the repertoire of political action. Characteristics such as party affiliation have taken the place of blood relationship, and someone can be politically sidelined without any bloodshed. Therefore, the lessons to be learned from the spectacular case of Mary Stuart should be known to contemporaries. It is more relevant than ever.

The Vigenère Encryption: In Search of the Indecipherable Cipher

At the latest after the tragic end of Mary Stuart, it was clear that there was an urgent need for a better encryption method. The greatest weakness of all cryptographic systems used up to that point was that they did not provide a sufficiently high security standard against statistical probability analysis. However, at this time, at the end of the 16th century, a French diplomat put together all the puzzle pieces that had gathered in cryptography up to this point and created one of the most significant encryption methods in the history of secret message transmission: the so-called Vigenère cipher. It was long considered absolutely uncrackable. Its name goes back to its inventor, the French diplomat and scholar Blaise de Vigenère, who lived from 1523 to 1596. One of his diplomatic missions took him to Rome for two years, where he came into contact with the thoughts and writings of the cryptographers from the Renaissance mentioned above in the vicinity of the Vatican. He studied, among other things, the writings and inventions of Leon Battista Alberti and Giambattista della Porta. These fascinated him, and since he was aware of the importance of secure encryption as a diplomat, he dedicated all his effort to developing a system that would offer a strength never seen before. A cryptographic standard work of this time provided the decisive inspiration for his system. In the *Six Books on Polygraphy* by the German Benedictine abbot Johannes Trithemius (1462–1516), a "polyalphabetic" substitution method was described for the first time, in which several alphabets were used compared to "monoalphabetic" methods (gr. *polys* = much, several). Vigenère picked up on this idea and developed it further. One of the basic principles on which the Vigenère encryption is based works similarly to the Caesar cipher—except for the fact that it has a much greater complexity. Instead of using just one alphabet, up to 26 ciphertext alphabets are used in the Vigenère encryption. Each alphabet is shifted one place to the right compared to the previous one. So for each individual letter of the plaintext alphabet, there are 26 different letters from the ciphertext alphabets available. The trick of the Vigenère cipher now consists in the following twist: How many of the 26 alphabets are actually used for encryption depends on a code word that must be agreed upon between the sender and receiver. We use such a code word in a similar function today, for example, when we use a password to encrypt a WLAN. The code word, also referred to as a "key", is selected in the case of the Vigenère cipher using the "Vigenère square". This consists of a table that represents all available ciphertext alphabets:

		Plaintext Alphabet
		A B C D E F G H I J K L M N O P Q R S T U V W X Y Z
Key		Ciphertext Alphabets
1	A	A B C D E F G H I J K L M N O P Q R S T U V W X Y Z
2	B	B C D E F G H I J K L M N O P Q R S T U V W X Y Z A
3	C	C D E F G H I J K L M N O P Q R S T U V W X Y Z A B
4	D	D E F G H I J K L M N O P Q R S T U V W X Y Z A B C
5	E	E F G H I J K L M N O P Q R S T U V W X Y Z A B C D
6	F	F G H I J K L M N O P Q R S T U V W X Y Z A B C D E
7	G	G H I J K L M N O P Q R S T U V W X Y Z A B C D E F
8	H	H I J K L M N O P Q R S T U V W X Y Z A B C D E F G
9	I	I J K L M N O P Q R S T U V W X Y Z A B C D E F G H
10	J	J K L M N O P Q R S T U V W X Y Z A B C D E F G H I
11	K	K L M N O P Q R S T U V W X Y Z A B C D E F G H I J
12	L	L M N O P Q R S T U V W X Y Z A B C D E F G H I J K
13	M	M N O P Q R S T U V W X Y Z A B C D E F G H I J K L
14	N	N O P Q R S T U V W X Y Z A B C D E F G H I J K L M
15	O	O P Q R S T U V W X Y Z A B C D E F G H I J K L M N
16	P	P Q R S T U V W X Y Z A B C D E F G H I J K L M N O
17	Q	Q R S T U V W X Y Z A B C D E F G H I J K L M N O P
18	R	R S T U V W X Y Z A B C D E F G H I J K L M N O P Q
19	S	S T U V W X Y Z A B C D E F G H I J K L M N O P Q R
20	T	T U V W X Y Z A B C D E F G H I J K L M N O P Q R S
21	U	U V W X Y Z A B C D E F G H I J K L M N O P Q R S T
22	V	V W X Y Z A B C D E F G H I J K L M N O P Q R S T U
23	W	W X Y Z A B C D E F G H I J K L M N O P Q R S T U V
24	X	X Y Z A B C D E F G H I J K L M N O P Q R S T U V W
25	Y	Y Z A B C D E F G H I J K L M N O P Q R S T U V W X
26	Z	Z A B C D E F G H I J K L M N O P Q R S T U V W X Y

At the Transition to Modernity: How Ancient Algorithms Became Modern Encryption Technology Through Mechanics

With stronger encryption, one primarily gains one thing: more time. Because it simply requires a certain effort to find out which method a message is encrypted with and how to crack it accordingly. The faster the transmission medium becomes and the faster a piece of information becomes obsolete, the more important this time advantage gained through encryption becomes. This fact became abundantly clear when two technical innovations revolutionized communication at the end of the 18th and beginning of the 19th century: first the invention of telegraphy and shortly thereafter the electromagnetic transmission of signals, the Morse code. The system invented by Samuel Morse and his colleagues is essentially nothing more than the transmission of the alphabet into electrical signals, which were ultimately reproduced acoustically. In Europe, the Morse method became the standard in 1851 and was soon used to spread messages in no time. The telegraph network also brought immense advantages in the field of trade, as it greatly facilitated the maintenance of business relationships over long distances. However, the system had a glaring weakness: to transmit a message, it had to be handed over to a telegraph operator who converted it and transmitted it over the network. This detour naturally poses a security problem, as the telegraph operators automatically read all the messages they transmitted. They could go to competitors with this valuable information, blackmail others with private secrets, or sell to spies from enemy states. By this point at the latest, the Vigenère encryption became the standard in business

communication. But—without going into detail here—
the Vigenère cipher was soon cracked. The British mathematician Charles Babbage, who first had the idea for a
programmable mechanical computer, found a system in
1854 that made it possible to extract the key from a text
encrypted with the Vigenère method.

In addition to the electronic transmission of signals, the
development of mechanical devices in particular shaped
the ongoing competition between cryptography and
cryptanalysis. The next milestone in the history of cryptography takes us to the USA. More precisely to Thomas
Jefferson, one of the founding fathers of the United States
of America. During this hot phase, all participants were
aware that something truly significant was at stake: the
founding of a state. This not only aroused enthusiasm, but
also many enemies. Jefferson knew that it was important
to keep certain information secret. He was therefore passionately interested in encryption methods and invented
the Jefferson wheel named after him. This is a device
that takes the idea of Caesar's shift to a completely new
level. For encryption and decryption, a mechanical device
is needed, consisting of a rod and a series of disks. Both
the sender and the receiver had to first be in possession
of such a wheel, secondly know in which order the disks
were to be arranged on the rod and by how many places
the respective disk had to be shifted so that the plain text
appeared again. However, Thomas Jefferson never actually used the cipher wheel he devised. It was not until
the period before and during World War II that the US
Army used a mechanical cipher machine, called M-94,
which implemented this principle. The key procedure was
changed daily to provide an additional measure of security.

The great advantage of mechanical encryption was
its practicality. With a cipher machine, messages can
be encrypted and decrypted very quickly. In the early

modern period, which was characterized above all by increasing speed in all areas of life, this was precisely the decisive advantage that decided victory or defeat in warfare. The real progress, which we will now encounter with the Enigma, consists in a combination of electronic and mechanical encryption. In addition, operating the Enigma was extremely simple—even though its encryption method was extremely complex.

The Enigma Principle and the Endless Race Against Time

In essence, the cyber war has already begun. Without the public taking much notice or much of the activities becoming public, numerous states launch thousands of attacks and defensive actions every day. There is a good reason why we learn so little about this war. Because for the committed hackers and state cyber warriors, it is essential that their actions do not become publicly known. Why this is so, I will explain in the following using one of the most exciting episodes that occurred during World War II. It's all about the infamous Enigma—a rotor cipher machine that the Nazis used to encrypt their communications during the second world war.

Since the Enigma is historically exceptionally significant, I would like to delve a little into the technical details to explain how the Enigma worked. The Enigma is an electromechanical cipher machine, in which both mechanical components and a battery-powered electronic switching mechanism ensure that the plaintext is encrypted. With it, all radio messages were encrypted that the Germans used for secret communication during the Second World War. At first glance, an Enigma looks like a typewriter that has an additional field in addition to the keys. On it, all the letters can be seen again, which can light up through a lamp located underneath. To understand the functioning of the Enigma, one must look more closely at three different mechanisms: the keyboard, the electronic wiring (plugboard), and the rotor system. Let's start with the rotors, which are sometimes also called rotors. These are located inside the machine and can only be seen through a small window on the top. The rotors are responsible for swapping the letters according to a variable principle. Each wheel has 26 numbers—each number stands for a letter of the alphabet. Once a rotor has rotated around its own axis, a small notch takes the subsequent wheel with it and brings it into a new position. Inside each rotor, there is also wiring that ensures that the letters are swapped with each other. An electronic signal that arrives at the "1", i.e., the "A", leaves the rotor at another point, perhaps at the "19", i.e., the "S". With each input on the keyboard, the three rotors rotate one after the other and at different speeds. Even simple words like "Anna", which would be "Dqqd" after the Caesar shift and leaves the double letters in the middle recognizable, have no similarity in structure to the original word after encryption with the Enigma. Not only that. Even if the same word appears several times in the sentence, it would look completely different at different points in the sentence thanks to the rotor system. A letter that is encrypted using the rotor system changes seven times on its way through the rotors. The "A" could become a "Y" on its way through the first rotor, a "Z" at the second rotor, a "T" at the third. At the end of the third rotor, there is a reflector where the signal is redirected, changed, and sent back through all the rotors. It could change from a "T" to an "R", then to a "K", which becomes a "B" again and finally a "Q". Immediately after a letter has been changed by the rotor system, the first rotor rotates one position further with the input of the next letter. If the next letter were again an "A", a different letter would come out at the end than the first time.

Let's move on to the next system, the electronic switching mechanism. After the electronic signal has wandered through the rotors and has already been changed several times there, it reaches an electronic switch system. There is a plug-in place for each letter, which looks and works similarly to a socket. Any letter can be converted into any other here by plugging a cable, which has a plug at both ends, into the designated plug-in slots. However, not all letters are changed here. Up to 13 pairs of letters are swapped again in this way. However, it should be noted here that the plugboard did not really increase the security of the Enigma. After "the bomb", which we will go into in great detail shortly, had cracked the encryption, the plugboard problem was only a minor brake. Finally, there is the keyboard, which sets the whole electromechanical procedure in motion. Each press of a key triggers both a mechanical movement—the rotors are rotated further via a rocker on which the keyboard sits—and at the same time closes an electrical circuit in which the pressed letter is variably changed between seven and nine times. The exact number of changes depends on the wiring of the switching mechanism. That's the basic principle. To make things even more complicated, there was not just one model of the Enigma, but a total of 17 different ones. Four different models were used by the navy, one for communication between allied states, another one by the secret service, and so on. In total, the German military had 30,000 Enigmas at the start of the war, thus having the most secure communication system in the world at that time.

To operate an Enigma, officers needed several pieces of information to set the machines to the correct starting position. Each Enigma machine had a total of five rotors. The first step was to select three of them. In a second step, these three rotors had to be inserted in the correct order. In a third step, the three—in later versions of the Enigma there were four or five—rotors had to be set to a specific initial value, i.e., a number between 1 and 26. In the fourth and final step, the number of plugs for the electronic switching system had to be determined and the connection between the pairs of letters established. From these four variables alone, there are 16,900 rotor positions and 150,738,274,937,250 different possibilities for the plug connections. In total, there are 10^{23} possibilities, or to be precise: 103,325,660,891,587,134,000,000 different keys, which corresponds to a key length of 76 bits. For comparison: AES encryption, the currently safest standard for data encryption, is based on a key length of 256 bits. At that time, the Enigma's encryption method was considered extremely secure, if not unbreakable for the time. And as if that wasn't enough, these key settings changed every day. For each machine, there were key tables or key instructions in the form of a book, also referred to as a code book. The responsible officers always carried these top-secret documents with them to extract the information for the respective day. The importance of both can also be seen from the fact that there were strict regulations for handling the Enigma and its code books. From the very beginning of the war, both the Enigma machine and the code books were considered confidential and should not fall into the hands of the enemy. Therefore, the Enigma machine and the key procedures had to be destroyed in the event of a serious attack, for example on a warship. As soon as it was hit and there was a chance that it would sink or the crew would be captured, the Enigma machine and the instructions had to be destroyed or thrown overboard immediately. This is also why, under the so-called Rainbow Order, 222 submarines sank themselves in Gelting Bay at the end of the war.

Given such efforts made by the Germans to secure their communication, it is understandable that they felt very safe. However, since the 1970s we know that this was not the case. Because the Allies—led by the British—were listening in. How did this happen? Given the description of how the Enigma encrypts messages, it is clear that it is not easy to crack the Enigma's code.

Anyone who had no information about the functioning of the Enigma and only received the radio messages encrypted with it would face a gigantic puzzle. A trained cryptanalyst would of course first check whether he could make progress with the so far very effective tool of statistical probability analysis. We have already learned above that certain basic conditions must be met for this. First and foremost, a sufficiently long ciphertext must be available in order to arrive at meaningful statistical statements at all. The Nazis knew this and had limited the number of characters per radio message to a maximum of 250 characters. Individual radio messages encrypted with Enigma machines have not been cracked to this day, which shows how good the Enigma system is. Even successful attempts often took weeks or months, which on the one hand shows how strong the encryption by the Enigma actually is, and that it still fulfills its central goal of gaining time. Because what use is a decrypted radio message about the exact position of a submarine if the information is several weeks old.

Now that the operating principle of the Enigma has been outlined in broad terms, the exciting question arises: How was it possible to crack such a sophisticated encryption system at all? The explanation alone reads like a thriller.

Since the First World War, the British had an intelligence department that was very much in the tradition of the Black Chambers. In the so-called Room 40, the world's best codebreakers were engaged in deciphering secret messages. However, since 1926, more and more radio messages were coming in that all their skills failed to decipher. The first Enigmas had been put into operation. The intelligence services of other nations also failed to crack the Enigma encryption. The Allies would have had no chance of deciphering even a single German radio message if it hadn't been for a fortunate chain of several events. Let's first remember the last chapter of the *Art of War* and the importance of spies, double agents, and in this case, their counterparts: the traitors. The former military employee Hans-Thilo Schmidt sold the first information about the Enigma to a French agent for 10,000 Deutsche Marks, thus giving the Allies their first clue as to how the radio messages were encrypted. It was only two pages from the instruction manual of the cipher machine, so much was still unclear. But gradually, Schmidt provided enough information for the Allies to make a first replica of the Enigma. An essential building block for deciphering the messages, which must be entered into an Enigma to make them readable again. Now it was up to the Polish intelligence service to take the first important steps in deciphering the Enigma. Poland had a keen interest in being able to read German radio traffic, as they knew they were in a particularly threatening situation. They were virtually encircled: on one side the Germans, who wanted their territories back that they had to cede to Poland after the First World War. On the other side Russia with its ambition to spread communism to the neighboring countries. However, Poland wanted to maintain its sovereignty at all costs. Accordingly, the Poles did everything in their power to crack the Enigma. This circumstance led to the

Poles initiating a paradigm shift in cryptoanalysis. The most successful codebreakers in the preceding centuries always dealt with language. Statistical peculiarities, conspicuous word forms, random guessing of words, and so on—all these methods attacked the encrypted messages at the level of language. The Poles quickly realized that this approach was pointless with the Enigma. Therefore, they decided to rely on scientists and mathematicians to solve the problem in this case. Thus, the task of codebreaking shifted from linguists to mathematicians. As luck would have it, they recruited the statistician Marian Rejewski (1905–1980). It would later turn out that he laid the foundations for deciphering the Enigma. His attack method was as simple as it was ingenious and exploited one of the weaknesses in the Germans' handling of the Enigma. Because at the beginning of each radio message, a so-called message key was transmitted. The message key consisted of twice three letters, which stand for a rotor position. For example: TBJTBJ. These first six characters were encrypted with the daily key. The rest of the message was encrypted with the rotor starting position TBJ. Repetitions are generally considered the enemy of secrecy. Rejewski exploited exactly this in his attack method. He analyzed dozens of intercepted messages every day and gradually got a picture of how the Enigma encrypted two identical letters each time. It took Rejewski about a year to develop a system (also called a bomb) that eventually allowed him to derive the daily keys from the radio messages and thus crack the Enigma encryption. However, the Poles achieved all this before the outbreak of the war. They monitored radio traffic for many years until the Germans increased the difficulty level of the Enigma in preparation for the war. Instead of the three rotors used until 1938, there were now five rotors to choose from. The number of plug connections also increased from six to ten.

Rejewski's bombs failed and he had to watch helplessly as Hitler organized the blitzkrieg and attacked Poland. The use of the Enigma was the key that made the lightning-fast attack possible. Because only the fast and secure coordination of all forces deployed made the military success possible. It is thanks to the intuition of the Polish head of the cipher office, Gwido Langer, that the groundbreaking findings did not get lost in the course of the German attack. A few months before the attack, he invited a number of French and British diplomats and cryptoanalysts to Warsaw and initiated them into their secret achievements. Since it was already suspected at this time that Poland was in danger, it was decided to hand over the replicas of the Enigma and Rejewski's bombs to the Allies. Just two weeks before the start of the war, these made their way to Paris and London via convoluted routes.

The importance of Poland's cryptanalysts cannot be overstated. It primarily consisted of shattering the reputation of Enigma as the perfect encryption machine. Without the successes of the Poles in cracking the Enigma, the Allied forces would probably never have attempted to continue decrypting German radio messages during the course of the war. Also, the realization that not necessarily linguists, but primarily mathematicians should work on the decryption of the Enigma, was invaluable. In the case of Great Britain, this meant that instead of continuing to decipher messages in London's Room 40, a new department was established to crack the Enigma. The newly recruited cryptanalysts worked from then on in Bletchley Park in Buckinghamshire, the headquarters of the Government Code and Cypher School (GC&CS). A major advantage over Room 40 was that there was more space for the new employees. And this was urgently needed. Because German radio traffic exploded from two million transmitted words per month to two million words per day. And so the number of employees also grew from initially 200 to over 7000. This large number of people was necessary primarily because speed was of the essence. The daily key changed at midnight. If it had not been cracked by this time, the work had to start anew. The cryptanalysts in Bletchley quickly learned to adapt Rejewski's bomb so that it could also break the encryption, which was now ten times as heavy. During the first years of the war, the British gained numerous strategic advantages in this way. Sometimes the German Enigma cipher operators made their work particularly easy. Out of laziness to think of a complicated daily key, they simply took three letters that were next to each other. Therefore, the cryptanalysts always first went through these simple message keys and often had success with it. Also, the people responsible for creating the key book did not always approach the task with the greatest imagination. Instead of constantly rearranging the wheel combination unpredictably by random principle, they sometimes used simple variations, making the life of the cryptanalysts easier. However, these human errors on the part of the Germans should not obscure the great effort and drama that took place on the side of the Allies.

One name in particular is associated with the decryption of the Enigma: that of the mathematician Alan Turing (1912–1954). His task in Bletchley was, among other things, to consider what would happen if the Germans no longer transmitted the daily key twice at the beginning of the message as they had been doing, but only once. They wanted to be prepared for this moment, because it was clear that they would then be completely in the dark again, as all previously used attack methods like the bombs would be useless. Therefore, Turing began to take a closer look at all previously decrypted radio messages. He noticed a peculiarity. Every day there was always a radio message at the same time, in which the current day's weather was transmitted. Since they could rely on the thoroughness and order of the German army, it could also be assumed in the future that the word "weather" would be included in the radio message transmitted shortly after six o'clock in the morning. Since all weather reports were similarly structured, they could even roughly know where in the sentence the word was. However, this insight was only a small starting point and not the key to a solution. Because unlike Rejewski, a general statement about the wheel positions could not be derived from a single word. It would only remain to repeatedly enter the word "weather" into an Enigma machine and change the settings by one detail each time until the correct setting of all elements had been found. To be precise, 159,000,000,000,000,000,000 possible settings would have to be tried out. The exact description of Turing's solution to this seemingly insoluble task would take up many pages of a book. His attack method was a further development of Rejewski's method and would not have been possible without his insights. It ultimately consisted of linking several Enigma machines together and connecting them via a complex circuit. In this way, he was able to drastically reduce the number of possible settings. The machine that was built according to his considerations was huge and measured two by two meters. It was also called the Turing Bomb in reference to Rejewski. Now events came to a head. Because at the point when the Germans actually started to transmit the message key only once at the beginning, on May 10, 1940, work on the Turing machine had already progressed so far that the first prototype was soon to be delivered. Just four days later, on May 14, the bomb named Victory arrived in Bletchley. The first results were a great disappointment. It took up to a week for the bomb to find a key message. So the work on the machine had to be continued under high pressure. It took a whole four months until the new, revised model was manufactured. One can imagine the disappointment among the cryptanalysts, who had played a central role in British warfare up to this point. They hardly managed to decrypt a message anymore and morale had reached a low point. When the new bomb was delivered—it was called Agnus Dei—the expectation was correspondingly high. And it worked. By the end of 1942, 49 Turing Bombs were in operation.

Despite all the success of the Turing machines and all the decrypted radio messages, it was always necessary to know at least one word and its position in the radio message. Without such a starting point, one was lost. In addition, there were certain areas within the German military that took additional security measures against which even the Turing bombs could do nothing. This was nowhere more evident than in the Battle of the Atlantic. In the submarines of the German navy, Enigmas were used that could choose from a total of eight rotors. Moreover, they were so cautious here that there were hardly any human errors as in other areas. The Enigma cipher operators, for example, meticulously ensured that there were no repetitions. This caution paid off: For a long time, it seemed as if the Germans could win the battle in the Atlantic and possibly even the war. All the more, the efforts of the Allies, and especially the British, were focused on gaining the upper hand here. It was clear that the cryptanalysts in Bletchley had no chance of cracking the radio messages of the submarine fleet without further help. The seemingly only way out was therefore to get hold of the German key books. There were numerous plans to steal or otherwise obtain one of these valuable documents. Despite great efforts, many of these attempts failed, until finally a few daring raids on submarines and smaller German weather observation ships were successful. In this way, they were repeatedly supplied with daily keys for a few months and could slowly achieve military successes in the Battle of the Atlantic.

However, the utmost caution had to be exercised, and this brings us to the second and for the context of this book decisive aspect in the decryption of the Enigma. Because the enormous effort that was made in Bletchley, and also its successes, must under no circumstances become public. Not even Alan Turing's parents knew that he was working as a cryptanalyst—even considered a genius in those circles—and they were always worried about his private and professional career. However, strict secrecy was absolutely necessary. As soon as the German military leadership would have had the slightest suspicion that the Enigma encryption might no longer be secure, all efforts and struggles would have been in vain. Therefore, it was crucial that the insights gained about the tactics of the Germans in the Atlantic in Bletchley did not lead to a series of obvious victories by the Allies. In every single case where decrypted information was used, a deception maneuver had to be devised first, which would explain to the Germans why they had suffered a defeat in this particular case. This was done, for example, by first sending reconnaissance aircraft to a position where it was known that German warships were located. Only then was an attack carried out. Alleged submarine sightings were also faked and sent as radio messages into the ether.

However, one maneuver failed in such a deception attempt. Through a decrypted radio message, they knew of nine German supply ships and their exact position. Since their destruction promised a great advantage, the allied military leadership agreed to attack the group, but not to sink all of them—the two ships *Gadania* and the *Gonzenheim* were to be spared. It was assumed that too much success would arouse suspicion on the German side.

With this assumption, the Allies were right. Because in the heat of battle, the officers on the destroyers of the Royal Navy decided that it was their duty not to let this opportunity pass and to attack and sink all boats. In fact, an investigation of this incident was initiated in Berlin, also with the aim of finding out whether the Enigma could have been decrypted. The investigation report speculated that there could be an English spy who had infiltrated the German navy and could have betrayed the position of the supply ships. Pure luck on the part of the enemy was also considered as another possibility. However, the case that the Enigma could have been cracked was ruled out as impossible. The Germans assumed until the end of the war that the Enigma code had not been cracked. Even after the war, the British kept their abilities to themselves and used them for their own purposes. They distributed numerous Enigma machines, captured from the German war loser, in their former colonies. Of course, they let the new users believe that it was the most secure communication system in the world and listened to their message traffic for many years. The many men and women who fought in their own way for the victory of the Allies in Bletchley, contributed significantly to shortening the war and saved countless lives, were dismissed after the end of the war and received no military or societal honor. Only in the 1970s, when the Commonwealth countries no longer used the Enigma for communication, did the British government and its secret service agree to reveal the secret of the decryption of the Enigma. However, the secrecy of achievements in the field of cryptanalysis is one of the most important lessons that can be drawn from the history of the decryption of the Enigma, in my opinion.

A Different Story of Cryptocurrencies

Let's now look from this perspective at a part of our post-modern world, where cryptography plays a major role. Because today, cryptographic techniques have a significance that goes far beyond the realm of military and intelligence communication. Starting with (ideally) encrypted WLAN networks to eavesdrop-proof messenger services on the smartphone, cryptography has arrived in everyday life. Cryptography is even at the center of the money and banking system today. The fact that this is the case is solely due to the historical development of encryption techniques. It is the logic of outbidding that ultimately led to the fact that essential aspects of the monetary system, which were previously fulfilled by institutions, can be replaced by a technology. To understand this, we must briefly ask why money has value at all. A seemingly trivial question, but the answer is complex. Because strictly speaking, money in none of its forms has intrinsic value. The metal of coins is not proportional to their monetary value. The fact that we attach great importance to gold today, but no longer to shells or iron, shows that it is a societal consensus to understand gold as valuable. Printed paper in the case of banknotes is counterfeit-proof, but ultimately no value arises from it. The same applies to plastic cards with magnetic stripes and digital numbers on computer screens. So where does the value of money come from? As so often, it is mainly about power.

What has become money in the course of history often has cultural-historical origins and a lot to do with conventions. In early tribal history and antiquity, money usually developed from cultic and religious contexts. Certain objects such as shells or coins subsequently became circulating money as exchange objects. However, their value was always also tied back to the issuing bodies: the priest or the temple in which they were minted. Many centuries later, the modern money system began to emerge from the Renaissance onwards, in which primarily banks and states issued money and guaranteed the value of money. In this context, bookkeeping, i.e., the written records of who owns how much money or who owes how much money to whom, played a significant role. The banks guarantee that this information is really correct and is not falsified or passed on to unauthorized persons. In modern times, the state then took the money monopoly for itself. This means that the value of money is guaranteed by the state, but at the same time, all other forms of money are not accepted as money. This is also why the destruction of money is considered a crime in many countries.

However, the economic and currency crises that became increasingly frequent in the 20th century have caused cracks in the idea that the state is a truly reliable guarantor of the value of money. A key date in this context is 1971. In this year, US President Richard Nixon abolished the so-called "gold standard". Until this point, the value of coin and paper money was tied to the value of gold, i.e., fixed exchange rates between all currencies and gold. This dissolution led to a shock in monetary, economic, and foreign policy—also known as the "Nixon Shock". Moreover, this event led to a massive rethink that continues to this day. More and more people began to ask questions like: How safe is the money in banks really? Are banks irreplaceable in their function? Are there alternatives to the state money monopoly? The inventor or inventors of Bitcoin and other cryptocurrencies answered this question very clearly: Banks cannot be trusted and there are alternatives for the secure storage of information. These two assumptions are at the beginning of the invention of cryptocurrencies. As their name suggests, these are cryptographically secured currencies. An asymmetric encryption process generates a public and a private key for each user ("public key" and "private key"). However, these are not owned by an institution. The public key is publicly visible, as the name suggests, and serves like an address or IBAN number. The private key is exclusively owned by the owner and thus proves that he is the owner and grants him access to it. If it is lost, there is no telephone support that one could call and ask for help. The private key consists of a 256-bit number, which is usually represented as a series of 64 characters. It consists of letters from A-F and the digits 0-9. A fictional example of a private key could look like this: F14B2A2BC6D87F1BBA1A577 3A3C389FF453212201DA91F80BF66FCA43AB28900.

Anyone who has already had experience with the purchase and ownership of currencies like Bitcoin knows that there is another security measure that allows access or reconstruction of the private key. The so-called "seed phrase" consists of twelve terms. You should definitely remember this as well, as it is also not stored by anyone. This seed phrase is a representation of the private key that can be remembered much more easily by humans than a random sequence of 64 characters. This seed phrase therefore also secures the owners of cryptocurrencies access to their tokens and allows them to trade with them. The level of security that these twelve terms (with some cryptocurrencies there are even more) offer is considered uncrackable as of today. But if we have learned one thing from the history of cryptography, it is this: Especially when it comes to power and money, a lot of time and energy will be spent on cracking an encryption that is considered secure. In the case of Enigma, the construction of just one Turing bomb cost the British taxpayer 100,000 pounds. The story of the deciphering of the Enigma has also taught us that achievements in the field of cryptoanalysis are kept secret. So it would be anything but a matter of course that we would know if it were already possible to break this highest standard of current cryptography. If a state or a company already had a sufficiently powerful computer capable of cracking the current standard of cryptography, everything would be done to ensure that this information does not become public. This does not necessarily have to be a so-called quantum computer, although this is currently considered to have the best chances of solving this task according to the current state of technology.

At the same time, the probability of a fight against cryptocurrencies like Bitcoin is very high. Both a look at the present and a look at history can teach us how states react when their sovereignty over money is disputed. Let's first take today's China and analyze how the post-communist state has dealt with Bitcoin so far. After countless attempts to ban all cryptocurrencies in the country, China has launched its own digital central bank money. The Chinese leadership knows that controlling money means power and control at the same time. China's behavior seems to suggest that there would be nothing worse for states than if the currency were in the hands of the citizens. So when a state like El Salvador voluntarily chooses Bitcoin over the dollar, it shows the signal that was sent to the USA. Because never in history have states willingly and voluntarily given up power. This is also shown by the example of the Wörgler Schwundgeld. In the small Austrian town, an experiment was started during the economic crisis of 1929, which was reported in newspapers all over Europe at the time and secured the place a spot in the books of economists. Like many other regions, Wörgl also suffered from the effects of deflation. Unemployment was high, the city lacked tax revenue, and debt was growing. Even the bare necessities were lacking money. Anyone who still had money preferred to save it in the bank rather than spend it. That's when Mayor Michael Unterguggenberger had an idea. He remembered reading a text by Silvio Gesell (1862–1930), a follower of the free economy doctrine, in which he had learned about the idea of free money. He proposed to the community to conduct a money experiment. Unterguggenberger's proposal was simple: People either had no money or did not spend it. So the state simply had to give them money. However, he did not want to give the Wörglers conventional money, but free money or Schwundgeld. The so-called free money is a currency that aims to always be in circulation. So anyone who hoards free money has to live with it becoming less and less valuable—hence the name "Schwundgeld". In the case of the Wörgler Schilling, this was ensured with adhesive stamps that were stuck on the notes when they circulated. At the same time, the Schwundgeld also lives from being valid in a limited space. This is intended to stimulate the local economy. Free money is usually a currency that is used in parallel to the conventional currency. Even today, locally valid money can be found in some cities, usually called Taler. In Wörgl, tax debts could also be paid with the Schwundgeld, which led to more and more people and businesses accepting the Wörgler Schilling. The success of the experiment was so enormous that people were already talking about the "miracle of Wörgl" at the time. Because Wörgl experienced a small economic miracle: People spent the money, unemployment fell, and tax revenues rose sharply. Only when the Austrian National Bank heard about the money experiment, which had found numerous imitators in the meantime, did it see its power threatened. After Unterguggenberger did not comply with the National Bank's request to "stop the nonsense", he was sued. On November 18, 1933, the Austrian Administrative Court ended the experiment and ruled that the Schwundgeld violated the law. Does this story also cast a shadow on the young history of cryptocurrencies? These too have set out with the vision of giving citizens back some control over money and taking it away from state power. Cryptography plays a new, crucial role in this context, which also leaves the outcome of this experiment open.

Considerations like these certainly always leave us somewhat in the dark. Because every actor in this field must ask themselves whether it is worth investing large sums of money, time, and energy in the development of, for example, quantum computers. Even if these are currently still secret projects of the military and companies, there comes a point when it inevitably becomes known that the next development step in the field of cryptoanalysis has been reached. Conversely, however, this only means that the hot potato is back with the other side and it is only a matter of time before the next, even better encryption technique is introduced.

Outlook: An Arms Race Without End?

The history of encryption techniques shows that it is a race between cryptographers and cryptoanalysts or codebreakers. A result of this dynamic is a technological arms race that never ends. What began with Caesar hiding information about warfare led to the modern encryption of ciphers to the point where we stand today, when we encrypt and send or decrypt messages via computer or smartphone. The crucial question that arises when looking at the history of encryption is: Do we know where we stand in terms of encrypting and decrypting codes? If we know it and the currently used encryption technique is secure, we can confidently trust that our messages and information are safe. If we do not know it and someone has already managed to crack the code, for example with the help of a supercomputer, we should think about where and how we store and send information. The more our lives shift into the digital realm, the more important the answer to this question becomes. Because decrypting encoded data and information today has a significance that is still underestimated by many observers. Even though it is often read that data is the new oil, its actual value is still not properly tangible. In addition, the use of artificial intelligence or quantum cryptography opens up new possibilities, for example in the field of social engineering through so-called deep fakes. These are artificially created actors who appear as if they were real people. But viruses and trojans are also getting better and could make even the best encryption techniques insecure in the future. No matter at which point of the endless arms race we find ourselves today, it pays to always stay on the ball. Only because Alan Turing had dealt with the question many years in advance of how to crack the Enigma if the key phrases were no longer transmitted twice, the Allies were able to maintain their lead.

But before we can continue towards the present and future of cyber warfare, we have to go back to the Middle Ages. Because the history of steganography and cryptography has shown two things. On the one hand, the relevance of the past: Even the most modern encryption is based on the "old" principles such as those of transposition and substitution. And on the other hand, that the development of technologies plays a crucial role when it comes to new tactics and strategies. Therefore, the next chapter focuses on the history of technology.

3

Stuxnet and the Poisoned Well: What Connects the Middle Ages with the Cyber World

After the Chinese and ancient origins of classical warfare, as well as their development and relevance for the present time, were presented in the two preceding chapters, the following will deal with the war techniques and tactics of the Middle Ages. When one hears Middle Ages, most people think of knights, castles, and martial weapons. And all three examples can be used for today's analogy in cybersecurity. For example, the massive walls took over an important defensive function of medieval fortresses. Analogously, in the digital age, we use a firewall as one of the most important bastions of a system to keep attackers from the outside at bay. Such defensive structures were of course much more complex in the Middle Ages, and technical systems and IT networks usually have comprehensive protective measures. The crucial point, however, is that the similarities do not end with the metaphor of the wall. Rather, the principles, functionalities, and methods of the

© The Author(s), under exclusive license to Springer Fachmedien Wiesbaden GmbH, part of Springer Nature 2024
P. Kestner, *The Art of Cyber Warfare*,
https://doi.org/10.1007/978-3-658-43879-1_3

centuries-old facilities can be found in modern security architectures.

The castle as a symbol of medieval defense

Hardly anything is as symbolic of medieval defense as the castle. The medieval castles were the centers of power. And since even then a lot was fought over the five typical drivers of conflicts—power, fame, wealth, honor, and desire—that were introduced at the beginning, they had to be built particularly securely. Even before the first stone is placed on the other, security begins with the choice of location. And even then the rule was: location, location, location! An elevated location or an area crossed by a river offered, as Sun Tzu already knew, additional protection against attackers. If you look at the structure of castle complexes from a bird's eye view or in the form of floor plans, another peculiarity becomes apparent. If these are completely built structures that do not work with local conditions such as rivers or rocks as natural barriers, then they are centrally structured. That is, in the center are the castle and the associated buildings, towers, houses, and squares. Around this area to be protected, there are usually several closed protective walls, walls, moats, or other fortifications. These can be ring-shaped, circular, or even in the form of a citadel, i.e., as a regular polygon. The precursors for this basic form can be found, for example, in Jerusalem, which was already surrounded by a ring wall around 1400 BC. Since Jerusalem was attacked, besieged, destroyed, and rebuilt many times, one could write an entire book just about the development of the fortifications. For this context, it should suffice to note that the medieval builders, who were all familiar with the holy city and its buildings, found numerous suggestions here. The false, but widely spread prejudice of the "dark" Middle Ages led to the fact that the building forms of that time were underestimated for a long time. In particular, the building of castles in the Middle Ages was almost perfected. The solutions conceived at that time met the latest security standards of the time and therefore still serve as a model to some extent today. If you look at the security precautions taken around the Munich Oktoberfest, for example, you can easily find parallels to the structure of medieval castle complexes. For several years, the area around the Theresienwiese has been divided by the police into three, sometimes even five security zones, also called "security ring". In the outer ring, no cars are allowed, in the second zone the executives can check the identity of the visitors and only in the third zone have you finally arrived. Additional security is provided by a construction fence that is erected around the Wiesn during the construction phase. There was also discussion about building a bridge that would lead over the site. The security concept is discussed and adapted anew every year. The temporary concrete pillars were followed by 180 permanently installed, retractable high-security bollards, which can certainly be associated with drawbridges or fall gates. Such security rings or zones are also found in the cybersecurity area. Here too, there are usually three zones that are switched on before the sensitive, private area. The outermost area corresponds to the publicly accessible internet. The first security zone consists of the services or computers that can be reached from there. In the second security zone, the isolation layer—also called DMZ, i.e., demilitarized zone—there are numerous technical measures that restrict access possibilities. For example, by checking identities, which in the digital space is done by issuing and checking certificates, additional firewalls, or the use of wired network connections (LAN). Only in the inner zone are there sensitive data or applications like the crown jewels in the citadel.

The aforementioned DMZs are already found in fortresses in Arab territories or in Jerusalem. Facilities that had multiple rings used the space that arose in between as a defense zone. If the attackers advanced into this area, they could be attacked by the defenders from both sides. However, a direct comparison with Roman defense facilities makes clear how sophisticated medieval fortresses were. The Romans used simple wooden fences or comparable stake constructions to protect their marching camps. Permanently used fortresses, castles or other military locations were also fortified with stone walls from around 100 AD, but usually had a square basic shape. These comparatively simple walls can hardly compete with the finesse of medieval castles. Security considerations already played a role in the selection of the location. That's why castles are predominantly located on elevated spots in the landscape, which allowed a wide view and early identification of attackers. Around the castle, as already mentioned, were the ring-shaped defense facilities with walls, moats or defense mechanisms such as towers, drop gates or machicolations. Some things that might appear to an untrained eye as construction defects were deliberately designed that way: castle walls that are wider at the bottom and thinner towards the top, for example, have not sagged in one direction over the centuries like the Leaning Tower of Pisa, but were built that way. This design not only made it difficult for intruders to climb up, but also gave the walls a high stability. Castle walls are not only inclined, but often also curved. This was not due to the mead consumption of the builders of the time, but gave the walls elasticity. The damage that the impact of a ball has on a straight wall, like those with which the Roman castles were fortified, is much greater than with round and beveled walls. These absorb attacks with a battering ram or catapults much better. This is ensured not only by the curved design, but also by an additional built-in buffer zone. Castle walls often consist of two walls: a steep wall inside and one outside. In between is a buffer area that was filled with gravel. This also makes the wall construction overall elastic. If a ball hits it, the wall can give way, is not so quickly penetrable and does not collapse immediately. The deeper reason for the vaulted masonry is therefore the war tactics of the time.

Access to castles was also made difficult. One often enters and exits via drawbridges, passages protected by drop gates, or underground secret passages. The safer the architecture of the facilities became, the more creative attackers and spies had to become. Just think of the secret messages that can be hidden in eggs. Steganographic methods cannot be stopped by any heavy drop gate when something as inconspicuous as an egg is carried through in a basket. Even if it is not immediately evident at first glance: the supply of food represents a massive weakness for the defense of a castle. Again, it starts with the location: When it came to choosing the perfect location for a castle, not only the considerations that have a meaning in terms of defense should play a role. A good location for a castle is also characterized by the fact that the supply is secured. Although a castle located on the summit of a 5000 m high mountain would be very difficult to conquer—it would also be almost impossible to regularly supply oneself with water and food. The same applies to modern times: An independent power and water supply with necessary cooling or in case of fire can also greatly increase the security of technical systems. And although a mountain peak is not necessarily considered an advantageous location for data centers, one of the safest cloud data centers is located deep within a Swiss mountain massif in the canton of Uri. This is a repurposed and formerly top-secret military bunker that was used for air defense. A few details about the equipment: armored doors and locks, which are controlled by security personnel, keep unwanted visitors away, the servers are cooled by a natural water supply and an independent air supply protects against attacks with chemical or biological weapons.

If one had to imagine a medieval castle as an idealized image, it would be located on an island, surrounded by four towers representing an alarm system in all directions, and a drawbridge as the only access. In the center of the castle, the crown jewels would be located within a structure in the citadel. This is followed by a first inner ring and an outer ring, each consisting of double-walled castle walls. All these protective mechanisms would have to be overcome by attackers visible from afar to get to the king's treasure. A direct adoption of this idealized system can be found, for example, in the field of IT security. The so-called "crown jewel protection" refers to the measures taken to protect particularly sensitive data from hacker attacks. In this case, the crown jewels are the most valuable information a company or organization has—this can be customer data, but also trade secrets such as patents, strategic plans, or insights from research and development. If an IT system is structured like a medieval castle, such data is definitely not stored in the area of the first line of defense. These are all computers that are directly connected to the Internet and thus represent obvious targets for attack. Ideally, no sensitive data should be found in the area behind it, the so-called back-office network, which is used only for internal purposes. Similar to castles, there are also walls (firewalls) and something like watchtowers within IT systems (ideally). Be it with the help of technical systems that can detect attacks, and/or through the use of a security team—it is important to always keep an eye on current events and react immediately in case of emergency. Analogous to the drawbridge, there are technical possibilities to abruptly prevent access to systems from the outside, or for example through zero-trust policies (portcullises) to deny access to all those who cannot clearly identify themselves. In the past, the real crown jewels were stored in the citadel, a small, self-contained fortress. Today, server safes or HSMs (Hardware Security Modules) are used for this purpose, which are secured by both physical protection measures such as video surveillance, security personnel, isolated buildings, as well as software tools and IT systems, and a complex security architecture that manages and regulates access.

However, even in this case, one should not be tempted to give in to this image of the castle and the feeling of security it conveys. Because a look at history is enough to see how the tactics have changed parallel to the further development of the building forms. When steep castles with moats spread, a war tactic was necessary: the siege. With this new tactic, it was possible to bypass the strengths of the castle. Because at a certain point, people knew that they could not destroy the walls. But instead of trying to destroy the stone walls, they shot dead animals over them with catapults. In this way, plagues arose and spread within the castles, or they hit the well with some luck. Once the well was poisoned, they could interrupt the vital water supply and make the castle inhabitants open the gates to leave the castle in search of new supplies.

Stuxnet and a Lesson from the Middle Ages

One of the most significant, sophisticated, and at the same time one of the most elaborate cyber attacks in history to date was carried out with the Stuxnet malware. The actual target of the malware was extremely pointed. It targeted gas centrifuges from Siemens, which the attackers must have known in detail. These are used in uranium enrichment plants. Exactly such Siemens centrifuges were also used in the two Iranian uranium enrichment plants in Natanz and Bushehr. The effect of Stuxnet was highly specific: The program targeted a physical weakness of the centrifuge rotors. These rotate at a high speed and under high pressure, close to vacuum—a very fragile matter. The attack took place in two stages. The first step was to increase the pressure in the centrifuges. This increased the load on the rotors, causing them to deform. In a second step, the rotational speed of the rotors was then increased to overdrive and further deform them.

What can be described in a few sentences is a highly complex task in reality. Because to get to the place in the first place, Stuxnet had to succeed in overcoming all security precautions of the involved IT systems. Most likely there was an insider or a careless employee who stuck a USB stick into a computer that was connected to other networks or passed on the USB storage. Gradually, the malware spread to the point where it could finally copy itself to the control unit of the gas centrifuges. Every time

Stuxnet succeeded in successfully copying itself to another computer, it sent the attackers all sorts of data about the hijacked system. Only after the program had managed to spread to the plants in Natanz and Bushehr could the actual attack take place. But even that is anything but simple. After all, the program had to manage to manipulate the control of the Siemens centrifuges unnoticed. And finally, the third and hardest step of all: It had to succeed in damaging the rotors through this manipulation of the control.

The fact that Stuxnet was able to overcome certain security barriers was also due to the special situation in which the Iranian nuclear program found itself. International sanctions prevented Iran from acquiring state-of-the-art equipment for its uranium enrichment facilities. Therefore, many makeshift solutions and bypasses of security precautions were used as standard. Gas centrifuges were constantly failing even before the Stuxnet attack and rotors had to be repaired. The insidious thing about Stuxnet, however, was that even when the malware had already taken control of the centrifuge control, nothing seemed amiss to the local staff. This was because the legitimate code continues to run, but is essentially isolated from the real control. Stuxnet initially records a few seconds of normal activity and feeds this in a loop to the isolated control program, which, however, appears to continue recording sensor signals and transmitting them to the operator in the control room. Since Stuxnet positions itself between the control code and the actuators/sensors, this is also referred to as a "man-in-the-middle scenario".

When Stuxnet was discovered and analyzed, the shock at its capabilities was immense. Not only was the program code found worldwide in hundreds of industrial plants. It quickly became clear what it was capable of. Without the operators noticing, it could increase the pressure in nuclear reactors or deactivate pumps in drilling towers. And all this with a program code that is just 500 kilobytes in size. Here are a few lines from it:

```
else if (DB8063.state==6)
{
FC6065(); //manipulate outputs
FC6079(); //replay recorded input image
FC6057(0×1F7F#84034020, 0×0000#87000230, var60.2);
if(var60.2==1)
FC6078(1, var50, 0×1F7F##84034020);
var56=var58=-1;
SFC41(var56); //disable alarm interrupts
if(var56 !=1)
          DB8063.error_flag=1;
SFC27(0, var2, var4); // update process outputs
(electrical)                       SFC42(var58);
//enable alarm interrupts
if(var58 !=0)
             DB8063.error_flag=1;
if(var2       !=0)          DB8063.error_flag=1
;                              if(DB8063.timer4
>=6m58s)
{
DB8063.state=7;
FC6078(2, var50, 0×1F7F##84034020);
          }
}
```

The analysis of the Stuxnet code took many years and is still relevant today. Because it is the world's first weapon based solely on program code. Moreover, this code can be rewritten, adapted, and further developed. Therefore, it is important to reconstruct the exact sequence of events in order to learn from it and prepare for comparable situations.

So what was the goal of Stuxnet? The political goal was clearly to hinder the Iranian nuclear program. On a technical level, it was to disrupt the gas centrifuges to prevent uranium enrichment. Unlike many other cyber attacks, in the case of Stuxnet, no data was deleted, stolen, or altered. Nor was it about extorting money. The ultimate goal was certainly the destruction of the facility without any clues as to the true cause and the attacker, of course. Since we still do not know with one hundred percent certainty who was behind it, there are also several versions of the narrative of the exact course of events. However, for the tactical success of the attack, it was important to give the impression that the control of the facilities was functioning perfectly. It is essentially the classic "camouflage and deception", because in the event of subsequent destruction, a "technical defect" would have been to blame and not a state or other third parties.

Stuxnet is remarkable for several other reasons as well. Firstly, because it managed to infiltrate a highly secure environment. Secondly, because the attack proved that a computer program can cause significant damage to physical infrastructure. Until this point, the feasibility of such an attack was always in question. Because it is considered one of the most difficult challenges to cause physical damage with software. But I would say there is another reason that distinguishes this attack and has so far been barely recognized or appreciated. Namely, Stuxnet is characterized by the tactical approach of its creators. Because they ultimately resorted to a medieval, largely forgotten approach. From confidential conversations with the developer of Stuxnet, it is known that he actually used history as a model for his attack tactic on the Iranian uranium enrichment facilities. The historical example that served as a model for the attack with Stuxnet is the so-called poisoning of wells. Earlier, we explained in detail why castles were so difficult to conquer. The security system of these facilities had to be bypassed in some way. The goal was to cause such great damage inside the castle that its inhabitants were forced to open the gates, leave the castle, and thus admit their defeat. One of these ways was one of the attack methods described above, the poisoning of wells.

Both the poisoning of the well and the Stuxnet attack have another commonality: the attack takes place with a time delay. If it is possible to poison the well secretly, none of the inhabitants know that something terrible is brewing, while the attackers can prepare well in advance. With Stuxnet, the time delay added another advantage: it was not simply possible to trace the attack back to an individual, an institution, or a state. Attacking only one installed part of a component of a nuclear power plant also had the advantage that no one had to smuggle anything into the high-security facilities. That's why Stuxnet is still considered one of the most dangerous cyber attacks in history. And even though there is a lot of information about the program code today and there are numerous reports about the attack, there is no official comment about the origin, the objectives, or the actors involved in the execution, only a lot of speculation. For political reasons, they even shied away from naming a responsible party. It is all the more important to keep historical knowledge alive and in consciousness, because from it one can learn enough to deal with the risks and dangers of such attacks: In both the case of the Iranian uranium enrichment plants and in medieval castles, other means had to be found to gain access to the secured systems. It is told that Henry the Lion, in 1168 during the siege of the castle Desenberg located on a mountain cone near Warburg, hired miners from the Harz. He had them drive a tunnel into the mountain. This allegedly hit the castle's well shaft, so the attackers could block the well. The defenders then had to give up. Every system has vulnerabilities. And since there is no completely closed system and there are dependencies or connections to the outside at some point, these points can be used for an attack. Be it in a medieval castle or a high-security building like the enrichment plants in Iran. Gaining unnoticed access to such a system is also a widely used tactic in cyberspace today. Even though the approach of the Stuxnet creators was sometimes described as innovative in the reporting, this is anything but accurate. Rather, this form of attack is many centuries old. The idea of attacking someone from within is a deeply medieval theme. Back then, dead animals were thrown into the water, today malware is smuggled into the interior of an industrial device. This example once again shows how closely the past and the present are connected.

Built Defense

How much architecture is capable of preparing for extreme situations can also be seen in the famous Indian tomb, the Taj Mahal. The mausoleum, completed in 1648, is surrounded by four outer towers, the minarets. What is not immediately noticeable: the four minarets are slightly tilted outwards. Why? In the area where the Taj Mahal was built, there can be earthquakes. If one is so strong that it could bring the towers down, they would fall outward and not damage the mausoleum. Many medieval castles are similar. There the tower falls outward—that's why many tips are tilted outward. In other words, it is a built security structure that protects the valuable interior of the facility. This principle is also found today in areas where the highest security standards are indispensable, such as in the military. Many are probably familiar from books and films like the *Da Vinci Code* with constructs like the "Cryptex", a small device that serves as a secret hiding place for secret messages. It is secured by a number combination. However, if you try to break open the box by force, you break a small vial filled with acid that destroys the document hidden inside the Cryptex. Comparable mechanical and electronic mechanisms can destroy hard drives or the data on them as soon as they are unscrewed from housings. Alternatively, there is the possibility of equipping hard drives with small amounts of explosives that will destroy all data (and probably a bit more) if a certain key combination is not entered within a predetermined time. A geographical variant is also conceivable here. With the help of geofencing and a built-in GPS chip, the use of certain data can be restricted to a predefined area. If someone tries to steal a computer or it leaves the area for another reason, the data on the hard drive and in the memory is deleted. Also, cutting off the power supply can trigger a hardware-side protection mechanism in the form of BIOS protection. Techniques like these are rarely standard solutions for the average consumer, but rather special developments used by intelligence services and the military.

Another characteristic of the defense apparatus of medieval castles are the battlements. Practically speaking, they served as a hiding place for archers, behind which the defenders of a castle could take cover. The gaps between the battlements, on the other hand, allowed the soldiers stationed there to shoot at the attackers. Beyond this purpose, they have a high symbolic value, as it was considered a privilege to be allowed to defend one's own seat. They therefore ultimately stood for power and are therefore found on numerous coats of arms. A very similar function is fulfilled by machicolations, from which hot liquid pitch was poured onto the attackers, or arrow slits, which initially have a narrow opening and widen towards the inside, so that the shooter can see everything, but the attacker has to hit a small slit. Elements like these stand at the transition between the defensive architecture of medieval castles and the protagonists of medieval warfare: the knights.

The Fall of the Knights

The epitome of medieval warfare is the knight. The knights in their armor were invincible for a long time. The ordinary infantry, with their primitive weapons, had no chance of competing with them. It would be almost like trying to take on a tank with a slingshot today. But in essence, it only took one technical invention to bring about the downfall of the knights: the crossbow. Even though the original form of the crossbow was already known in China and ancient Greece, this knowledge was lost after the fall of the first high cultures. It was not until the Normans in medieval France rediscovered this form of weapon around 1000 AD and developed it into an effective weapon of war. Finds and pictorial representations prove that the Normans used crossbows against their opponents, the Anglo-Saxons, in the Battle of Hastings in 1066. The importance of the crossbow cannot be underestimated—at least for the battles on the home battlefields. Even the defense system of the castles needed an update after the invention of the crossbow and other firearms like cannons. The aforementioned battlements are a particularly visible and symbolically charged feature. Others, however, if they have been preserved, may remain hidden to today's viewer. This is because they were designed to be exactly that. They are distance stones, which were hidden at regular intervals in the landscape in such a way that they appeared to be random parts of nature. From the castle, however, they were clearly visible and served their purpose. As attackers approached the castle, the bow and crossbow shooters knew their exact distance thanks to the hidden markers. Since they had calculated the flight path in advance, they could adjust their bows to the exact angle and repel the attackers. All the strengths that armor could have in direct combat were thus eliminated. And even a large army of knights was no longer of any use against a castle where people were stationed with crossbows. On the contrary. The armor even became a disadvantage for the knights because they became too cumbersome and could not dodge the fast arrows. One of the most important insights that the medieval contemporaries had to learn is therefore: A new weapon system can change the entire conduct of war from one day to the next and necessitates a change in tactics.

In the end, the downfall of the knights was of course a somewhat more complex process, which was not only due to their inferiority on the battlefield, but also went hand in hand with economic and political decline. In particular, the fact that Muslim troops conquered Palestine in 1291 and drove the Christian knights out of Jerusalem and the Holy Land is considered a severe defeat that contributed to the loss of power of the knighthood as a whole. The plague, which raged in Europe from the 1340s onwards, also left its mark. Not necessarily because the plague also claimed its victims here, but because it deprived the courts and castles of their economic basis. The knights, who did not produce anything themselves, were dependent on the yield or the taxes of the peasants who cultivated their fields. But despite all these parallel events, the importance of the penetrating power of the crossbow should not be underestimated. It posed such a great threat that the use of bows and crossbows in fights between Christians was already banned by Pope Innocent II at the 2nd Council of Lateran in 1139. The argument was made both with the range and the penetrating power that these weapons had against the armors. Therefore, they were henceforth considered unchivalrous, although they could still be used against heathens and non-believers. However, they continued to be used on the battlefield despite the ban, and so Richard the Lionheart died in 1199 from a crossbow bolt.

By the way, one did not necessarily need superior weapon technology to fight against knights. If one does not have such techniques as the crossbow at one's disposal, one can also gain an advantage with the help of Sun Tzu, i.e., with tactics. If one faces an army of knights, one can, for example, make them run through mud. To do this, of course, one must bring knowledge of the terrain and the weather. However, if one succeeds in doing this, one has a helpless, immobile, and cumbersome team in front of one, which one can throw on their backs like beetles and simply defeat.

But back to the history of technology. Just as the invention of the crossbow had a resounding success, so was the invention of gunpowder groundbreaking. Konstantin Anklitzen was the real name of a man who, according to legend, changed nothing less than the course of human history. In many Christian religious communities, it is customary for people who enter these communities to change their name as part of a ceremony. This was also the case with Konstantin Anklitzen, who joined the Franciscan Order in the 14th century. From that day on, he bore the name Berthold Schwarz. More or less by chance during the alchemical experiments he conducted, he discovered the black powder named after him in 1359. He mixed saltpeter, sulfur, and charcoal together and placed the mixture in a vessel on a stove. Fortunately, he left the room afterwards and was not directly witness to the explosion of the gunpowder he had just invented.[1]

In a way, this rhymes with the invention of dynamite in 1866 by Alfred Nobel, the Swedish chemist who later established the Nobel Prize. Even though he himself denied it, the discovery of the formula for the explosive is very likely also due to chance. Nitroglycerin, the explosive base, is a very viscous substance with a devastating effect. It is much more dangerous than black powder because the explosive power is many times greater. Before Nobel managed to find a stable mixture ratio that could be ignited in a controlled manner, the research, extraction, transport, and inexperienced use of nitroglycerin claimed numerous victims. In experiments, Nobel even blew up his own house. His brother and four employees were killed in the process. To transport the highly explosive substance safely from A to B, Nobel and his employees used a flour made from fossil diatoms as padding material (so-called "diatomaceous earth"). When a transport container nevertheless broke, some of the glycerin leaked out, but was absorbed by the diatomaceous earth and did not explode. Nobel had thus found a way to store the explosive oil and added soda as a chemical stabilizer. He filled everything into a cylindrical protective shell and in 1867 he patented the mixture ratio that would bring him unimaginable wealth. Dynamite changed the world. Positively, because it made massive construction projects like the Panama Canal or the Gotthard Tunnel possible. But also negatively, because it made terrorist attacks possible. Numerous assassinations were carried out with dynamite—in 1892 alone there were

---

[1] Even though Schwarz may not have known it, the actual invention of gunpowder dates back to the 9th century. As early as the Chinese Empire around 1000 AD, there are written records of saltpeter-containing firebombs.

more than 1000. This form of attack was so "popular" that a term was even coined for assassins who used Nobel's invention: dynamitards. The most prominent victim of a dynamitard was Russian Tsar Alexander II in 1881. Nobel himself was shocked by these consequences of his invention and became a pacifist. He saw the dangerous potential of a weapon that makes it possible to kill one's opponent in fractions of a second.

Such attacks, as enabled by dynamite, are also found in cyberspace. When it comes to the effect and the process of a controlled explosion, one could think of logic bombs, for example. This is a computer virus whose "detonation" is linked to predefined conditions. A prerequisite could be that a very specific person logs into a system at a certain time, then starts a special application or prepares a transaction. The damage that a logic bomb can cause is usually defined in advance and can be both very targeted and enormously large. Starting with intercepting and deleting all data, encrypting the system, and even demanding ransom.

From the Middle Ages to the future and from the crossbow to the cyber troop: A brief history of technology in cyberspace

The history of the Middle Ages can therefore also be told as a history of technology. Without a corresponding infrastructure (castles) and weapon techniques (crossbow, black powder), the power and rule of knighthood would not be explainable. From medieval history, we learn that the development of new techniques can not only be decisive in war, but can also go hand in hand with the rise and even the fall of entire peoples and cultures. A historian from the year 2500 could just as well look at our time and conclude that without the invention of a certain infrastructure (Internet) and certain weapon techniques (computer viruses, Trojans, etc.) the flowering and perhaps also the downfall of certain nations and countries would not be understandable. Let us therefore look at cyberspace, its origin, its development, and its significance from this perspective.

We have already heard about the early beginnings in connection with Enigma. Even though there were earlier precursors and systems, the year 1837 marks the starting point of the development of a technical communication infrastructure that characterizes the nature of our modern world. With the invention of telegraphy in conjunction with Morse technology, we humans had for the first time a system that allowed us to speak and exchange information with each other in at least approximate real-time over long distances. If we briefly recall the hardships of Pheidippides, the first marathon runner, or think about the risks and time involved in sending letters that were transported by horse and stagecoach, it quickly becomes apparent what an advantage it was to be able to send a message over several hundred kilometers in a matter of minutes. This development did not make this possible overnight. But when, for example, the first functioning undersea cable was available in 1866, connecting the European continent with the USA, 50 letters could already be transmitted per minute. It was not until 1870 that large parts of the world were connected in this way. By 1900, one could already access 14 cable lines to telegraph from Berlin to Beijing. From this point on, it was essentially possible to transport messages from one end of the world to the other within a manageable period of time. The path to the development of the Internet was still a very long one from here, but one can already speak of a kind of proto-Internet. For this reason, the telegraph network was later also referred to as the "Victorian Internet", as it exhibits—regardless of the topology—similar basic characteristics as the Internet. Both enabled world-wide communicative networking through an interactive medium. The effects triggered by both networks are also similar: Global information exchange formed the basis for the intensification of exchange in the field of international relations, a flourishing of international trade, and an increase in stock market activity. To this day, there is the term "stock ticker", which goes back to a telegraphic device invented in 1867. The telegraph operator E.A. Calahan developed the first ticker device, which was intended to make current stock prices accessible outside the stock exchange building. The device was a combination of a telegraphic receiver and a printer, which continuously output the current stock prices on a continuous paper using two printing rollers. Under a typical loud rattling and ticking, numbers were output on one endless band and letters on the other. Due to the limited form of representation, abbreviations with three to four letters became established. This form of displaying the prices is still used today. The stock ticker represented a small revolution in stock trading, as it made it possible to transmit current prices of the New York Stock Exchange to smaller exchanges without significant time loss. In this way, the different stock exchange locations were communicatively linked, increasingly eliminating local price fluctuations. The stock ticker thus represents the first real-time mass medium, as it mechanically duplicated information and made stock prices available to a large circle of recipients. The invention of the stock ticker is also significant for another reason, as it did not simply make communication more efficient. Once again, it's about power: Before the stock ticker existed and made information about the prices accessible to a wider public, there was only a small, exclusive circle of initiates who traded with companies and goods listed on the stock exchange. There were strict regulations for those who had access to the books in which the business figures and prices were recorded. The stock ticker made it impossible to maintain this degree of secrecy and for the first time in history allowed a wider public to participate in stock market speculation. But the ticker did much more than just democratize stock market activities. Precisely because it constantly spat out new prices and price changes, it promoted the increasing dynamics of stock trading. Only when there are new prices every few minutes are short-term speculations on rising or falling prices possible. This then also brought other all too human characteristics and drives to the fore: greed, fear, and hysteria. With the spread of the tickers, the negative consequences of increasing stock market activity also became apparent. People spoke of "ticker fever" and "tickeritis" to describe the behavior of people who had succumbed to the ticker. The parallels to today are obvious. Certain markets, such as the trade in cryptocurrencies, no longer have fixed trading hours. And even though the devices have changed and the view of the ticker is much quieter than before, there are many parallels that connect our time with the past. The pace imposed on us by today's devices no longer knows any ticking, but it is more tiring than ever. It knows no break, no day, and no night. Information is available in real time at any time. And even if the nervousness is no longer audible, you can see it frothing up at any time on various social media sites. With a view to the past, however, one must always ask what power relations are expressed in it, whether things are really fairer today and our digital media have brought about more democracy, and how today's devices shape our behavior. Because one thing is clear: Just as power manifested itself over the ticker back then, it does so over today's technology. And even if the medium has changed, the tactics often remain the same.

And even the technologies that seem so different at first glance can be arranged on a common timeline. Because the history of telegraphy also includes its further development within the framework of wired and wireless message transmission, which ultimately led to the emergence of cyberspace. According to the German Ministry of Defense, cyberspace consists of all communication technology connected to the internet and includes all processed information. Reason enough to deal with the historical development of this communication technology and technical information processing. The following list could probably be supplemented with numerous dates, but the following highlights provide a rough orientation about the most important development steps of cyberspace:

1941: Konrad Zuse develops the "Z3", the world's first computer.

1946: The first hacker group, Tech Model Railroad Club (TMRC), is formed at MIT, modifying software and hardware to make them better and/or faster.

1956: The first transatlantic telephone cable TAT-1, with a length of 3600 km, goes into operation.

1957: "Sputnik", the first satellite, is in space.

1964: Thomas Kurtz and John Kemeny develop BASIC, a programming language still in use today in a modified form.

1969: ARPANET, the first computer network, is set up in the Pentagon and the first message is transmitted between two computers.

1972/73: The File Transport Protocol (FTP) is developed and a year later in 1973, Vinton Cerf and Robert Kahn develop the Internet Protocol TCP.

1975: IBM introduces the first portable computer.

1981: Wau Holland and Klaus Schleisiek found the Chaos Computer Club (CCC).

1984: The first email is received in Germany.

1984: Development of the Domain Name System (DNS).

1985: The Windows operating system makes its breakthrough.

1989: First drafts of the markup language HTML (Hypertext Markup Language) are published.

1990: The birth of the World Wide Web: Tim Berners-Lee makes the first website available.

1991: 100 countries are connected to the internet.

1993: Over 1.3 million computers and over 10,000 networks are interconnected via the internet, through which 1% of the global information flow runs.

1997: The search engine Google goes online.

1999: The first smartphone with a camera comes onto the market.

2000: 51% of the global information flow runs over the internet.

2004: Social networks like Facebook emerge, spread quickly and usher in Web 2.0.

2007: 97% of the global information flow runs over the internet. Apple introduces the first iPhone.

2009/10: The Stuxnet computer worm attacks 1000 Iranian uranium centrifuges.

2013: China is suspected of building a cyberwar unit, primarily focusing on attacks on the USA.

2015: A cyber operation against three Ukrainian power distribution stations results in a one to six-hour power outage.

2016/17: Cyberspace is officially declared an attack space at the NATO summit, Germany receives its first cyber attack force and the Cyber and Information Space (CIR) becomes an independent military organizational space.

2021: SpaceX, Elon Musk's space company, puts the Starlink network, which consists of 48,000 satellites in the final expansion stage, into operation.

2022: The first countries, China and Russia, discuss completely disconnecting from the internet.

With this short overview, my intention was not so much to trace a complete history of the development of cyberspace. There would certainly be a lively debate about the exact starting point. Rather, with this overview, I want to show how a short period of time and seemingly small events are enough to create an epochal technological innovation. Who would have dreamed in the 1960s, 1970s or 1980s that a niche topic, which ultimately only "nerds" were interested in, would become a new military strategic area, joining land, sea, air and space. It is also remarkable that the military has initiated, accompanied and further advanced the development of the internet and cyberspace from the very beginning. The list also makes it clear that the issue of security has been concerning us in this context for a long time. Although the term hacker was not initially negatively connotated and it was not about criminal, but experimental activities that playfully tried to expand the field of possibilities. Basically, they just wanted to understand how things worked, took apart model railways and circuits and put them back together. Part of the group later also dealt with computers and programming languages. In a kind of manifesto, which they called "Dictionary of TMRC Language", they also formulated far-sighted theses such as: "Information wants to be free."

However, those who only look at the history of technology do not see the complete picture either. Because cyberspace is not just made up of technical devices and infrastructure, which also includes distant things like satellites and a growing number of networked, almost invisibly small or hidden things. Two other crucial components are added: On the one hand, a software layer, which includes programs, firmware, and platforms, and on the other hand, data, ranging from cat pictures to PINs. These virtual components of cyberspace are absolutely crucial. Because hardly anyone would bother to break into a highly secure system if there were not valuable information stored there. The technical side of the coin is therefore just as important as the lessons from history to understand the implications of developments in this area. Because such transitions can be observed again and again over the centuries. Only after the transition from horses as the main means of transport to the automobile was a scenario conceivable in which the Germans overran Poland in the Second World War, whose army consisted of an impressive number of cavalry soldiers: 70,000 cavalrymen, who were divided into eleven brigades. While one side was already organizing the action on a large scale with tanks and vehicles, the other was still largely relying on pre-industrial methods. But no matter in which century such a technical revolution occurs, certain conditions always remain the same. The battle of good against evil, the pursuit of power, or proven procedures and tactical advantages that result from a certain formation or positioning. Knowing these can decide victory and defeat.

Part II

Modern and Hybrid Warfare

After the classical origins of warfare from antiquity to the Middle Ages were illuminated in the first block, the following will focus on the methods and thinkers of the modern era. For this transitional period not only marks the passage to our modern times, but is characterized by significant changes compared to antiquity and the Middle Ages. Here too, there are numerous approaches and events that are still relevant today and from which instructive insights can be derived. The beginning is made by one of the most important strategists and thinkers in military history: Carl von Clausewitz. He lays the foundation that still allows us today to discuss, think about, and act accordingly in relation to modern and hybrid warfare.

Part II

4

"The End Justifies the Means" or: the Legacy of Carl von Clausewitz

In war and love, everything is allowed.
Origin unknown, falsely attributed to Napoleon

What is the essence of war? Is really "everything" allowed in war? Such philosophically tinged questions about war may seem a bit strange at first, but they are nonetheless justified. Because when looking at the history of human civilization, it must first be noted that wars and military conflicts over the centuries were more the rule than the exception—and, although it is regrettable, this will very likely continue to be the case in the future. Whether intended or not, wars have thus contributed to the fact that there are reorganizations on the map, peoples and cultures mix and replace each other by conquering and incorporating territories. Often, the relationship between states that have made peace with each other after the war is much closer than before, as can be observed very vividly in Europe. When asked about the nature of war, i.e., what

© The Author(s), under exclusive license to Springer Fachmedien Wiesbaden GmbH, part of Springer Nature 2024
P. Kestner, *The Art of Cyber Warfare*,
https://doi.org/10.1007/978-3-658-43879-1_4

characterizes or constitutes war, it is also about the laws and rules by which a war operates. What is allowed in war and what is not? On the one hand, war was long understood as the exception to the rule. In a state of emergency, certain otherwise applicable laws, basic rights, norms, and conventions are suspended. In most cases, so-called emergency laws or exceptional rights apply. Even Roman law had such constructions, and the philosophers and thinkers of the time dealt with the theory of the state of emergency. Especially in modern times, when the question of sovereignty was discussed in the creation of the modern state, the question of the state of emergency played a crucial role. "Sovereign is he who decides on the state of emergency," summarizes the controversial thinker Carl Schmitt later this constitutional development. The sovereign—this can mean both the modern state, the people, or a sole ruler—is thus not only responsible for defining the laws and rules but can also decide on their abolition. War is thus the very opposite of the state order, interrupting, abolishing, and renegotiating boundaries and conditions. When we talk about the sovereign (in the sense of ruler, head) or sovereign (in the sense of superior, self-confident, or independent), it is always also about power—one of the oldest forces shaping human history, and, as mentioned in the introduction, one of the five driving forces from which people repeatedly start conflicts and wars. But what is someone who has power allowed to do? Or rather: Is there something he is not allowed to do? In the constitutional discussion, war is interpreted as a form of force majeure to obtain legitimation for military action. One of the most important thinkers of modern times is Carl von Clausewitz (1780–1831), who is sometimes also referred to as the "war philosopher". According to von Clausewitz, the essence of war consists of three characteristics: first, hatred and enmity, second, the application of military force, and third, the political purpose pursued with the war.

War According to Clausewitz

"The end justifies the means"—This much-quoted sentence is probably the best-known thesis of Carl von Clausewitz. It comes from his work *On War*, which he wrote between 1816 and 1830 and which was published posthumously by his wife in 1832. It is one of the most influential and at the same time one of the most controversial works in the field of strategic and tactical thinking, but also of power philosophy and military ethics. Numerous generals and leaders are known to owe their successful campaigns and strategies to reading Clausewitz's work—starting with Field Marshal Helmuth von Moltke during the German Wars of Unification, through numerous German generals in the context of both World Wars, to US war strategists in the Vietnam War. The crucial question is what exactly Clausewitz's work contributed to this. Because it is no coincidence that we know mainly quotes from *On War* today. Rather, it is the case that everyone more or less constructs "his" Clausewitz to some extent. This has several reasons. First, because the work has a very complex genesis. Since this is key to understanding Clausewitz's thinking, it will be discussed in more detail shortly. Second, *On War* is a rather bulky text that most people probably have not read in its entirety. Third, we are dealing with *On War* as an incomplete and unfinished work. The fact that we have it in this form at all is solely due to the efforts of Marie von Brühl, the wife of Carl von Clausewitz.

To understand Clausewitz, we must therefore take a closer look at the genesis of his work, which in turn is closely linked to his biography. Clausewitz worked on his manuscript mainly under the impression of the Napoleonic Wars. The convolute from which *On War* consists largely contains analyses of individual battles, where it is not always clear whether the insights that Clausewitz drew from them can really be generalized. From notes and letters, we know that the author was well aware of the weaknesses of his work and therefore intended to rethink and revise the entire text fundamentally. How far he got with this revision is unfortunately not known because he died over it. According to a widespread opinion, he only managed to revise the first chapter.

But let's start at the beginning: Carl von Clausewitz was born on July 1, 1780, as the son of a family of pastors and scholars. His father—himself an officer in the army—sent his son to the military at the age of 12. Just a year later, Clausewitz took part in his first campaign. At the age of 15, he already held the rank of lieutenant. His qualification for the war school a few years later in 1801 ultimately paved his way into European history as the author of the comprehensive work *On War*. The war school was a significant station in Clausewitz's life because he met his mentor there. For he was under the command of Lieutenant Colonel Gerhard von Scharnhorst, who later even became a paternal friend. It was Scharnhorst who established a new form of military education at the Prussian war school. From then on, theory and history were considered prerequisites for successful action by officers.

The first setback in his life and a significant event regarding his thinking was the defeat of the Prussian army in the Battle of Jena and Auerstedt in 1806. Clausewitz then went as a staff captain and adjutant into the Fourth Coalition War and had to surrender along with the battalion of the wounded August von Prussia. The reason for the loss: The approach and organization of the Prussian army were based on rigid structures. Against the highly mobile French troops, they had no chance. The battle lasted only a single day. This traumatic experience gave Clausewitz food for thought and also the time to do so. For he was taken prisoner of war. During his French captivity from October 1806 to September 1807, he asked himself: How could it be that the proud Prussian army had lost to the French? From that moment on, he admired Napoleon and his abilities as a general and even referred to him as a "war god". Of course, he could not freely admit his admiration, as it was still the archenemy, for whom he simultaneously developed a hatred.

Initially, he wanted to learn from the defeat and help Prussia to victory against Napoleon with a new theory of strategy, tactics, and psychology of warfare. For a long time, he believed, along with others who gathered around Scharnhorst, that he could reform the Prussian army. But with the conclusion of a defensive alliance of the Prussians with France against Russia in 1812, he lost faith in the Prussian monarchy and became a nationalist. Still, in the same year, he left the Prussian troops and committed himself to Russia. Von Clausewitz advised the Russian Tsar in the battle against Napoleon to use the Russian territory defensively in the depth of space, which brought him initial successes in strategic warfare. The deterioration of supplies due to the stretching of troop supply in combination with occurring diseases led to a rapid decimation of the French troops. He analyzed the experiences in the Russia War and recognized glaring weaknesses in Napoleon's warfare. If this strategy of rapid subjugation had previously worked, it led to failure in Russia and essentially repeated itself in World War II.

In 1810, Carl von Clausewitz married Marie Countess von Brühl, later: Marie von Clausewitz. The connection with her is also significant in several respects for understanding Clausewitz—not only because of the publication history. For the marriage to her was anything but a matter of course. Clausewitz was born as Carl Phillip Gottlieb Clausewitz, without a noble title. At that time, it was not yet common to look for a suitable partner beyond one's own social boundaries. However, Clausewitz remained persistent and also proceeded strategically in this area of life, so that in the end, he succeeded in convincing her and her family of the marriage. For Clausewitz, this connection was associated with a social rise and also with access to education and contacts. Through Marie, he also met Goethe, for example, and was able to study numerous paintings of past battles and events in private collections. This explains why Clausewitz included numerous major battles in his analyses in *On War*. Among these are, for example, those of the Thirty Years' War and the War of the Spanish Succession.

After his service for the Russian side, he was only allowed to return to Prussia in the rank of a colonel in 1814. However, his professional career took a hit. Any further promotion was denied to him, and only after several years, which he spent teaching at the General War School, was he finally promoted to the youngest general of the Prussian army at the age of 38. But Clausewitz was driven by ambition and wanted to achieve much more. From 1816, he worked intensively and continuously on his work *On War* alongside his teaching activities until 1830.

From at least 1827, Carl von Clausewitz devoted himself intensively to the topic of warfare and considered it in terms of its purpose and the means used for it. The famous phrase "The end justifies the means" is often used in connection with cynical power politics and is considered a principle of so-called Machiavellianism. According to this political theory, any means is allowed for the preservation of power, regardless of law and morality. However, this assessment does not do justice to the true meaning of Clausewitz's work.

It is clear: For von Clausewitz, dealing with war was always more than just a purely aesthetic occupation. He was drawn to practice. At the age of almost 50, despite his already existing health problems, he decided to return to active service. He took over the leadership of a Prussian observation army. He did not live to see the publication of his main work, as he died on November 16, 1831, in Breslau from a combination of cholera and heart attack.

It was his wife, Marie von Clausewitz, who further developed his complete works after his death and published them in Potsdam in 1834, with far-reaching consequences. This can be most easily demonstrated by the sentence "War is merely a continuation of politics by other means," which is also found in *On War* and is one of the most famous and frequently quoted statements. The catch with this Clausewitz quote is: it did not come from him. Clausewitz always avoided making such definitive statements. The sentence actually comes directly from his wife Marie. When she opened the estate, she saw that it was a sometimes completely chaotic collection of seemingly unrelated papers and analyses. However, having spent the last thirteen years together and having discussed his main work extensively, she believed she was more familiar with his thinking than anyone else, so she organized the texts and added headings and other missing components.

The Theory of War According to Clausewitz

The distinction between absolute and real war is the most important starting point in the theory of Carl von Clausewitz. This theory describes the difference between the planned war on paper and the actual war events, which are influenced by various factors. In other words, Clausewitz refers to the theoretical nature of war as "absolute war". Furthermore, he distinguishes three tendencies, which he assigns to certain entities such as the people or the government on a further level of abstraction. He calls this theoretical framework the "wondrous trinity". Ultimately, it is a model that helps to explain what factors really make up war and its development. The first side represents violence, hatred, and enmity. According to Clausewitz, one way to understand war is to see it as a blind natural instinct (also one of the five driving forces) of man. Therefore, this instinct is assigned to the people on the level of abstraction. The second characteristic element that makes up a war is the battle. Accordingly, the commander and the army are assigned to this on the level of abstraction, as they are the executing organs of this understanding of war. The battle is characterized by a game of probability and chance and the operational and tactical leadership of the armed forces. Thirdly, war can be understood as an act of rational intellect. On the level of abstraction, this side of war is assigned to the government, for which war is a political tool. These three dimensions—war as a blind natural instinct, war as free creative activity, and war as an act of reason—are not to be understood as static or strictly separate from each other. Rather, they interlock, overlap, and appear in different forms throughout history and reality.

As a definition and planning tool, Clausewitz introduced another level of abstraction, the purpose-goal-means relation. The variables means and goals are dependent on the overarching political purpose. However, the purpose can also change during a war and is therefore not a static size. Due to the close interrelationships of the three variables, a change in purpose also requires a rethinking of the goals and means.

The political purpose is described by Clausewitz as the overthrow of the enemy. The enemy is to be forced to fulfill a certain will and to achieve this, the means of war, i.e., violence, is used. Peace should then be sought when the effort is judged to be greater than the purpose pursued with the war. The original motive and the measure for the war is thus the purpose for von Clausewitz. The smaller the overarching political purpose, the smaller the effort and the means used will be. This circumstance is particularly relevant for cyber warfare. Because if it is possible in the future to achieve large and even small political goals with very little effort, one can easily calculate the state of the world in a few years. Because in cyberspace, it is essentially the case that a handful of skilled attackers are enough to cause considerable damage. Therefore, troop strength, technical equipment, a faster communication infrastructure (lines), digital mobility, unrestricted access to already existing information are the future, not to be underestimated variables.

Once politics has decided on the purpose, the goal must be defined. According to Clausewitz, a warlike act consists in rendering the enemy defenseless, which also coincides with Sun Tzu's idea. I also consider this definition to be groundbreaking when we will later deal with the evaluation of cyber attacks as a warlike act. Many activities that we can observe so far in cyberspace are not yet evaluated as a warlike act—if this were the case, we would already be in a permanent state of war with a large number of states today. But more on that later. Back to Clausewitz: Once a goal is achieved, the attacker can force his opponent to fulfill his will, i.e., make him surrender or demand other concessions. However, it is important that the situation is more disadvantageous for him than the demanded sacrifice. Moreover, the disadvantages must not only be temporary, as the opponent will break free from the role of the defeated at the next opportunity. There is no absolute sharpness of separation between the purpose and the goals.

Identifying the enemy's focal points is the essential step. The enemy's focal point can be the starting point of the enemy's army or the capital of a state. If smaller states have allies, i.e., allies, as an essential part of stability, the focal point can be precisely on these. If there is a popular armament, the main leader and public opinion should be targeted.

However, defeating the opponent is not always the top priority. In these cases, the goal of the military action can either be the conquest of a small part of the enemy's land or the defense of one's own country until a better opportunity arises. Demonstrating strength or conquering territories is often enough to achieve the goals demanded by politics through negotiations. Clausewitz emphasizes that wars of lesser intensity must be conducted with great care so that the fluctuating balance does not turn into a disadvantage and the half-war does not turn into a major one. The less intense the war appears, the more political it becomes. Here, politics dominates the action. The scope of action for the army and the commander-in-chief is limited in this context.

The third element of the purpose-goal-means relation are the means. Their use is determined by the political purpose and the goals that are to be achieved with the use of military actions. The means expended are in relation to the political purpose and the corresponding goals. For a precise definition of the means, von Clausewitz formulated a mathematical formula:

Resistance of the opponent = size of the means x strength of the willpower

This formula includes two different factors: estimates and numbers. The size of the means can be determined by numbers. However, the willpower of the opponent or his mental and emotional forces can only be estimated. In addition, frictions, coincidences, and probabilities play a significant role. The longer the war lasts, the more these three factors influence the course of the war. The importance of the quality of the warlord, the extent of the means, and the virtue of the army is emphasized here. However, the means are not just the pure strength of weapons and troops, but the means are determined by the political purpose.

The purpose-goal-means relation is a core component of the strategic thinking and action of Carl von Clausewitz's theory and, together with the "Wondrous Trinity," it forms the basis for a comprehensive and holistic strategy.

In reality, the war plan deviates from the actual course of the war. Small delays, errors, and misunderstandings can occur. Carl von Clausewitz refers to the sum of these as frictions and distinguishes four types, which can affect the morale of the soldiers and the course of the war.

The **internal friction** arises within the armed forces themselves due to human weaknesses, which are caused by friction losses and mistrust of their own leadership. Through anticipatory planning and good training, the potential of internal friction can be minimized.

Weather changes, the surprising actions of the opponent, or the appearance of an unexpected geographical obstacle, represent points of the **external friction.** The actions of the warlord play a major role here in counteracting this friction.

Clausewitz sees the "fog of war" as particularly dangerous. In this case, false information triggers a **tactical friction,** which can be minimized by the commander and his good training.

The sum of internal and external frictions does not represent a separate type of friction, but is described as **general frictions** to reduce the blur.

As previously described, the influence of frictions increases with the duration of the war. To recognize this in time and to reduce it by timely intervention, good training and sensitization of the field marshal and the armed forces are necessary. To achieve a balance of frictions, it is important that rational decisions according to the purpose-goal-means relation are supplemented by unpredictable, frictional and emotional elements and the enemy's counteraction. Clausewitz describes here the development to the martial genius, who, in addition to a war-accustomed army, is an important support for successful warfare. For the martial genius, the tact of judgment is important, which is based on natural talents and can be increased by acquiring knowledge and personal experiences. Through the collaboration of knowledge, the field marshal intuitively makes the right decisions. Moreover, it is essential that the field marshal, despite success and power, continues to make structured and clear decisions. Nothing hinders the success of the field marshal more than if he makes bad and hasty decisions with a bold and conceited behavior. For Clausewitz, the influence of the people also plays a role in the moral potency of the martial genius. As an example, the French army is mentioned, which was driven by the enthusiasm and zeal of the French Revolution. However, Clausewitz assigns the people a subordinate role. More important to him is the esprit de corps of the armed forces. Through constant practice, the talents, habits, and norms for the soldiers should be easily retrieved and used.

Clausewitz therefore points to the necessity of good and stable training for the army as well as for the field marshal. It is a fundamental building block for the stability and provision of means in a war. It is also important that a certain preparation and analysis of the geographical conditions take place in order to minimize external frictions. However, there is no 100% security here, as the fog of war and the uncertainty about the correctness of the information always play a role to a certain extent. With this, Clausewitz adopts the principles of Sun Tzu and modernizes them.

Types of War

In the following, I would like to go into a distinction in more detail, which was briefly mentioned above. Because the war theory of Carl von Clausewitz distinguishes war in two different ways and manners:

- War of the first and second category
- The Small War and the People's War

The first distinction has already been encountered above. The first type of war is purely theoretical in nature. Clausewitz also refers to it as absolute war, which is characterized by its strong motives and extreme violence. It encompasses the existence of all nations. The more the subjugation of the enemy comes to the fore, the more there is a congruence between the warlike goal and the political purpose. The difference to the first type of war lies in the second type, in that this type reflects the war in reality. Here, the war ends without an existential decisive battle and its nature is rather limited. The enemy is neither subjugated nor put into the predicament of defenselessness. Therefore, minor conquests and diplomatic means lead the enemy to sign a peace treaty at the negotiating table. The first and second types of war are political in nature, as the use of violence is intended to bring the enemy to a certain end state. Absolute war is characterized by the absence of one's own escalation of violence, as each action of the enemy is met with a compensatory counteraction. This results in an unlimited state of violence. Absolute war is characterized by three interactions. The first interaction leads to the tendency of escalation in the use of violence in war. Here, both sides try to outdo the previously used violence by increasing it. The task of the enemy is the goal of the second interaction. Here, the enemy is to be put in a situation where his situation is more disadvantageous than the demanded sacrifice. The third interaction describes the formula from which the resistance power of the warring party is derived. This consists of the product of the size of the available means and the strength of the willpower. To a certain extent, a lack of means can be compensated by willpower.

These three interactions accelerate an escalation. This happens when they are simultaneously maximized by the use of all available means. According to Carl von Clausewitz, they characterize absolute war, which, however, does not occur in reality due to the lack of logic. The factors of time, probability, and chance have a strong influence and have a moderating effect in reality. There are situations where one faces an overpowering enemy who cannot be defeated in an open field battle. To defy these situations, he introduced the "Small War" and the "People's War" as methods.

The characteristic of the "Small War" in contrast to the "People's War" are small, mobile units. The order of magnitude here is twenty to forty men and it is usually locally concentrated for a certain period of time on the periphery of the enemy's operations. The tasks of these small units are versatile and primarily aim at hindering the rapid advance of the enemy. To wear down the enemy, they rely on delaying resistance, ambushes, and pinpoint attack actions. In the 17th and 18th centuries, the Small War was developed as "petit guerre" or guerrilla. The Small War is opposed to the type of People's War. For this to be successful, various aspects must be fulfilled. On the one hand, a wide field with geographical challenges such as forests, swamps, and mountains is needed. Furthermore, in addition to the support of the population, a decentralized location outside a battlefield must also be given. It is important that the enemy does not gain control over the land. The distinction between Small War and People's War is an important starting point for the argumentation and description of hybrid wars, which is becoming increasingly important today and in the future.

Later, there will be extensive discussion of the reevaluation of new forms of war. But it should already be mentioned in this context what historical role Clausewitz's thinking plays here. With the formation of the sovereign state and the international system after the Peace of Westphalia of 1648, certain rules apply as to when one speaks of a war. Not every violent conflict is therefore considered a war. To be defined as a war, closed groups of armed forces must be involved, which are organized and centrally directed over a longer period of time. The current definition refers to the simplified form. Accordingly, a war is a violent conflict fought with weapons. The Working Group on the Causes of War (AKUF) at the University of Hamburg provided another definition:

a) two or more armed forces are involved in the fighting, at least on one side of which are regular forces (military, paramilitary units, police units) of the government. Today, this is attempted to be undermined with mercenaries or "special paramilitary organizations" (such as Blackwater);

b) on both sides, there must be a minimum level of centrally directed organization of the warring parties and the fighting, even if this means nothing more than organized armed defense or planned raids (guerrilla operations, partisan war, etc.);

c) the armed operations take place with a certain continuity and not just as occasional, spontaneous clashes, i.e., both sides operate according to a planned strategy, regardless of whether the fighting takes place on the territory of one or more societies and how long they last.

Wars are considered ended when the fighting is permanently stopped, i.e., for a period of at least one year, or continued only below the AKUF war definition. The AKUF thus not only created a comprehensive definition that is still used today, but also followed the theoretical considerations of Carl von Clausewitz with it. However, his thinking did not stop with the considerations of classical war, but contributed much more. This is particularly evident where the definitions of the AKUF stop: in cyber war or other disputes and conflicts in the digital space. Even for the new wars, Clausewitz's framework of thought and key concepts can be used to better understand them.

Clausewitz and the New Wars

The interesting thing about Clausewitz is precisely that he does not provide a complete theory of war. Rather, he provides his readers with a vocabulary, key terms, and analyses of past and then-current wars, which should stimulate independent further thinking—an aspect that Clausewitz shares with the author of this book. At the same time, however, this method of thinking and writing makes *On War* so fruitful in the analysis of new forms of war, of which Clausewitz could not have had the slightest idea—such as cyber warfare. However, there are other examples that can illustrate Clausewitz's foresight. For instance, Clausewitz served as a basis for understanding asymmetric wars, conflicts without strictly running front lines, and other disputes without clear warring parties. Phenomena such as international terrorism, partisan wars, or indeed cyber warfare can be analyzed and better understood with the help of Clausewitz.

In today's world, there are primarily three forms of war that can be analyzed and represented with Clausewitz. The classic, symmetrical state war is characterized by a war between two or more states. A coalition war is also a state war. According to Clausewitz's definition of a people's war, this can be continued as a partisan or guerrilla war when the country is already occupied and the government is disempowered. After the Peace of Westphalia in 1648, a monopolization of violence took place, and this was the beginning of state wars. Only the state had the power and the right to declare and wage war. In addition, there was a striving for supremacy by the larger states in Europe, which provided a balance. State wars are characterized by a certain symmetry, hence they are also referred to as "symmetrical wars", which makes the war particularly legalized. This symmetry leads to a stabilizing function at the political level. The balance of power could be estimated to a certain extent reliably, and a comparison was possible. During the Cold War, coalitions could prevent the military superiority of the opponent. The classic image of war has changed significantly, and with the collapse of the Soviet Union, interstate wars have lost their importance.

The new image of war is characterized by multilateral interventions in civil wars. Privatization displaced the state's monopolization of violence. This creates an asymmetry. Many political scientists refer to this new form as

"New Wars". September 11, 2001, is probably the day that remains in everyone's memory. There is hardly anyone who cannot remember what they were doing at the moment they learned of the attacks on the World Trade Center. Since then, military research has focused on these asymmetric wars and the new wars. On a theoretical level, the essay by William S. Lind, titled "The Changing Face of War: Into the Fourth Generation", was an important research basis. Lind understood the fourth generation of wars as stateless wars, where the characterization according to Clausewitz as an extended duel no longer applies. The New Wars are based more on ideologies or religions with a stateless character. Moreover, these wars cannot be described as classic civil wars and not as a military confrontation within state borders.

Mercenaries, warlords, and terrorists now determine the course of war by undermining laws and definitions. They finance their livelihood through asymmetric warfare or use it to achieve their own goals, which brings us back to the beginning with the five driving factors. These can also be of an economic or political-religious nature. While previous forms of war were economically based on the mobilization of war production, the new wars focus on the plundering of resources, mineral resources, and the appropriation of rents. In cyberspace, this corresponds to the theft of intellectual property and know-how, gaining access to critical infrastructures, for example, to prepare for other wars or attacks. Western states are currently trying to contain conflicts here. In doing so, they invest primarily in armament technology, for example, to keep their own losses as low as possible through air strikes. This point, in particular, demonstrates very clearly why it is so important to understand the new wars on a theoretical level: Before terrorism was re-evaluated with the help of Clausewitz, it was assumed that individuals were at the level of criminals and organized in gang structures. If terrorism is understood in this way, the political and state measures and consequences are quite different than if terrorism is understood as a new form of war that is directed against a state as such and is carried out by small, decentralized cells. A military response to a terrorist act can only be given if the terrorists are interpreted as actors within an asymmetric war.

Technologies for gathering information may have developed, but terrorists today act and react with the opposite: That is, if they are being eavesdropped on, they only pass commands from mouth to mouth, on paper, or via dead letterboxes. To defeat a technically superior enemy, they therefore rely on non-technical tactics. Today's technically savvy conflict parties are dealing with an enemy from the past who is not dependent on digital communication paths. Therefore, the understanding and awareness for the evaluation and interpretation of information must change. This change has long been recognized by Hollywood and incorporated into the new narratives. In the film *Body of Lies* (directed by Ridley Scott, 2008), set in the Middle East, a technically highly skilled war is depicted. Every action of the CIA agent Roger Ferris (played by Leonardo DiCaprio) is observed by drones and guided by his colleague Ed Hoffman (played by Russell Crowe) from Washington. Time and again, they reach their limits because their opponents are tactically one step ahead or let them run into the void with very simple means. At one point, Roger Ferris reflects: "By now, our enemy has very much realized that he is fighting against guys from the future and that is as brilliant as it is threatening. Whoever lives like in the past and behaves like in the past, is very hard to discover for the guys from the future. If you throw away your cell phone, don't write emails, pass all instructions face to face and hand to hand, you close yourself off from any technology and disappear in the crowd."

New forms of warfare developed from the partisan war. However, it is no longer the partisan, but a mobile and globally acting actor. This actor is no longer bound by any rules of war and uses the infrastructure in the enemy's center. What counts are body counts, and these are achieved by attacks on soft targets such as civilians with cheap weapons.

In the case of classic terrorism, which also existed in the past, the target of an assassination was the representative of the power wielder and the civilian population was accepted as collateral damage. The new terrorism, however, is directed against the civilian population. There are no clear front lines, and instead of battles, the actors rely on massacres, displacements, and rapes, mostly based on ethnic differences. According to the state of Low Intensity Conflicts (LIC), no Western or highly armed country can afford a costly military operation for an unlimited period of time. Nor can it afford to simply end a war once it has started. The wars in Afghanistan or Iraq were about holding territory. To protect the capital, various tactics are used. These range from classic military operations to state building or nation building. The combat operations are thus kept away from the center.

It's different with the jihadists or the Taliban, who wage a war of territorial gain. Their goal is to take over the space of the periphery with asymmetric means, and then to operate their own kind of "state building". This is done, for example, by proclaiming an emirate based on Islamic law (Sharia). The use of suicide bombers shows the opponents their vulnerability and sends the message that further costs can be expected. In the sense of Clausewitz's definition, it is an act of violence with the clear aim of forcing the opponent to do something. To achieve a balance and a re-symmetrization, the participating states carry out various special operations and covert missions, for example in cyberspace. The combination of modern and pre-modern traditional motives and forms of warfare is a key feature of the new wars. The theoretical framework and the wondrous trinity can also be applied to the asymmetric or new wars, as Clausewitz already described the asymmetry of war.

The Hybrid War as a "new" Form of Warfare

In particular in the USA, the term "hybrid war" emerged in the context of military dealing with new forms of war and their evaluation. This form of war relies on the full range of conventional, criminal, terrorist, and asymmetric means. This can be carried out by both state and non-state actors. However, since the Department of Defense initially did not recognize a new form of warfare, terms such as "hybrid war" or "hybrid warfare" were not officially used. Today, terms such as "hybrid warfare", "hybrid threats" or "hybrid elements" are much more common.

Due to the increasing merging of forms of warfare, future conflicts will be multi-variant or multi-modal. Moreover, it will no longer be limited to individual challenges, with approaches such as conventional combat, irregular combat, and terrorism. Rather, warfare will involve a combination of different tactics, and these may even be used simultaneously. Other ways to destabilize a government also include smuggling, drug trafficking, and illegal arms trading. The boundaries between war and crime are thus increasingly blurred. For this reason, this criminal approach will also find its application in hybrid warfare.

Hybrid forms of warfare can already be observed in the past. The transformation of regular forces into irregular formations, for example, already took place in 2003 with the Fedayeen in Iraq. Former loyal mercenaries of Saddam Hussein had joined the armed resistance against the US troops. Critical infrastructures, whose failure has a lasting impact on supply, significant disruptions to public safety, or other dramatic consequences, were the targets of a hybrid attack. The complexity and vulnerability of the global economic and trade flows made them a suitable target. Not only terrorist groups, but also state groups try to find and attack such vulnerabilities. Banks and companies, such as Bank of America or American Express, have long been targets of attacks. Evidence of attacks by intelligence services or special cyber units of other countries' militaries have already been found in abundance. Among these countries are also China, Russia, North Korea, and Iran. Iran, in particular, has openly supported terrorism for many years. In addition to the radical Islamic Hamas, Hezbollah is also financially and militarily supported. Iran was described as "the most active state sponsor of terrorism" according to an analysis by the US Department of State.

However, it must also be critically asked how "new" the classification as a hybrid war really is. Because certain elements of what is called hybrid warfare can also be found in history. Just think of the episode about the Trojan Horse, which was already mentioned above in a different context. With the trick of the soldiers hidden in the belly of the horse, a military victory was achieved. On one level of observation, it is a tactic of camouflage and deception. Viewed differently, a cultural given is exploited here to gain an advantage on a military level. Because there is the custom of not being able to refuse a gift, especially such a large one. But it is precisely this mixing of different dimensions or levels that is at the core of hybrid warfare. This raises the fundamental question again: What exactly is hybrid warfare?

A Definition of Hybrid Warfare

Hybrid warfare can thus be described as a specific form of warfare. It is characterized by three features and their interaction: 1) the multidimensional action space, 2) operating in gray areas, and 3) the creative combination of means and methods. Depending on how strongly these features are pronounced, the degree of hybridity can be determined.

Let's start with the multidimensional action space. Hybrid war is characterized by the fact that actions are not primarily and not exclusively located in the military sector. Rather, numerous other action spaces are added, in which actions are taken or which are combined: politics, economy, critical infrastructure, society, or culture. A form of warfare is called hybrid when it is no longer conducted purely with armed violence, but primarily with non-military means. The different dimensions thus become independent battlefields.

Operating in gray areas or at interfaces is the next characteristic of hybrid war that we will look at more closely. This is about transition areas such as between war and peace, friend and enemy, civilian and military, truth and lie, legal and illegal, state and non-state. The fuzzy gray areas between such categories are characteristic of hybrid warfare. They are difficult to grasp and are therefore particularly suitable for actions. Because there is no clarity here or old orders are deliberately questioned, the opponent is incapacitated or at least paralyzed in his decision-making ability.

The third characteristic of hybrid warfare is the creative combination of various means and methods as well as tactics and strategies. Also, aspects that are otherwise considered separately are brought together here. In this way, new approaches and hybrid mixtures are constantly being created that are innovative and surprising. For example, elements of disinformation and propaganda can be combined with means of economic warfare and diplomatic efforts. Or military confrontations with a societal culture war and economic blockades. The combination of conventional war and guerrilla tactics is also conceivable. Here too, the goal is to operate in gray areas. Precisely through the combination of means and methods, an exact assignment to one or the other area is made difficult. The combination possibilities of not only means and methods are inexhaustible. The orchestration and different expression of all three characteristics of hybrid warfare also allow for endless design possibilities.

So, is Cyberwar a Form of Hybrid War?

If we now try to understand cyber warfare as hybrid warfare, it is first necessary to note that technologies already play a larger role in warfare today. In the information age, propaganda primarily takes place on social media. The possibilities that arise from the use of artificial intelligence and automated systems also characterize recent conflicts. New technologies enable a new dimension of warfare. However, since cyberspace does not exist separately from the physical world, it is not a new battlefield. Rather, cyberspace extends the existing dimensions by another one, has numerous interfaces, and is therefore ideally suited for hybrid warfare.

Last but not least, it should be noted that cyber warfare as a form of hybrid warfare and its connection with military means and methods do not mutually exclude each other. In this context, three motives can be identified that speak for such a combination: First, if the actors intend to use their own military potential within the framework of hybrid warfare, for example to intimidate, threaten or blackmail their opponent militarily. Second, military strength can support hybrid action on other levels. If military means are used at the same time, cyber operations can be successful. Third, it is about securing what has been achieved, i.e., the opponent tries to make up for the hybrid attacks and the terrain gained there with military means.

To clarify why cyber warfare is also located at the threshold of hybrid warfare, the relevance of Clausewitz should be briefly made clear at this point. Clausewitz described war as an "act of violence to force the opponent to fulfill our will". The legitimate question, however, must be whether this still applies to cyber warfare in the 21st century. An answer depends first on how one defines cyber warfare. Today we do not yet encounter it in a pure form—the cyber attack on the electronic health system of Latvia in 2018 also made it clear that the central act of violence that triggers and defines a war must still be of a physical or military nature and does not take place in cyberspace. However, in recent wars, individual elements of cyber warfare can be identified again and again, which can theoretically already be interpreted as acts of violence with some justification. After all, the measures and actions that state actors carry out in cyberspace also represent serious threats to the security of states and the people who live in them.

What has been missing so far in this context, however, is the possibility of a clear and immediate assignment of these acts of violence. If one were to apply Clausewitz's thinking to cyberspace, this act would have to be based on an offensive or defensive military strategy within the information field, which is approved or carried out by a state. It would therefore also have to aim at the immediate disruption or control of enemy resources. So far, there has not been such an act of violence that could be immediately and clearly assigned or that had an immediate effect in the history of war. Or in other words: All previous cyber attacks have not yet led to a war. Hackbacks are also legally prohibited in many countries. Attacks in cyberspace have so far often been used as disruptive elements or for gathering information in advance of an attack. The exact state of the discussion will be discussed later. However, it can already be revealed that as of today, the shot of a soldier would have more consequences than the attack of an entire cyber army on another state. An example of this are the attacks by Russia on various neighboring countries that have been ongoing for more than a decade. None of these acts of violence, which were often directed at critical infrastructures, triggered an official war between two states. Precisely for this reason, the dangers emanating from cyberspace today are to be assessed as much more serious than many people and especially politicians do. It can be assumed that the capabilities that states are developing in this area go far beyond what has been observed so far and that the decades of true cyber warfare are still ahead of us. What cyber warfare will look like is also not yet certain from today's perspective. It is only clear that it has little to do with what we know from previous wars or what is used in parallel. There will not be the images on television that we are used to from current wars. This is also due to the sensationalism and logic of the press, which often only shows atrocities that secure their attention. In contrast, cyber operations take place in the background, even if they prepare such acts. A rocket strike gives a better picture for the media than a stolen database. First of all, this is because the preparations for this can take years and can remain completely invisible. The same applies to the execution of a cyber attack. Last but not least, there is no guarantee and no obligation that such an attack will ever be made public or that a state will admit to it. Cyber warfare could become a very quiet, unspectacular, yes—from the outside—even almost boring affair, which is rather to be located in the area of espionage, sabotage and propaganda support. However, the latter does not apply to the damage caused. This is shown by the NotPetya attack, which is believed to have originated from Russia and was directed against civilian infrastructure in Ukraine. At first glance, "NotPetya" was a ransomware, which encrypts the data on a system and only decrypts it again against the payment of a ransom. The enormous impact and effect of NotPetya became apparent on 06/27/2017, when ATMs failed throughout Ukraine, card readers like in the subway no longer worked and the IT systems of banks, companies and authorities were no longer usable from one moment to the next. There were chaotic conditions throughout the country. There were also numerous victims of the attack outside Ukraine. For example, the entire computer system of Maersk, the world's largest container shipping company, was affected. Even the radiation monitoring system of Chernobyl fell victim to the malware. The pharmaceutical company Merck alone, whose production completely collapsed, estimated its loss at 830 million euros. The damage caused by NotPetya in total amounts to almost 10 billion EUR. NotPetya was particularly successful because it is a so-called "worm". This refers to software that can replicate itself and thus spread to hundreds of thousands of computers around the world without human intervention. NotPetya was a very sophisticated virus that exploited a security vulnerability in Microsoft Windows and could gain access to all computers in a network. In contrast to Petya, a ransomware that was really about extortion, NotPetya's goal was not to make money, but to cause maximum damage. Although a ransom demand was also displayed with NotPetya and the payment of a certain amount of Bitcoin was demanded. However, the data in the background had long been destroyed or made unusable. Hence the name *Not* Petya, or "Not-Petya". But despite the immense damage that Russia had caused through this attack in Ukraine and around the world, nothing happened on the political world stage at the time. According to official information, only one country remained free from any damage caused by NotPetya: Russia.

The Definition of Tactics and Strategy According to Clausewitz

In Clausewitz's thinking, the ability of the armed forces to fight was the basis of warfare. Therefore, the battle had a central significance. The means used for this played only a subordinate role compared to the purpose pursued. However, the question arises: What would Clausewitz say about an attack like the one by NotPetya? Is it a legitimate tactical means used in battle? Certainly not one of symmetric warfare. Because according to Clausewitz, tactics are defined as the "doctrine of the use of armed forces in battle". In contrast, strategy is "the doctrine of the use of individual battles for the purpose of war".

Therefore, his thoughts on guerrilla warfare, which Clausewitz also called "small war", are more revealing in this context. He understood this as a form of warfare suitable for conducting a people's war. It does not have to be army against army in an armed conflict, but other actors, such as guerrilla fighters recruited from the people, can also be involved in a war. Even though Clausewitz is credited with being the first to fully describe this form of war, it is still not sufficient to fully describe and understand cyber warfare. Because for Clausewitz, the guerrilla fighters in the tension field of attack and defense took on the role of defense forces. Their advantage was that they were inconspicuous and could maneuver flexibly until they could go on the tactical offensive for the purpose of defense. Clausewitz did not foresee that such forces would be used for the purpose of attack.

But even if Clausewitz does not provide a clear description and classification of cyber warfare, his key concepts nonetheless help to delineate the theoretical field and to describe and classify the behavior and approach of the new actors. The extent to which Clausewitz's impact extends beyond his time is also demonstrated by his application in the field of economics. His theories and works have long been part of the curricula of economics and business administration. Clausewitz is also indispensable in many management schools and books. An example of this is the book "Clausewitz. Thinking Strategy", published by the Strategy Institute of the Boston Consulting Group. In addition to the work of Sun Tzu mentioned earlier, Clausewitz now also belongs in every bookshelf of military personnel or business leaders.

5

The Shift of Powers, Borders, and Resources

Nothing is as constant as change.
Heraclitus

On the one hand, one could rightly argue that it is a constant in human history that power relations have always changed, borders have shifted, and new resources have been tapped and used for wars. On the other hand, this very fact provides the occasion to ask the question at the transition to the present: What is really new and what is as before? Let's consider the situation where only man stands against man on the battlefield. Here one could clearly suspect that this form of power struggle no longer exists. And even though recent wars such as those in Afghanistan, the Syrian war, and the Ukraine war have shown that even the oldest techniques and tactics still play a certain role, a closer analysis reveals a highly complex, asymmetric situation on the battlefield. When armies still faced each other, the numerical ratio of both sides was paramount. If

© The Author(s), under exclusive license to Springer Fachmedien
Wiesbaden GmbH, part of Springer Nature 2024
P. Kestner, *The Art of Cyber Warfare*,
https://doi.org/10.1007/978-3-658-43879-1_5

1,000 men stood against 10,000 men, the army leader had to come up with a lot to still achieve a victory. Think of the advice from the 13 chapters of Sun Tzu. And already in the chapter about the Middle Ages, we learned how the invention of techniques shakes this logic of numerical ratios. What was the invention of the crossbow back then is the use of remote-controlled drones today. As a result, there are now acts of war in which no human being needs to be involved on site. This person can sit hundreds of kilometers away at a computer and remotely control the drone or carry out a hack. Being aware of this development can be all the more shocking when you see war scenes reminiscent of those from past centuries.

The point here, however, is different: With the advancement of technology and modern warfare, power relations also shift. A small, economically very weak country like North Korea has a position to play on the world political stage, not only because of its nuclear weapons. It only needs a few, but highly specialized hackers, to cause targeted unrest around the world. Another example is the hacker groups named APT28 or APT29. APT stands for the attack method "Advanced Persistent Threat" mentioned earlier, which is particularly used by states. There are numerous such groups that are assigned to different states: APT39 is presumably Iran, APT40 and APT41 are probably China, and APT32 could be Vietnam. There are also hacker groups like APT5, where it is still unclear whether and which country they can be assigned to. Often these are a collection of not even 20 people. In the case of APT28, there are likely to be many more now, as it can be assumed that the Russian government generously provides this troop with financial resources. The striking power of APT28 is now so notorious that the entire IT world fears it. Their approach is like that with a crowbar. In every system they penetrate, they override everything, cause immense damage, and disappear again without cleaning up. The group is often used for political and economic attacks and is available for any dirty job. It used to be a small special unit, today a troop with massive strength. The reputation that precedes them—brutal, but also brutally good—unfortunately proves itself in practice too often. The group has several other names and is sometimes also called Fancy Bear, Tsar Team, or Strontium. The fact that so much is known about the procedures of the individual hacker groups is anything but a coincidence. Here again, a brief reminder of the decryption of the Enigma helps to understand why this aspect is so important. The procedures can be used to identify the identity of the hacker groups. Each group and each hacker has a certain signature to some extent. This circumstance helps enormously with forensics. The parallel to the decryption of the Enigma: Even then, a key was the human factor. The peculiarity of certain radio operators, always sending a radio message at the same time or using characteristic formulations or the speed at which they were morse, helped enormously with decryption. Hackers are also people and they too are looking for recognition, money, and fame— the old, typical motives for conflicts: wealth, power, fame, lust, and honor. This also improves their order situation.

If these typical behaviors did not exist, it would often be difficult to assign responsibility for cyber operations. Because: Code is code. It is independent of the country in which it is written and which is behind an attack. Sometimes tricks are deliberately used—think of Sun Tzu or the tactic of camouflage and deception—to make it difficult for the attacked and forensic scientists. Just because Russian code appears in malware does not mean that the attackers come from Russia. A Dutchman can also write Russian, Chinese, or Vietnamese code lines. It is much more difficult to imitate procedures. That's why they are the real possible fingerprint.

Many hacker groups also often have no political, ideological, or physical home. Like the virtual new-work nomads, they too can move anywhere in the world and offer their services like freelancers for payment to others. In this way, a virtual mercenary has emerged, where a small hacker army can simply be bought. For this reason, access and availability of resources represent a significant difference between then and now. While it was still decisive for war a few centuries ago who had the necessary resources, these are now available at any time. Let's remember from here once again the formula that Clausewitz set up to calculate the means, which was:

Resistance of the opponent = Size of the means × Strength of the willpower

It is noticeable that the size of the resources was a crucial factor in this equation. However, this looks very different today when we look into the world of cyberspace. What role do resources then play? If someone is planning a large-scale attack on the critical infrastructure of a hostile country, it is a valid option to simply steal the resources needed for this. Just think of the numerous, well-known raids in which Bitcoins worth hundreds of millions of dollars were transferred to fraudsters. For most actions, this is more than enough budget, because after all, unlike in earlier times, you don't need to feed an army of 20,000 men. Today, an army of bot computers, which need to be hijacked via malware for a major attack, is sufficient. These can be switched off the day after the attack and resold. Attackers in cyberspace can act quickly and flexibly. Digital mercenaries can be active in Ukraine today and in Kuala Lumpur tomorrow. Whether in the past or today—this is not possible with a classic physical army. Agility is not only something that is preached in many companies, but a lived reality of cyber warfare. But this is only one aspect in which it differs from the wars of earlier times.

National borders and zones of influence played a significant role for many centuries when it came to strategic marriage politics among the nobility and royal houses or wars were waged. However, in cyber warfare, borders no longer apply. This does not mean that there will no longer be conflicts over the course of national borders or the struggle for national identities. The recent wars of the present prove the opposite. However, for the central actors of cyber warfare, it no longer matters where in the world they are. The presence of a technical infrastructure is more important to them than the country in which they are located. They can plan and use their efforts flexibly. For observers and those affected, both pieces of information contained in this description are important. Because this means on the one hand that the drivers leading to conflicts will remain unchanged in the future. They can be recognized early on and thus the course and developments can be estimated. On the other hand, this means that it will become more difficult to clearly identify the position of the enemy. The classic, symmetrical course of war could therefore someday be a thing of the past, because the course of war in cyber warfare will become confusing. The latter can happen with full awareness of the participants, because this also brings tactical advantages. The temporal course will also become increasingly blurred, as actions in cyberspace can take a lot of time or be prepared for a long time. Confessions can also be waited for a long time, as it is of tactical advantage to leave the attacked in the dark about who attacked him at all. Again, the bridge can be built to the decryption of the Enigma. It was of absolute importance not to reveal too early that the code of the Enigma had been cracked. The less the opponent knows about one's own abilities and successes, the better. That's why the British had to let a passenger ship, which the Nazis planned to attack, sink during World War II. Because by deciphering intercepted messages encrypted with the Enigma, the Allies knew about the planned action. However, they decided not to protect the target of the attack, as they would otherwise have revealed that they had the ability to crack the codes of the Enigma. The British thus consciously accepted collateral damage in order not to jeopardize their medium and long-term goal with a short-term action.

The Nature of Cyber Warfare

This part of the book is generally about exploring what is new about cyber warfare and what (old) known aspects from earlier times can be found in it. In other words, it is about determining the nature of cyber warfare to some extent, much like Clausewitz did in his work. The question, however, is whether this is so easily possible. Because if borders no longer play a decisive role, this means that cyber warfare presents itself as a borderless struggle. Does everything dissolve here so that nothing can be recognized anymore? Not quite. Because just because national borders no longer play the role they once did, this does not necessarily mean that no order can be recognized at all. Clausewitz himself called war a "true chameleon," "because it changes its nature somewhat in each specific case." To grasp the nature of cyber warfare more precisely, we must deal even more intensively with its real formation. According to Clausewitz, there were three constants or axes by which the nature of war could be determined.

So let's ask: What are the means, the goals, and the purpose of cyber warfare?

Digital Weapons and the "Silent Arms Race"

Let's first deal with the means of cyber warfare: digital weapons and digital infrastructure. A key characteristic of cyber warfare is therefore the digital armament time. In general, armament refers to the military measures taken to maintain military resources and prepare for operations such as attack or defense. Looking at the military development of different states and alliances, a distinction is also made between armament and disarmament. The geopolitical ambition of individual countries can also be read from the expenditure on military armament—in this respect, such information always also has a communicative aspect. In particular, the USA, which spends by far the most on armament (in 2021: 801 billion US dollars), thereby signals that they are ready to defend their world supremacy by all means. China, on the other hand, which has been catching up in terms of its armament expenditure for many years, is now in second place (with 293 billion US dollars in 2021).

The situation looks quite different when we turn to the digital arms race. Different insofar as information about armament expenditures is not communicated to the outside world to the same extent. Also, progress in the field of cyber defense and cyber forces is not recognizable through reconnaissance flights or satellite images. Much information only exists because it came to light more or less by chance, was uncovered through intensive espionage, or was made public by whistleblowers. Deliberate disinformation, for example, to be deliberately underestimated by the enemy, should not be forgotten here. From today's perspective, it seems clear that we are mainly dealing with four cyber superpowers. The USA is at the forefront, followed at some distance by China, Israel, and Russia. But the EU and NATO do not need to shy away from this comparison, but can certainly play in the top league. These countries have capacities of several tens of thousands of cyber soldiers who are available at any time. In addition to such digital warriors, a technical infrastructure is also needed. This, in turn, can be seen from space, because the data centers, some of which have several hundred thousand servers, produce so much heat that they can easily be located with satellites equipped with infrared sensors. However, there is no way around such data centers of this magnitude. Because these capacities are necessary to carry out the time-consuming guessing game to determine the sources of attacks. Because only if the exact origin of an attack could be clearly identified, which has so far happened very rarely, can targeted countermeasures also be taken. The question "Who against whom?" is crucial for cyber warfare and will encounter us more often.

The decisive factor at this point is above all that the digital arms race takes place in silence. The less the other side knows about one's own capabilities, the better. At the same time, of course, there is a kind of digital saber-rattling. Especially smaller players who want to appear bigger and more dangerous—they probably have read their Sun Tzu well—use this method deliberately. But there is another aspect to the digital arms race that is often forgotten. Preparing for attack and defense also involves testing the weaknesses of potential enemies for future attacks or countermeasures. Sometimes this is also referred to as an "active response". According to statements by military experts, the Bundeswehr's arsenal, for example, includes malware that can disrupt, manipulate or disable the communication systems of the enemy army, such as radios or mobile phones, in foreign deployments. In addition, there is the method of overload attack, in which a system is bombarded with requests until it is brought to its knees. The use of digital weapons in the first sense, i.e., by injecting malware, can only be successfully carried out in practice if both the software and the technical device used by the enemy have been analyzed in advance for possible attack options and security gaps. This must happen in silence and long in advance so that the element of surprise is not lost during actual deployment. Whether and how such attack methods can be used in the case of Germany and NATO depends on other factors as well. Because the discussion about the use of digital weapons is still in its infancy. There is neither a consensus within the Bundeswehr and alliances like NATO, nor a legal basis from the country or cross-border legislators. How far other countries have progressed in the development of such weapon systems in the meantime can only be speculated. It is known, however, that states like Israel have been using a digital weapon since 2007 that can manipulate enemy air surveillance systems. With the malware, the control system of a radar can be altered so that certain flight movements are not displayed. This allows unnoticed air operations for reconnaissance or attack purposes.

Quite apart from the technical possibilities of digital weapons and the consequences that result from their use, their development in the course of the silent arms race is not without problems. As mentioned, the possibility of using such systems must be tested, enemy systems analyzed, and the defense case rehearsed. There is a risk that too much forward defense could also be considered an attack and could hardly be distinguished from it de facto and de jure.

If we remember what was said about hybrid warfare in the previous chapter, then the invisibility of power and progress corresponds with the silent arms race. For the pursuit of goals within the framework of hybrid warfare, it is of great importance that the change of the status quo, for example through propaganda, sabotage or other cyber operations, takes place gradually, almost in slow motion. Power thus manifests itself inconspicuously, almost invisibly in very small steps. Even if the goals are pursued in the long term and the actions sometimes only have an indirect effect, the essential thing is that it happens covertly. It is a "stealth operation at a snail's pace" that combines the factor of time with the factor of invisibility. It is a success for the actors of cyber warfare if they remain undetected for as long as possible. Therefore, they strive to move below the threshold of violent acts and escalation and not to become visible in the process.

What is the Goal of Cyber Warfare?

In the next step, we must deal with the war objectives in the Clausewitzian manner. It must be critically questioned whether cyber warfare has a goal or can even have one. In the rarest cases, cyber warfare is located at the level of the battlefield, although every tank today is a mobile supercomputer that must be equipped with its own cyber defense. Against the background of hybrid warfare, it is rather to be considered that cyber operations aim to open up gray areas and distort, delimit, or at least shift the lines of the battlefield. Therefore, in cyber warfare, everything can ultimately become a target: the cohesion of a society, the critical infrastructure of a country, the morale of an actor, the legitimacy of political objectives, and so on. All domains—starting with politics and diplomacy, through the economy and finance, to the critical infrastructure of a country—can be considered as potential targets. Many activities discussed under the term cyber warfare can therefore hardly be subordinated to a uniform goal. If the motivation is merely to inflict the greatest possible damage on the enemy, this naturally contributes to the desire to be superior in ideological, economic, or individual terms. But is the demonstration of power really a goal? Or is it not rather a constant and a timeless driver of conflicts in general. Because what will remain the same in the future is the question of the balance of power: Who is the powerful one here? Who wants power? Who wants fame, honor, or money? And even if these questions have remained the same, the answers today and in the future can be fundamentally different.

It is quite different with the cyber warriors. A single person has the power to threaten an entire company or even challenge an entire state. However, he does not need nearly as many resources as a state has to spend on building and maintaining an army. So we are dealing with a completely new power constellation that we have to learn to deal with. What does it mean to be "powerful" in the future? Fame and honor are terms that are charged very differently today than in the past. We must also ask whether the drivers like lust will have different effects. For example, a new kind of pleasure is currently being observed in cyberspace, namely that of causing damage. There are subcultures where it is considered glorious to harm large corporations that are seen as a symbol of bad capitalism. Here we are dealing with a kind of retelling of an old narrative. The digital Robin Hood takes from the rich, without necessarily giving the booty to the poor. These have rather a symbolic gain, which they enjoy. Leaks also play an important role in this context. These are also a booty that is distributed to the general public. Large, powerful states like the USA had to record a major image damage after Julian Assange and Edward Snowden had uncovered the approach of the American military as part of the Wiki-Leaks.

To get closer to the question of the goal of cyber warfare, it must therefore be more precisely about the question: "Who against whom?". A goal in the sense of Clausewitz can only be meaningfully spoken of if it is states on both sides. In this context, the intelligence services and the divisions that carry out actions in cyberspace on behalf or in the name of states must be subjected to a closer look. The United Nations names three goals that such activities can pursue: 1) Online espionage, 2) acts of sabotage, and 3) attacks on critical infrastructures. So it's about information gathering, disruption or interruption of communication systems, or the disabling of facilities and systems such as power plants, the electricity or transport network, or the water supply. In the context of today's definition, cyber warfare cannot yet exist as an independent phenomenon, but it is a side show that can be used to achieve higher-level goals (such as territorial gain or change of power)—however, it would be the perfect "preparation tool" for this. Cyber attacks are therefore just a new form of warfare and represent an extension of the war away from the demarcated battlefield into the boundless digital world.

How much the old boundaries still have a meaning in reality and where we currently stand in terms of the evaluation of cyber operations became clear in July 2020. For the first time in the history of the EU, cyber sanctions were imposed against individuals from Russia, North Korea, and China. Specifically, the sanctions were travel bans and the freezing of assets. All measures available to the EU are below the threshold of armed conflicts. So even malicious and serious cyber operations like the Bundestag hack, NotPetya or WannaCry are not considered acts of war. Why is that? First and foremost, because currently, due to the legal basis, it is not allowed to "strike back". And with the other justification, we are moving far away from Clausewitz's thinking. It may not surprise many when it comes to bureaucracy at the EU level. When the EU imposes cyber sanctions, they must be lawful—after all, every person against whom sanctions are imposed is granted the right to bring an action for annulment before the European Court of Justice. To ensure legality, a careful and comprehensible investigation is therefore necessary first, with which the perpetrators of a cyber attack can be clearly identified. This takes a very long time and brings further difficulties. The attribution of cyber attacks should be coherent and consistent in technical, legal, and political terms. However, attribution is a sovereign act for which the individual EU member states are responsible. As so often, there are very different approaches, technical and intelligence capabilities in each country. The EU's task is to coordinate all the different activities around forensic evidence collection, to collect these, and to exchange the knowledge gained from them.

Does Cyberwar Have a Purpose?

Just as a reminder: According to Clausewitz, the purpose dimension of war is about "forcing the opponent to fulfill our will". The crucial question is who is meant by "us". Clausewitz himself discusses this at the political level. The purpose of war is therefore conditioned by political will formation and is therefore also linked to the people. Without a political will, there can be no meaningful talk of war. If we follow this definition, there can be no cyberwar in a vacuum. This automatically means that cyberwar activities are tied to certain state or political actors. Let's take a closer look at these.

To return to Clausewitz one last time: An important factor in his thinking was the structure between the commander-in-chief and the standing army. He contrasted this with the activities of individual groups or fighters in the context of partisan warfare. However, if we systematically look at the actors in cyberspace, we initially find all possible groupings. There are units assigned to the army, such as the Bundeswehr's Cyber Command, as well as groups like Fancy Bear, APT29, APT30, APT40, etc., which operate more or less freely, can be hired.as mercenaries, or are presumably assigned to individual states. Interestingly, the size of countries or states is becoming increasingly irrelevant. Otherwise, it would be hard to explain how a small and poor country like North Korea can appear on the geopolitical world map as one of the main opponents in cyberspace. But as we know, Sun Tzu anticipated this 2500 years ago by demonstrating tactics and ways to achieve victory against apparently superior opponents. New, inconspicuous actors like digital nomads or mercenaries or digital warriors are therefore also part of the spectrum of possible war participants, as the line between crime and warfare is blurred. The consequences of this will be the main topic of the next chapter. However, for this context, it should be noted that a key characteristic of events in cyberspace is the need to identify the authorship of warlike activities and the motivations behind them. Only in this way can we make a meaningful distinction between criminal activities, vandalism, or cyberwar, under which not everything that happens in terms of violent acts in cyberspace can be subsumed.

Cyberwar and Cyber Diplomacy

The fact that this is not just about pure mental acrobatics, but about a necessary confrontation with a new reality, becomes apparent when we take a closer look at the opposite side of cyberwar: peace. To secure peace, we will also need something like cyber diplomacy in the future. Otherwise, there would be—if you want to react to malicious activities in cyberspace at all—only the possibility to respond with similar means, which would lead to a spiral of violence and further escalation. Cyber diplomacy is an attempt to extend current diplomacy by another dimension of cyberspace and to cover the dangers and possibilities in this area in order to react in a peaceful way to the increased threat situation. A precise technical, legal, and political classification is a prerequisite for this. To get an idea of where we currently stand: The Five-Eyes Alliance, a coalition of the intelligence services of the USA, Great Britain, Canada, Australia, and New Zealand, is considered the gold standard—if it is exclusively about the aspect of attribution. Some call this secret service alliance the "most exclusive club" in the world and it almost sounds a bit like an invention from a James Bond film. However, this partnership between the mentioned countries has existed since 1946 as a continuation of the cooperation that arose during the Second World War. The speed of identification and assignment of responsibility could be seen in the context of the Corona pandemic. Just a few months after its outbreak, a comprehensive dossier was available, making serious accusations against China, such as cover-up attempts by the Chinese government and the theory of the origin of the virus in the laboratory. The truth of these accusations is not the issue here, but rather the speed. Even though the Five-Eyes Alliance has little to do with cyber diplomacy, it shows how quickly it is possible to identify the perpetrators of cyber actions. For comparison: After individual EU states were attacked in the context of cyber attacks like the Bundestag hack of 2015 or NotPetya 2017, it took many months and sometimes even years to clearly evaluate the actions and impose appropriate sanctions. Whether the signal effect of these countermeasures really fulfilled their purpose is debatable. But the example also illustrates the new standards at work here. To deal with a changed threat situation, which requires little more than a group of skilled hackers and laptops, a tremendous effort must be made in terms of personnel, technology, and finance. Since 2013, we know from the revelations of Edward Snowden that ethical boundaries are also being crossed. As part of the NSA's surveillance of internet traffic, which also contributes to the Five-Eyes Alliance, the entire internet data traffic was monitored and evaluated with the PRISM program. Even though the goal was to detect and pursue suspicious activities, the digital communication of millions of innocent and unsuspecting citizens was also monitored. With this dragnet technique, it is inevitable that data from law-abiding citizens will also be intercepted. Since then, the question of what security in cyberspace means has been completely redefined. In recent years, in the development of cyber security strategies, such as those pursued by the EU since 2013, one thing has become more than clear: new wars require new rules.

6

New Rules for a New War

I'm thinking about something much more important than bombs.
I'm thinking about computers.
John von Neumann, 1946

Today, every war is considered to be in violation of international law. Any threat or use of force between the member states of the United Nations and their international relations is fundamentally prohibited. The only exception to the rule is the right to self-defense and violence committed within the framework of sanctions decided by the UN Security Council. However, the assessment of wars and violence has not always been this way. Also due to Clausewitz and his reception described above, war was long considered a continuation of politics by other means. This only fundamentally changed in the course of the 19th century. Since then, a number of international conventions have been concluded. They regulate compliance with humanitarian international law in the context of armed

© The Author(s), under exclusive license to Springer Fachmedien Wiesbaden GmbH, part of Springer Nature 2024
P. Kestner, *The Art of Cyber Warfare*,
https://doi.org/10.1007/978-3-658-43879-1_6

conflicts and serve to protect people who are wounded, prisoners of war, and civilians who do not participate in the fighting. The history of humanitarian international law is interesting in itself, but also provides valuable insights for our context.

Already in the course of the 20th century, the nature of warfare changed fundamentally time and again due to technological developments in various areas. Therefore, the conventions also had to be constantly adapted and expanded. After the experiences of the First World War, for example, the use of chemical and biological weapons was banned in the Geneva Protocol of 1925. So, it is not the first time in history that the rules for war have to be renegotiated due to a technical or scientific development. Also, in view of the hitherto unimaginable destructive power of the atomic bomb, a long debate ignited about how states should behave in the future. One result of this dispute is the Nuclear Non-Proliferation Treaty, which the five nuclear powers USA, Russia, China, France, and Great Britain signed in 1968. Recently, this was supplemented by the Treaty on the Prohibition of Nuclear Weapons, which, however, was not negotiated or signed by some key states and is therefore not of great importance. It is important to note here that this chapter is far from being concluded. But at least as epochal as the exploration of nuclear energy and its civil and military use is the invention of the computer and subsequently the emergence of cyberspace. The quote from John von Neumann from 1946 shows how early he was aware of the epochal significance of the computer age. The dropping of the two atomic bombs on Hiroshima and Nagasaki was only a few months ago. Because in the coming decades, a completely different order and rules were negotiated on the world stage. During the Cold War and the time of the Iron Curtain, questions about dealing with nuclear weapons or nuclear powers were almost exclusively in focus. Cyberspace, which also gradually emerged during this time, was—if at all—only a marginal or accompanying phenomenon. Its importance was not recognized for a long time. This has fundamentally changed today. While dealing with nuclear energy and the use of nuclear weapons is still highly relevant and perhaps even more explosive than ever before, it is also becoming apparent that we are facing a completely different and novel challenge with cyber warfare, which should not be overshadowed by this. Today, completely new questions arise, for example with regard to the increase in non-state actors who play an increasingly important role in warfare alongside states in cyberspace. This calls into question existing categories of international law and they must be renegotiated. We also need to ask what counts as a "weapon" or "armed attack". Both the automation of weapon systems and the development of pure software weapons must increasingly be included in the debate. Because the human factor in warfare, which has always been crucial in the assessment of acts of violence, is increasingly being pushed into the background. Therefore, we will deal with two questions here. First, the question of why we need rules for war at all and how these have been historically spelled out. And secondly, the question must be addressed of what technical innovations cyber warfare brings with it, for which new rules are sensible or even necessary.

Why are There Even Rules for War?

Fundamentally, war is the exact opposite of rule-compliant behavior. Laws and norms that otherwise apply are suspended in war. War is a state of exception. And yet, there are internationally recognized agreements and rules for this as well. The most well-known example today is probably the Hague Convention of 1907, also called the Hague Convention, which was supplemented in 1949 by the Geneva Convention. But modern humanitarian international law has a long history. One of the central figures in this context is Hugo Grotius (1583–1645). He founded the science of international law as a separate field of research and with his *Three Books on the Law of War and Peace(De Jure Belli ac Pacis libri tres)* he laid the foundation in 1625 for the distinction between legitimate and illegitimate wars as well as international law, of which he is considered the "father". At the same time, he developed arguments for the so-called "just war" (lat.: *bellum iustum*). This legal historical discourse reaches far back into the Western tradition and deals with the question of whether and under what conditions a military conflict is legally and ethically legitimate. For example, if a state is attacked by another, according to Grotius, it should be legitimate and therefore just to defend oneself with military means. Thanks to Grotius, the legal and contractual argumentation of the underlying justifications has been based on natural law since modern times.

Another important milestone that led to today's international law is the Thirty Years' War, or rather the political order that was negotiated in the peace treaties of the Peace of Westphalia in 1648. If one follows the development of humanitarian international law further, two peculiarities can be observed that can still be seen today: On the one hand, treaties are usually concluded or expanded when a war has just taken place. On the other hand, it is noticeable that the worse the atrocities during the war were, the more the focus is placed on the protection of the civilian population. It is therefore no coincidence that, for example, the Geneva Convention was significantly expanded after the Second World War and has since provided comprehensive "protection of civilians in times of war" as well as other persons not directly involved in the war. However, since cyberwar, as described above, does not have an event character, but proceeds silently and operates specifically in gray areas, it is questionable whether there will be such a moment in the future that provides the occasion to think about changing and adapting the rules to the new circumstances. Therefore, I would like to give the impulse here to initiate the discourse today on how cyberwar is to be classified under international law and what measures can be derived from the means and methods of cyber warfare. And already the chairman of the Diplomatic Conference of Geneva, Max Petitpierre, said in 1949 that it is pointless to conclude agreements between warring parties during wartime. Therefore, war must be regulated in peacetime. So where do we stand today? Perhaps history can provide a clue here as well. Because we have already experienced a situation that is somewhat comparable to the silent arms race. In the Cold War, as the term suggests, there were never any real combat actions. We were dealing with a stalemate situation. At that time, this could help to maintain peace. It was clear to all participants at the time that no one wants to press the famous "red button" first. Because one can be sure that the other will then do the same.

In many respects, this is also the case with cyberwar at the moment. When a state or another organization develops a cyber weapon, this fact is usually kept strictly secret. The reason is simple. A malware can only be used once. As soon as an attack is known and the code is made public, the other side and all other potential opponents can work on the solution for defense, defense and counterattack. Therefore, we experience—as in the Cold War—extremely rarely a show-off. In the digital arms race, there are also no weapons parades and no digital saber-rattling. Rumors and leaks represent a new possibility for power demonstration. Also like in the Cold War, we are currently experiencing a new peak in espionage activity and the activity of the secret services. Because although there is hardly a stage for the power demonstration, it is clear to all participants and insiders: The threat situation in cyberspace is enormous. Of course, we are still dealing with an unresolved and problematic situation with regard to the nuclear threat. But perhaps this is exactly the state we have to get used to in cyberwar. More than ever, the saying is true: "Peace is only a pause between two wars". Because the times of peace are completely blurred by cyberwar. How can one speak of peace when there are regular cyber attacks that no one admits to? How do you even define victory and defeat in cyberspace? Is there such a thing as digital destruction and what could it look like? Questions like these are essential to prepare for the worst case. The protection of the civilian population and critical infrastructure is not only a question relevant under international law, but also a very practical one that politics, the economy, but also every individual must ask themselves. While this question will be dealt with more intensively later, the focus will initially be on the classification of cyberwar under international law.

On the International Legal Classification of Cyberwar

Generally speaking, there is a consensus within the international community that international law applies to cyberspace. What is still lacking is a uniform legal understanding of the impact and political as well as legal significance this has for individual international legal norms.

The context in which cyberwar is embedded here should be treated with caution for another reason. Because strictly speaking, cyberwar, even though the term appears in the word, is not yet a war in the actual, legal sense from an international law perspective. The Stuxnet attack on the Iranian nuclear program, which was described above in connection with the Middle Ages, is perhaps the cyber attack that comes closest to violating the prohibition of violence. The latter is regulated in Art. 2 para. 4 of the Charter of the United Nations (UN Charter). The paragraph in its wording:

> "All Members shall refrain in their international relations from the threat or use of force against the territorial integrity or political independence of any state, or in any other manner inconsistent with the Purposes of the United Nations."

The problem already arises with the first two words of the paragraph. Because how are incidents to be assessed that cannot be clearly attributed to a state? There is still an urgent need for action here, for example by establishing internationally valid rules on how the perpetrators of cyber operations can be clearly identified (attribution). Of course, we are not at the beginning here. Initial efforts in this direction have been made since 2013 at EU level and in the United Nations forum. Together they are in search of cyber norms that can be anchored in international law in order to be able to represent and enforce a valid international order for the cyber and information space (CIR) on this basis. For example, it was agreed in 2015 that the response to a cyber attack should always be proportional. In other words: A counter-reaction is only legally legitimized if a cyber attack has exceeded a certain threshold in terms of scope and effect to be comparable to an armed attack. In cases where the prohibition of violence is violated and physical destruction of objects or loss of human life occurs in the course of an armed attack, Art. 51 of the UN Charter guarantees the right of self-defense to attacked states. It reads:

> "Nothing in the present Charter shall impair the inherent right of individual or collective self-defence if an armed attack occurs against a Member of the United Nations, until the Security Council has taken measures necessary to maintain international peace and security."

In view of such serious consequences that a cyber operation such as Stuxnet could trigger, it must be said at this point in time that cyberwar cannot yet be evaluated as a war in the actual sense from an international law perspective. But this does not mean that this situation cannot change in the future. Just think of the great damage and the high number of victims among the civilian population that a cyber attack on a nuclear power plant could have. Even if governments have not yet classified cyber operations in this way or even discussed this case, there is nothing in international law to prevent cyber weapon attacks from being classified as acts of violence. Where exactly this threshold lies, how to explore and measure the gray area in which the hybrid cyber war is fought, these tasks remain today.

The reason why these associated questions arise can be well answered by history. Because in the context of the emergence of international law and the humanitarian rules for war, there were always two camps. One camp argued from the side that war belongs to the history of mankind and it must be asked when a military conflict and violence is justified and when not. This was associated with the question of who is a party to the war and which life must be protected despite the war. Over time, the so-called peace movement emerged from the other camp, which has been actively trying to participate in the negotiations since the 19th century. Its concern is to establish an order with international agreements such as the Geneva Conventions that prevents war and aims for a peaceful coexistence of a community of states. Even in Article 1 of the UN Charter, it says that the purpose of the founding of the United Nations is "world peace" and the preservation of international security. Both lines of thought can be found in the discussions to this day. They unite the question of how brutal and sprawling a war may be and whether there should not be limits that hostile parties should adhere to in order to spare innocent life. The aim of this long dispute was to find a consensus that certain civilian objects such as hospitals or groups of people such as children, medical personnel, old or disabled people should not be attacked during a war. The destruction of the livelihood of the civilian population and the torture of prisoners is also prohibited according to the existing rules. Anyone who does not adhere to them commits a war crime and can be prosecuted accordingly before the International Criminal Court (ICC) based in The Hague. However, the whole story also includes the fact that important states such as the USA, Russia, China and Israel have not signed or ratified the corresponding agreement, so that the ICC is not responsible for them. Whether it is a coincidence or not— this means that the four cyber superpowers that the world currently knows belong to the circle of these states.

Despite such significant restrictions, the history of the conventions must be considered a success. After all, 196 states have now ratified the Geneva Conventions and thus committed themselves to the protection of wounded soldiers, prisoners of war, shipwrecked persons and the civilian population. In addition, the development has shown that with the further development of weapons and other military technologies, an extension of the international treaties became necessary. Not only in view of the new risks and dangers in the cyber and information space, but also because of the recent wars, the question must be asked whether it is not time to critically question and possibly expand the existing "rules of war".

The Cyber War and the Transformation of Armed Violence

Even though the tactics, strategies, procedures, and motives leading to wars and conflicts remain constant or at least similar throughout history, the means and techniques change quite significantly. This has effects on both the course of conflicts and their end. For example, we are increasingly seeing that a war can no longer be won with purely military means. As national borders no longer play the role they used to, wars between two states may in the future also present themselves as purely internal conflicts. The influence of private individuals or private companies on the course of war, as was partly observed in recent conflicts, brings a new quality. Precisely for this reason, the battlefield is increasingly expanding into other areas and levels, which were extensively described above in connection with hybrid warfare. Therefore, it is becoming increasingly difficult to define the boundaries of what belongs to war. Even if the definition does not yet include this, more thought must be given in the future to the extent to which economic and trade wars, propaganda and disinformation, and other forms of cyber warfare must be understood as part of what constitutes a war. Because it is already foreseeable today that, firstly, conventional weapon systems and military equipment such as tanks, air defense systems, radios, etc. will be equipped with technology themselves, making them part of cyberspace. In addition, secondly, new intelligent and autonomous weapon systems are being developed, the effects of which on the battlefield have only been guessed at or visualized by films like *Terminator* or *Star Wars*. And finally, thirdly, pure software weapons and concerted cyber operations are targeting areas that were previously separate from the war. These three developments alone make it necessary to fundamentally reassess war and armed violence. So how can the protection of civilians and critical infrastructures be ensured in the future when they become the target or the scene of cyber warfare? Since cyber warfare and cyber operations have so far not been formally assessed as war or do not violate the prohibition of violence, the Geneva Conventions do not necessarily have to be observed. This obviously leads to malicious actors focusing precisely on this area and making the cyber and information space the scene of conflicts more than ever.

Cyber as the Fifth Dimension?

So what exactly is this cyberspace? The times when a war is characterized by a demarcated battlefield and its consequences can be measured by it are over. Rather, we must deal with and understand the boundless digital world. Because today we are on the threshold of an era in which the military conflicts are transferred to the internet. Therefore, cyberspace has sometimes been portrayed as the fifth pillar, but as already hinted at, cyberspace is actually *in* many other areas. So we need a more precise definition of what cyber warfare is and where perhaps the boundaries of what is referred to here as "cyber" lie.

For a long time, the military was divided into three action areas or dimensions. The ground troops or the army operated on land, the navy in the water, and the air force secured the airspace. A few years ago, space was already recognized as another dimension and added to the others. When the increasing threat from cyberspace became apparent, this logic was continued and cyberspace was added to the others as a fifth dimension and treated accordingly. Therefore, the Bundeswehr now has cyber units that sit in front of the computer keyboard and perform their service in this way. But slowly the realization is gaining ground that this understanding falls far short. The navy will have to deal with the cyber dimension just as much as the army and the air force. Because cyberspace encompasses all other dimensions. If frequency jammers are used to disrupt army communications, they need to know how to respond.

This division into different dimensions or separate areas does not only concern the military. Companies also need to learn not to perceive cyberspace as a separate dimension. Specifically, this means that companies do not need a department for cybersecurity, but all departments and essentially every employee need an understanding of security in cyberspace.

The Weapons of the War of the Future

Why this is so becomes clear when we look at the weapons of the war of the future. As we have already seen, a lot can be deduced from weapon technology. In World War II, the development of the atomic bomb was crucial for the end of the war and the subsequent international legal discussion. I am sure that the same will be said in the future regarding the development of computers and software weapons. Let's ask ourselves: What can cause more damage—a 250 kg bomb or a USB stick or maybe just a mouse click? While this question may have been easy to answer a few years ago, the situation is quite different today. All you have to do is consider how many human lives would be at risk if it were possible to attack nuclear power plants with a software weapon and trigger a nuclear meltdown.

We are only seeing the beginnings of this development today, and it is all the more important not to view cyberspace as something separate from the rest of the spheres. The advancing automation and digitization affects, above all, military and weapon technology. Fully autonomous weapon systems may soon be able to select and eliminate targets without human intervention. If there are machine errors or a misjudgment, the (international legal) question of the originator and those responsible arises here as well. How and when is forensic evidence provided here? What happens in cases where software is deliberately manipulated and civilian casualties are accepted or even provoked? Later we will deal intensively with the question of propaganda. But even here, the overall situation in the information space is further complicated. If a massive information offensive is launched on the net as part of covert military operations, blurring and reversing all contexts, what does an appropriate counter-reaction look like—both in military and legal terms?

We already have some practice dealing with disinformation campaigns and propaganda from the Cold War. However, its return in the form of fake news also takes on a new dimension. Because information and secure information exchange are the foundations of modern society. Phenomena such as the Querdenker movement or large-scale and concerted actions to manipulate elections go far beyond the mere factual level and the exchange of opinions. To go a step further, we must think primarily of developments that are associated with the possibilities of artificial intelligence (AI). Just think of the so-called "deepfakes". These are purely digital constructs of human identities that blur or even cross the boundaries to reality. An appropriately trained AI can analyze, modify, and output a video of a real person as a new, fake version. There are already impressive examples circulating on the net that demonstrate the capabilities of AI. The speeches of famous personalities and politicians like Bush, Obama, and Trump are used to put words in their mouths that they would never have said. However, this is just one variant of what is referred to as deepfake. Chatbots that pretend to be humans will be able to communicate with others in a way that is indistinguishable from a conversation with a human. A deepfake can appear as a profile on social media, showing real-looking people who do not exist. How real this can look, anyone can see for themselves. On the website https://thispersondoesnotexist.com/ any number of photos of people can be generated who do not exist. In the background, an algorithm runs that was trained based on an image database containing hundreds of thousands of real images. The neural network—a method from the field of artificial intelligence that uses the functioning of the human brain as a model—learns to understand what a face looks like through feedback. Anyone can see the success of this method for themselves. The combination of all different fields—image generator, manipulation of video streams, and conversation skills—shows what we need to prepare for in the future.

The Automation of War

The development and deployment of robots on the battlefield are probably familiar to most from movies like *Terminator*. Recently, considerations dealing with this new reality have indeed played a role in serious political discourse. Autonomous vehicles or AI-controlled robots have long been part of everyday life—sometimes more, sometimes less gracefully. But no one seriously questions whether, but only when such autonomous systems will surpass human capabilities. Therefore, it is overdue to understand the significance of this development and to deal with its consequences. The civilian use of such technologies is one side. The other is their military use. What are the (international) legal, ethical, security policy, and practical implications of autonomous weapon systems in strategic and military terms? There has been little public comment on this so far.

One of the most famous scenes from the movie *War Games* by John Badham from 1983 shows a self-learning supercomputer playing the game Tic-Tac-Toe against itself until it realizes that it cannot win. In this way, it is taught the absurdity inherent in a nuclear war between two states. This scene may contain much more truth than the film-makers of that time were aware of. It is not unlikely that in the cyber war of the future, algorithm will fight against algorithm and machine against machine. Humans are basically no longer needed. Drones are already being used today, which still have to be controlled by humans, but could do this autonomously. Anyone who wants to get an impression of the capabilities of robots only needs to watch the videos regularly published by Boston Dynamics, a leading robotics company that researches and develops walking robots that can move completely autonomously.

Who can be held legally responsible if such autonomous systems cause civilian casualties? Is it the manufacturer? The government of the country for which a system is in operation? The general who activates the autonomous system or provides it with target data? The "Automatic War" or the "automated war", which arises in the course of the development of automated weapons, autonomous aircraft, and drones, blurs the boundaries between computer games, simulation, and reality. We need a new way of thinking for it. Beyond the question of human casualties, we also have to deal with a new war logic in which there are no more human losses, in which it is only a pure material battle, or fought as a war between bytes, in which the superiority of an opponent or a stalemate is recognized, which no longer has to be fought out in reality.

The Mathematics of the New War

A central change to be discussed in the age of cyber warfare is the mathematics of war. Until the recent past and even in the face of the power of the atomic bomb, which makes it possible to wipe out entire countries and continents at the push of a button, a simple mathematical reciprocity of power relations applies. In a battle where 1000 men fight against 1000 men, the outcome is open. In a ratio of 100,000 to 1,000, the numerically inferior side has to come up with a lot to balance this imbalance. In cyber warfare, we have reached a point in history for the first time where this no longer applies. The damage that can be caused by individuals is no longer directly related to numerical superiority or inferiority. The previous calculations by which military power was measured are now void. While the size of the military budget previously gave a good idea of the striking power of a military force, this is no longer a measure of power today. Today, intelligence is pitted against mass. An individual can cause more damage than 1000 soldiers or 100 tanks. These considerations lead us into another gray area that needs to be renegotiated. When deciding on targets in conventional warfare, the international legal distinction between civilians and civilian objects and military and military targets should always be taken into account. However, this distinction does not rule out that there can be civilian casualties. In this case, we speak of collateral damage. There is no uniform, internationally valid definition of what is considered collateral damage. However, it is already foreseeable today that we need a new understanding of it. Because generally, international law is interpreted in such a way that conflict parties should choose those means and methods that largely avoid unnecessary suffering in the civilian population. Everything that was said above about hybrid warfare is diametrically opposed to this.

Real-Time as a New Challenge

But it's not just the old logic that the stronger one devours the weaker one that no longer applies. Not just because of the techniques and tactics of camouflage and deception, as taught by Sun Tzu. Today, it is more the case that the faster one devours the slower one. What this means becomes clear when we take a closer look at the history of reporting systems. This is characterized by a constant acceleration. And the pinnacle of speed in cyberspace is real-time. Today, this becomes a real information technology and interpretive challenge. Because any real information advantage can decide victory or defeat in a serious case. Therefore, let's ask ourselves what exactly the reporting chain looks like, how it used to work, and how it works today.

Let's think back to the marathon runner who has already shown us the way to cryptography. He was sent off with the goal of passing on information. In addition to the dangers and risks that could lead him astray, there are those that can compromise the information itself, such as through extortion. Also, the time itself, which lies between sending and receiving, is a problem. The information could be long outdated, irrelevant, or revised. In the next evolutionary step, runners were therefore replaced by riders. Information could also be transmitted over long distances in a short time with signal fires or smoke signals. Their disadvantage: They were widely visible and anyone who knew their code could read them accordingly. Also, the complexity of the messages was limited by the medium of transmission. The closer we get to modern times, the more sophisticated the messaging technology becomes. The invention of radio must be considered a technological breakthrough in this context. With it, it was for the first time possible to transmit information of a certain size in encrypted form over long distances in a short time. This allowed both the knowledge gained about enemy troop movements to be quickly passed on to gain a tactical advantage, and at the same time to coordinate one's own troops to implement the advantage. However, these are merely the technical side and the theoretical advantage. From our reading of Clausewitz, we know that reality can be quite different. On the one hand, human factors as well as aspects of power and hierarchy play an important role. Information passed within a system is not just value-neutral facts. Often they are adapted to the personality of the recipient. We know this especially from experiences with dictatorships or choleric or narcissistic autocrats. Negative news is then often glossed over or distorted in some other way when communicating upwards. After all, no one wants to risk their own career. On the other hand, the physical reality must be taken into account. Moving an army means organizing a large mass of people. The factor of 10, 1000, or 10,000 makes not just a quantitative, but a qualitative difference. What does it really mean when I move people of this magnitude from A to B? The logistical and time effort must not be neglected even today in the context of conventional warfare.

Things look very different in the area of pure cyber warfare. If only small hacker units are operating here or if operations are carried out with remotely controlled or autonomous weapon systems, the availability and distribution of information in real time can become a risk. Or in other words: The authenticity of the information becomes absolutely crucial. False or incorrect information can decide over the life and death of innocent people. Soldiers who have to control drones from containers and liquidate targets on command report how stressful the uncertainty about this is. Not knowing whether you have just killed an innocent civilian or a potential terrorist is a mental and physical torment for those affected.

Today, reconnaissance is often carried out via drones and the evaluation of satellite images. Even if this gives the impression of objective truth and reliability, in reality it often looks like there is a certain residual uncertainty. The ancient methods of camouflage and deception are therefore more relevant than ever. One of the most impressive scenes from the already twice mentioned film *The Man Who Never Lived* shows exactly this problem. It takes place in the desert and it's about the agent Roger Ferris (Leonardo DiCaprio) being handed over to the other side and waiting there for the moment of handover. Several thousand meters above him hovers a drone that sends live images of the scene to Washington. The viewer is repeatedly taken into the perspective of the control room. It is a room full of agents and with numerous screens, which is supposed to show the technical superiority. But the members of the terrorist network use a simple trick that all the technology can't cope with. They arrive with four cars and keep driving in circles around Ferris when they arrive. They stir up dust so that the camera can no longer see. Then the handover takes place. Ferris is forced to get into one of the cars. In the next scene, all four cars drive off in different directions. In the control room, you hear the question several times: "Which car should we follow?" But there is no answer to that.

It is precisely this silence that brings the challenges of real-time to the point. It is the hesitation, the ambiguity, and the uncertainty that characterizes the moment of the absolute now. The more the now-time is drawn into the war events, the more difficult and confusing it becomes. The far-reaching implications become apparent when we realize what it means if a cyber attack will trigger the beginning of a war in the future. Because then what we have already described above in connection with the problem of attribution comes into play. There will inevitably be a time difference between the cyber attack and the moment of proof or evidence of who is responsible for the attack. This time gap is characteristic of cyber warfare. It can give one side a practical tactical advantage. But it also symbolically represents a power vacuum that we need to examine more closely.

The Current Situation: Power Struggle and Power Vacuum

We are currently experiencing a situation that makes it even more difficult to conduct an open discourse. Because on the one hand, it's about a power struggle and at the same time about a prevailing power vacuum. A power struggle can be observed on many levels. It starts with the approach within the EU when it comes to attributing cyber attacks. Security policy, which also includes the attribution of cyber attacks, is the responsibility of individual member states. Here, the Enigma principle comes into play again: Even if a state and its intelligence service have the ability to precisely identify who was responsible for a cyber attack, they are very hesitant to share this information. After all, they do not want to reveal their methods and sources, nor do they want this information to fall into the wrong hands or compromise it. This is just one of many examples that show how much mutual distrust still exists in this area and how attempts are being made to expand and consolidate one's own power position. Because it is not yet finally clarified who the new superpowers in cyberspace will be. Even more: It is currently unclear who will be the superpower of the 21st century on the big world stage. Because even the USA, which without a doubt has taken the top position in the past decades, is currently losing influence in many areas and faces major economic, political and social challenges. At the same time, contenders like China, India, but also the EU as a group of states, sense their chance and try to seize it. Such a competition for power, influence and global dominance, however, also brings with it the danger that new wars and conflicts will be waged. In addition, the entire world must adapt to new conditions—be it in terms of climate change or due to digital change.

From what has been said so far, it has already become clear that the lines of conflict will be new and different than usual. In addition to state actors, private companies and individuals will increasingly be drawn into such conflicts. States that want to expand their economic dominance will not shy away from using all available means to engage in industrial espionage or steal all data they can get their hands on. That's why we need internationally binding rules for cyber warfare. Otherwise, we are heading towards a time when chaos reigns, unpredictable interstate conflicts can break out at any time, and every individual could be drawn into cyber warfare.

The Montreux Document as a Model?

Since the 1990s, a trend has been observed that could also be relevant to our context. Private military and security companies were increasingly involved in armed conflicts. Therefore, the Montreux Document was drafted on the initiative of the International Committee of the Red Cross. It was adopted by 17 states in 2008, but is not legally binding under international law. Nevertheless, the Montreux Document could serve as a model or at least as a starting point for the necessary adjustments and changes to international law. For it includes, among other things, proposals for procedures and methods to deal with private security companies and negotiate questions of their liability. In this context, it was also clarified whether and how they can be held accountable for possible crimes under national jurisdiction. This discussion must now be continued and expanded. What about private companies or individuals operating in the field of cybersecurity? If services or technologies they offer are used for war purposes, it is essentially a comparable case to private security firms deployed in war zones. In this context, the distinction between warrior, soldier, and mercenary must also be revisited and discussed. What significance do these terms have in the context of cyber warfare? Do only people who use digital resources as weapons fall under this definition, or also bots and bot farms?

In this context, however, the role of other private companies must also be discussed. Large corporations like Google or SpaceX have the power to interfere in warfare. The fact that Google is very much aware of the significance its own data and associated services can have for conflict parties can be seen from the fact that the company recently deactivated a feature of Google Maps in Ukraine. The live tracking feature, which evaluates data on the current traffic situation in real time, allows users to avoid traffic jams, for example. What serves a practical purpose in everyday life can be abused in war. Information about traffic volumes also provides insights into when, where, and in which direction refugees are currently leaving the country. They or the infrastructure they use could quickly become victims of attacks. To protect their safety, Google decided to deactivate this feature throughout Ukraine. Information about how busy certain public places or shopping centers are is also currently unavailable there for the same reason. Besides these security concerns, however, the data also has a military and intelligence level. Even though this was not part of the official announcement, there are also reports about how completely different traffic jams were displayed on Google Maps in the first days of the war. The troops invading the country were also captured by the search engine giant. This shows how quickly a private company can be drawn into a war situation today.

Another company and a closely associated private individual also made headlines in the context of this war. Elon Musk announced early on that his company Starlink's satellite network should maintain Ukraine's internet supply as a replacement for the destroyed infrastructure. With this step alone, he made both himself as a person and his company a potential target for cyber attacks—but also for very real attacks on satellites in space, if a warring party has such capabilities. For as noble and commendable as the gesture is on one hand, it cannot be denied on the other hand the central tactical function that the transmission of data and information has in the context of wars. Cutting off the enemy's supply of supplies and information has always been an important goal of war tactics. Regardless of the purpose for which the network provided by Starlink is used, however, the international legal dimension should be considered here. If the Montreux Document were applied to this case, the company itself would be responsible for ensuring that the rules of international law are complied with in the use of the services provided. Thus, we have two examples of companies that have become part of a war situation, which illustrate the spectrum of possible reactions and implications. However, this is just a small taste of the many entanglements of private business and interstate conflicts.

On the Relevance of the Geneva Conventions

The Geneva Conventions are an important measuring tool with which similarities, but also differences between cyber warfare and conventional wars can be captured. On the one hand, a change in the type of weapons and warfare as well as in the course of conflicts can be observed. At the same time, we see that the Geneva Agreements have not lost any of their relevance—because at their core, the wars of the present and the future are still being fought over the same constants as in the past. And as in the past, the parties involved fail to maintain the required humanity. Therefore, it is to be feared that the further development of humanitarian international law will only take place in the context of peace negotiations and new agreements after new conflicts have made clear why we need new rules for the new war. But who knows: Maybe the next war will be fought again with slingshots and clubs. Or it will be a war in which only avatars beat each other up.

Necessity of a New Language

Another adjustment that will become necessary, and is already being partially altered, will be in the area of military language. The chapter on propaganda will go into more detail about the power of language. But even at this point, it must generally be asked whether the current language and the terms used are still contemporary or to what extent they need to be adapted to the new reality. Language, and especially military language, has far-reaching implications. If formulations here are even slightly off, a dangerous scope for interpretation can be opened.

The boundaries and possibilities of attributing attacks are increasingly blurred by technological development. The role of intelligence agencies is increasing, while the use of conventional armed forces is simultaneously declining. The question of international law, which is casually phrased as: "Who 'kills' whom?", is becoming increasingly difficult to answer in cyber warfare. To illustrate the current and future extent and the associated new reality of this development, techniques and tactics of cyber warfare will be presented in the following chapter.

Necessity of a New Language

Part III

The Art of Cyber Warfare

While the first two sections of the book dealt with the history and thinkers of antiquity, the Middle Ages, the modern era, and the modern age, with the third section we move into the present and future of cyber warfare. Because as much as we can learn from history for cyber warfare, it also challenges us to rethink certain aspects. What technical innovations are relevant and what do they mean in tactical terms? What do these developments mean for each individual? And how can we deal with the propaganda that is a central accompaniment of cyber warfare? Here too, we can draw on the past: What distinguishes today's propaganda from the past? And what do the previous war-like activities in cyberspace teach us?

7

Techniques and Tactics of Cyber Warfare

Our only chance of long-term survival is to expand into space. The answers to these questions show that we have made great progress in the last hundred years, but if we want to continue beyond the next hundred years, the future is in space. That's why I advocate space travel.

Stephen Hawking

A long time ago in a galaxy far, far away…

Star Wars, Intro

Every Star Wars fan will immediately hear the fanfares and the sound of the entire orchestra at these words, with which each of the films begins. Not for the first time, we use the world of science fiction as an opportunity to learn something about our present world and the future. Because the race for space has long since begun—both in a civilian and military sense. Cyber warfare will also be conducted there, as it is, as just explained, an integral part of all

© The Author(s), under exclusive license to Springer Fachmedien Wiesbaden GmbH, part of Springer Nature 2024
P. Kestner, *The Art of Cyber Warfare*,
https://doi.org/10.1007/978-3-658-43879-1_7

dimensions. It is even quite conceivable that cyber warfare in space will take its actual course, as we will see shortly.

As early as 2020, the Bundeswehr responded to this situation by establishing an operations center for air and space: the "Air and Space Operations Centre" (ASOC). In it, the Bundeswehr combined several of its capabilities to account for the growing military importance of space as an operational dimension. Space operations are therefore not yet part of the Bundeswehr's everyday life. Many technologies needed for monitoring and conducting air operations are also needed for missions in space. In addition, there are already relevant technical infrastructures there that are already in use today and can hardly be imagined without in the lives of all people. Satellite networks enable both civilian and military navigation, as well as communication, data transmission, and reconnaissance. Therefore, space-based satellites are also considered critical infrastructure and must be protected accordingly.

Because even if many people are not strongly aware of it, the technological arms race has long since begun and is of enormous importance. Many people will immediately think of the project to colonize Mars. Although this project has received the most media attention, it is by no means the only planned project beyond our planetary borders. For example, numerous mineral resources such as titanium, platinum, aluminum, or other rare earth metals are stored on the moon. Permanent moon stations are therefore already being planned, as are mining projects to extract the resources located there. The motivation behind such large projects is quite simple: it's about unimaginable amounts of money and therefore also about greed. The first company to succeed in mining resources on the moon and transporting them to Earth would instantly have a valuation in the range of over a trillion dollars. Added to this is the symbolic gain in fame for having been the first to achieve it.

A number of companies, especially from the USA and China, have already begun to build satellite networks in the orbit of our planet. Starlink, one of Elon Musk's many companies, is doing exactly that with the greatest success so far. His ambitious goal is to bring 48,000 Starlink satellites into a Low Earth Orbit (LEO). A single satellite enables a data connection with a bandwidth of 17 gigabits per second. For comparison: A USB-3.1 connection manages 10 gigabits per second. If the entire constellation of 48,000 satellites is in the sky, this would result in a capacity of 816 terabits per second, which is about eight times the performance of a fiber optic cable. A Chinese state-owned company also announced that it wants to build its own constellation following a similar principle to Starlink. The operation of such satellite networks is as follows: Thousands of satellites are gradually placed in low Earth orbits, enabling seamless access to the Internet on Earth. But this not only builds an additional infrastructure that makes connections safer, partly faster, and more resilient. It also allows more people than ever before in history to access the Internet at all. This means a massive political and economic shift in power and also a change in the configuration of power relations. Even though for many inhabitants of the Western world the Internet has become a basic need like access to water and clean air, it should not be forgotten that there are still 37% of the world's population (that's about 2.9 billion people) who, according to the United Nations, have never used the Internet in their lives. Critical infrastructure is never just critical infrastructure—especially when it comes to access to the Internet. The first fully functional satellite network will represent an extreme concentration of economic and political power. The possibilities for political influence are enormous. A company or a state that controls this infrastructure could also decide who has access to the Internet and who does not, and under what conditions information exchange takes place. It is easy to imagine that this is reason enough to attack the newly emerging satellite networks both physically and with means of cyber warfare. What is noticeable so far in this development: Germany and Europe have so far played no role. This also means that they have no say or leeway in shaping the newly emerging digital infrastructure or in co-determining the legal framework according to their values. Whether it is still possible to catch up with the lead of other companies and states through cooperation or negotiations is completely open. However, this should not obscure the importance of these projects. Nothing less than a geopolitical reordering is at stake. An open, free, and globally accessible Internet is not a matter of course and anything but certain.

The Importance of a Global Internet Infrastructure

The power emanating from communication satellites makes them a potential target for attack. Space also gains relevance because, for example, intercontinental missiles initially leave the atmosphere and spend a short time in space before they begin their target approach. As soon as there are weapon-capable satellite systems there, which is only a matter of time, they could be attacked there, for example, by an EMP system or laser-based weapons. An EMP (for English "electromagnetic pulse", or in German: "elektro-magnetischer Impuls") is a weapon system that—like a lightning bolt—briefly emits strong electromagnetic radiation. All electronic components, circuits, and boards are destroyed in the effective field of an EMP. The dimensions of effectiveness attributed to EMPs in the *Matrix* films do not yet exist in reality, of course. But perhaps there will be interesting areas of application for this technology in the future. Because an EMP is a true electronics killer and thus a quite effective weapon in cyber warfare. However, because it requires so much energy, it is currently an impractical tool. An alternative to the EMP are electronic jammers, which can cause a lot of damage with much less energy expenditure. At this point, where we are thinking about the specific ways in which hostile states can fight each other in space, we have to ask ourselves: How far are we really from the galaxy where good fights evil in Star Wars?

The global internet infrastructure that is currently being created is not the first of its kind. As early as the 19th century, a globally operating communication system was created with the telegraph connections. Its emergence and use illustrate the importance of such an infrastructure. Because even telegraphy had an impact on the balance of power between states. States used it from the beginning to expand their administrative and military scope of action. They promoted the expansion of the telegraph network in order to receive information about developments in the colonies more quickly and to be able to react to them. Then as now, the reliability and security of the infrastructure are of crucial importance when it comes to its use for administrative, diplomatic, intelligence, or military purposes. Earlier, I claimed that cyber warfare could begin in space. To assess the historical significance of the global internet infrastructure, let us briefly recall the beginning of World War I. At this time, the German Empire was one of the four largest cable powers in the world with its stock of submarine cables. One of the first actions of the British High Command after the outbreak of World War I was to interrupt a large part of the German Empire's international cable connections. These were not put back into operation until 1925, many years after the end of the war. The tactical significance of technical innovations in the field of communication infrastructure should therefore not be underestimated.

Technology and Tactics of Cyber Warfare

Just as "cyberspace" and "space" are closely linked through technology, there is also a connection between the tactics of conventional warfare and future cyber warfare. However, we see again how old terms and definitions are being put to the test. Let's briefly recapitulate the forms of warfare according to the textbook and how they are changed by cyber. Interstate wars are probably the prototype of the classic war, in which, according to Clausewitz, the use of military means serves to achieve political goals. Here we will see how the technical transformation of even the classic form of war will strain its definition. But let's first continue through the forms of war. Closely related to the classic war is the so-called active, hard or kinetic warfare. This refers to all forms of direct military violence used to cause physical damage, up to the death of enemy soldiers. In contrast to interstate wars, civil wars are internal conflicts, which can also be about territorial claims, but can also be a struggle for resources, social oppression or other reasons. Civil wars are characterized, among other things, by the use of military means, but also by guerrilla tactics or terrorist attacks. In addition to interstate wars and civil wars, the "new wars" have emerged since the late 20th century. Their course is often described with the term asymmetric warfare, because there is a great imbalance between the warring parties. A paradigmatic example of this is modern terrorism in its form after September 11,

2001. Also considered new wars are those conflicts that are about resources, such as in Somalia, Sudan or Congo. It is no coincidence that the deployments of the Bundeswehr in Afghanistan, Mali or South Sudan are usually not referred to as war. Regardless of what has been said so far, what we have defined above as hybrid warfare must be considered. Even though the terms hybrid and asymmetric are often used synonymously, they mean very different things in practice. While asymmetric wars simply refer to those where the warring parties are characterized by an inequality in terms of their military, weapons technology or numerical strength, hybrid warfare refers to a mixing of different levels and dimensions in which action is taken, operating in gray areas and the creative use of a wide variety of means and methods with which the war is waged.

Apart from all these forms of war, there are still the soft wars, which do without the use of weapons. They are called soft because they are fought in the field of culture or religion, for example. In the USA, since a famous appearance by Colin Powell, then American Secretary of State, at the World Economic Forum in Davos, there has been the term "Soft Power". He explained that measures like the Marshall Plan would also be suitable for achieving strategic goals that would otherwise be enforced with hard means.

At this point, we exclude soft warfare, although it will become more than clear in the chapter on propaganda that cyber warfare also causes significant changes here. But since this is mainly about technology and tactics, we can see that all other forms of warfare are in principle open to technological innovations and innovations, which in turn must lead to a reassessment of tactics. This view was anything but common sense for a long time. Old beliefs are often overtaken by reality. In the *White Paper 2016*, one of the most important basic documents of the Bundeswehr, it reads: "The effects of cyber attacks can correspond to those of armed conflicts and escalate into the non-virtual world. Although it is not foreseeable that there will be an interstate conflict fought exclusively in the cyber and information space, operations in the cyber and information space are increasingly part of military conflicts today." However, cyber warfare and all the diverse elements that belong to it will affect all forms of war in one way or another. The cyber and information space cannot be considered separately from all other spheres. Starting from the political level, which formulates strategic goals based on information and communicates them via a technical infrastructure, to the level of the military, with the reporting system and software-controlled weapons and defense systems, down to the individual who moves on the net or relies on the technical infrastructure around it. The more we are aware that the digital dimension lies like a veil over everything, the more all previous considerations about the theoretical definition of wars and the practical tactical formations must be reconsidered.

The Difference Between Warriors and Soldiers in Digital Urban Warfare

This form of cyber warfare is one where the soldiers will never be seen. But does the category of soldier play a significant role in cyber warfare at all? In many modern wars, we can observe that there are always numerous volunteers from all over the world who support one side or the other. Hackers can cause damage in various ways. For example, they can leak and publish secret documents, paralyze or shut down networks or websites. However, all these actions are not acts of war in the sense of Clausewitz. But if they are skilled attackers who manage, for example, to uncover the secrets of important institutions like banks or to penetrate the systems of armed forces and steal information there, which they publish on the internet, this can indeed cause considerable damage. However, these are actions that can take several weeks or even months and may serve as preparation.

Here, let's refer again to Clausewitz and his briefly mentioned treatise on "small war". There, he already contemplated new forms of warfare and the so-called partisan technique. This form of warfare is also found in cyberspace. The digital urban warfare is as chaotic as the real one. Harmless environments can become battlefields. Actors who just looked like normal users a second ago transform into an attacker. Often, these are the infamous teenagers who, according to the cliché, sit in the basement of their parents' house all day in front of the computer. Indeed, it can be observed that script kiddies, as they are called in cybersecurity jargon, train with computer games and simulations what they then put into practice. At hackathons, they show their skills that they have trained over many years. The boundaries between game, simulation, and reality are increasingly blurring. Just as virtual, artificially created worlds are becoming more real, the real world is increasingly permeated by the virtual world. Consider also the emerging metaverse. Depending on which technology and variant will prevail, the real world will be merged with the digital world using virtual or augmented reality glasses. Games like *Capture The Flag*, which exist both as a real field game and in virtual form, symbolize this fusion. In both the real and virtual variant, it's about devising tactics on how to steal the opposing flag. However, each team must also think about defense and secure their own network or base or flag accordingly. But the game can quickly become serious. Because state players are increasingly being used as digital mercenaries for this new form of urban warfare. They camouflage and at first glance do not differ from the millions and billions of other people on the net. In an emergency, however, they can appear and act behind a "door" or in a harmless-looking network. Such sleepers can be inactive for years and behave absolutely inconspicuously. At the decisive moment, however, they can tip the scales. If a state actor relies on digital partisans or sleepers on a large scale, a new form of digital terrorism could emerge, in which a sleeper can be activated at any time and cause locally limited damage from within, for example in the form of leaks or the passing on of confidential information.

But even the conventional urban warfare so far could run completely differently in the age of cyber warfare. Partisan or urban warfare is one of the most dangerous approaches to taking or attacking a city. Because it always involves high losses and is a fight for every single meter. Doors are kicked in, window panes are thrown in with grenades, and traps are set. Sometimes it is necessary to lie in wait for several days in the tightest space and under the most adverse conditions just to catch a hidden sniper. Even the most capable armies in the world shy away from this form of combat. Urban warfare is therefore always the last option to be considered. At the same time, it is tactically used by the other side for this very reason, to inflict high losses on the other side.

However, urban warfare in the digital village could run completely differently in comparison. Before a single shot is fired, a fleet of mini-drones equipped with thermal imaging cameras would first fly through all streets, alleys, and houses and draw a pretty accurate picture of how many armed opponents there are, where they are located, and whether it is an accessible or locked house. Then the radio signals in all parcels are evaluated to see where a lot of communication is currently taking place at critical points. In the next step, digital jammers would ensure that the opponents can no longer communicate with each other. All of this did not exist in this form before and is technically more or less feasible today. Anyone who has ever used Google Maps is certainly familiar with the live function, which can be used to read how busy certain cafes or doctor's offices are. However, this does not end urban warfare. Rather, it is transformed into a battle of technology. Because the other side will also equip itself accordingly and with techniques and tactics of camouflage and deception ensure that the clear picture that the other side is trying to get is clouded again. But the trend is clear: losses will be massively reduced, urban warfare defused, and partisan warfare completely changed. The art of hiding and the tactics of camouflage and deception will therefore gain immensely in importance in the digital age. Because once the drones have flown over an area and collected information, only tactical questions remain.

So let's turn to the tactical level, which means taking a closer look at the battlefield. We have already seen how quickly a transition from one paradigm to the next can take place and what effects this has in connection with the Middle Ages. The age of knights, equipped with armor, sword, and ax as the dominant weapon system, was followed by the bow and crossbow—and the downfall of chivalry. The new weapon technology was also responsible for questioning all previously valid considerations for attack and defense and finding a new practice. Therefore, we must also look at the various new weapon systems today to see whether and to what extent the previously valid beliefs and convictions are still suitable.

The New Technology of War

Anyone who wants to fully understand the future of cyber warfare must go far beyond the level of codes, software, and programs. Just as these are worthless without the computers on which they are written and used, other machines that run on software should not be overlooked. These include—to name just a few—robots as well as drones, tanks, weapon systems, radar systems, and satellites, but also cars, smartphones, production and agricultural machinery, centrifuges, and the largest system of all, the power grid. Precisely because these represent a combination of software and hardware, they could become targets of cyber attacks. But if we go one step further, we come to software-controlled machines that bring entirely different implications.

Even in the context of international law, there were initial points of contact with autonomous weapon systems. In technical jargon, this is also referred to as a UMS, for "Unmanned Military System". An alternative, also common term for this type of weapon is borrowed from English and is "Lethal Autonomous Weapon System" or LAWS for short. The latter emphasizes the purpose of this deadly weapon system once again. The crucial point here is that neither the selection nor the combat of the target requires human intervention. This requires a combination of sensor technology, computing power, and software capabilities. The latter are based on algorithms from the field of artificial intelligence. A question that immediately arises here is whether and how humans can have any control at all. Air defense is already partially based on these principles today and operates fully automatically. However, the airspace is not exactly a complex area of operation, which is why it is technically quite simple to develop autonomous solutions. The public debate has mainly revolved around armed drones. But what if the warfare of the future is dominated by walking, driving, and flying robots, tanks, or drones that can both move autonomously and fire? At this point, the moral, ethical, and legal questions should be left out for once and the practical and tactical consequences should be asked—after all, we want to know what the war of the future looks like.

A first change arises from the fact that decision-making processes in the use of LAWS are transferred from humans to machines. We don't even have to venture into the realm of science fiction and imagine robots like the Terminator. Because even today, decisions that people make are increasingly data-driven. Starting with the selection and collection of data, its filtering and processing, and its processing by algorithms—all these processes are relevant points that could ultimately lead to a decision about life and death. Where exactly do you draw the line as to whether it is still a decision made by a human? Especially in the case of wrong decisions, the blame is quickly shifted to the machine, which shows that algorithms already have a share in the development of action options today. It is quite legitimate to question whether the person making a decision based on certain data can really understand how it came about.

The transfer of competencies from humans to machines is an inevitable side effect of the digitization and automation of our world. It is a regularly observed phenomenon that assistance systems or learning programs are initially inferior to humans during their training phase. But once they have mastered a specific skill that they have acquired through a self-collected database, they are far superior to humans in this specific area. Just think of the successes of AI programs in games like chess, Go, or poker. In the evaluation of medical images, where cancer cells have to be distinguished from healthy cells, a correspondingly trained

AI can already keep up with doctors and even surpass them in some cases. The railway also increasingly relies on the suggestions of an AI when schedules are disrupted by irregularities and track allocations have to be replanned ad hoc. Autopilots for controlling airplanes or cars will also surpass human ability in this activity in the coming years. As soon as a certain problem of reality can be solved with logic, such learning systems are capable of developing a rule-based solution. In some areas, it is even sensible and advantageous to have autonomous systems in use. A remotely controlled drone must abort its mission as soon as the communication connection between it and the control center breaks down. However, aborting a mission can endanger the lives of other soldiers in action or civilians in the worst case. Here, autonomous drones that can carry out their mission independently are tactically advantageous. Since drones will be used more and more in swarms in the future, remote control by humans will no longer be an option due to the complexity and the amount of data that needs to be transmitted. The development of LAWS is also being driven forward for another reason: the arms race. If the opposing side uses such weapon systems, one must be able to respond appropriately to these potential attacks for tactical reasons alone.

The Cyber War as a War Without Humans

Following the automation of weapon systems, which could occur in this or a similar way, comes the idea of the "Automatic War", that is, the complete automation of warfare. This new way of thinking about weapon violence, in which there are no human losses, can also be understood as a pure material or pure byte war. Where does this development lead? Let's exaggerate this scenario for the sake of clarity and conduct two thought experiments. The first starts quite positively. We assume that the cyber war of the future is one in which no people have to die at all. Let's imagine an idealized and staked battlefield. On this battlefield, the robots, drones, and tanks of two warring opponents meet to fight each other. There are no more human losses because the war is fought exclusively between machines and their electronics. AI-controlled robots must face AI-controlled tanks and drone swarms. Although this war will still cost billions and can only be financed by the most powerful states, it will also be a virtual power struggle between one AI and another. In a next step, one can even virtualize the kinetic dimension of warfare and conduct the power struggle exclusively in cyberspace. Then, at some point, it will only be machine vs. machine or, thought one step further, algorithm vs. algorithm.

The second scenario, which is supposed to illustrate the tactical changes in cyber warfare, can best be described as drone warfare. Let's imagine a warring party deciding to attack the enemy with drones. What options are currently available for this? A solution as crude as it is effective is to equip drones with an explosive device and send them on a kamikaze mission. In other words, it automatically heads for the set target and crashes there. As a rule, not just one, but several drones are sent on their way for this purpose. With modern air defense, it is usually possible to shoot down a large part of such a fleet, but some always manage to reach their target. One reason for this is the now sophisticated autonomous flight capabilities, which also include evasive maneuvers. Since drones sent on a kamikaze mission do not return anyway, material losses do not matter as long as at least one reaches its target. Those who want to reduce their costs or have little money in the war chest anyway, resort to the cheap versions from the electronics market. Some would be surprised at how great the effect of even such small devices is in doubt. But let's move this scenario further into the future. What happens when not only one side sends drones, but both? And how does the tactic change when not just individual drones, but a drone swarm is sent?

Robots and drones will populate the battlefield of the future. The war becomes a war of technology companies and technological progress. Above all, swarm intelligence, which is formed after the model of nature to coordinate large amounts of devices with a simple set of rules, will provide tactical advantages. To recognize the potential of drone swarms, one only has to look at the technical spectacles on New Year's Eve. Drone shows are the new fireworks in various metropolises of this world. However, the massive release and coordination of drones serve much more than just a short light show. While their operation is still centralized today, according to a fixed program, the future belongs to decentralized control. Only the goal of an action can be defined, while the drone swarm will independently find the optimal way from A to B. If 500 drones are enough today to conjure impressive images in the night sky, we don't need much imagination to imagine with what creativity an attack can take place. The only requirement then is: The drones of a swarm must not fly into each other. Anyone who has analyzed or even observed the flight of bees or birds knows with what variety and precision, but also with what power comparable beings in nature act. The beauty that we can gain from bird flight quickly turns into sheer horror when a swarm of mini-drones, equipped with small amounts of plastic explosives, attack the same target one after the other and at a furious speed from a swarm. But it doesn't have to be the suicide mission right away. Even in the field of air reconnaissance, drone swarms will soon be able to provide a degree of detail in information that, in relation to tactics, makes a difference literally between day and night. Anyone who has already had experience with the technical capabilities of drones that can now be ordered on Ebay or Alibaba has a faint premonition of what will soon become standard in the military sector. Mimicry, or the imitation of nature, or in short: camouflage, will provide the ultimate advantage here. Drones that look and behave like dragonflies, birds, or bees can communicate with each other and scout out areas without anyone noticing. One does not even want to imagine what will happen when drones or robots are equipped with AI capabilities or autonomous weapon systems like the LAWS. Even today, the militaries of all countries urgently need to deal with the question of how to gain a tactical advantage in such scenarios or what can be done against such weapon systems.

In cyber warfare, which has taken on such forms, the only thing that really helps is to hack the enemy in real time in order to bring the drones down or to take control of the drone swarms and send them straight back where they came from. Of course, we are not there yet today. At the moment, only brute force helps. If necessary, drones are brought down from the sky with a club or with classic weapons. In the future, however, only the combination of speed and skill will count. Whoever hacks the fastest wins on the battlefield. This is then the reality of real cyber warfare. Scenarios like these must basically be assumed when undertaking the task of setting up a cyber army today.

A Market for Vulnerabilities

No system is one hundred percent secure. Every software and hardware has security vulnerabilities. Anyone who knows such a vulnerability can exploit it. They can be the decisive gateway through which an attack occurs. Companies are aware of this risk and strive to close all security gaps as quickly as possible within the framework of software patches or updates. An operating system like Windows or a software suite like Microsoft Office, which are used by millions of people every day, should be secure. A security gap promises not only a successful attack, but also enormous reach and correspondingly maximum damage. Companies, governments, and various interest groups are aware of this and therefore organize so-called bug bounty programs, or "software error bounty programs". Prizes are offered for every error (referred to as "bug" in English) and every security gap that is found by participants in the code. Such bug bounty programs are manufacturers' countermeasures to the so-called "stockpiling", i.e., the accumulation of security vulnerabilities. This is exactly what actors such as hacker groups in the darknet do, who systematically and specifically look for ways for future attacks. Of course, such security vulnerabilities are kept secret by them in order to exploit the element of surprise for the attack. That's why this type of cyber attack is also referred to as a "zero-day exploit". Because in an attack that exploits such a vulnerability, software manufacturers or their developers have exactly zero days to fix the error and avert damage. In view of this threat, it is not surprising what value such unrecognized security vulnerabilities have. Companies like Microsoft value the discovery of a novel error between 10,000 dollars in the case of Office programs and 100,000 dollars for the Windows operating system. Zerodium, a company that specializes in zero-day exploits, even pays bounty sums up to 2.5 million dollars. The threat of cyber warfare does not always have to serve as a backdrop. The area of organized crime is enough to make the motivation behind such programs understandable. The economic damage that can be caused by a zero-day attack is enormous. Not all companies and organizations that are affected make it public, so we have to rely on estimates. But according to these, the annual damage caused by cybercrime worldwide is in the order of hundreds of millions of dollars. Despite these comparatively high amounts from the manufacturers, this knowledge can sometimes earn significantly more in the darknet. States or intelligence services also pay much more than the manufacturers. Here, greed comes into play again and sets its own market dynamics in motion.

We live in a capitalist world and in view of such sums, it is not surprising that a market for such security vulnerabilities has emerged. Not only manufacturers pay a lot of money for vulnerabilities in programs. In the darknet, trading platforms have emerged where zero-day security vulnerabilities can simply be bought with a click of the mouse. This, in turn, allows smaller states, organized groups, or even individuals who may lack the resources and skills to organize large attacks, to cause tremendous damage. A legitimate way to get to the vulnerabilities are the aforementioned bug bounty programs. In contrast to the black market or the darknet, this is also referred to as the "white market". The black market for vulnerabilities and other illegal goods and services is gigantic. It goes without saying that there are no official surveys and statistics here and there will continue to be none. But estimates suggest that several billion dollars are turned over here every year, so that this black market exceeds the sales volume of the worldwide trade in arms, drugs, and human trafficking (estimated: 500 billion US$). Of course, far more is sold on the black market for cybercrime than just zero-day gaps. Botnets (automated, networked malware), stolen credit card information and identities, hacker services, and exploit kits, with which the purchased vulnerabilities can be directly exploited, are also part of the range.

Understanding the market for zero-days is crucial for understanding the overall threat situation in cyberspace. Because the black market customers include not only the stereotypical hacker and cybercriminal, but also governments, intelligence agencies, and companies. The exchange between business partners is, of course, characterized by the utmost discretion and secrecy and takes place exclusively via encrypted channels. The fact that zero-day vulnerabilities are particularly in focus here is also no coincidence. They are among the most expensive digital goods that can be purchased on the black market for cybercrime. The reason: With the help of these vulnerabilities, not only can a large number of people or systems be effectively attacked. Rather, they represent a way to carry out an attack with extreme precision. A few years ago, for example, a vulnerability was made public in the press that impressively demonstrated the potential inherent in it. It was a zero-day vulnerability of iPhones, with which it was possible to take control of the entire phone by simply sending or receiving an SMS. No action was required on the part of the user. This vulnerability, known as CVE-2016-4657, was a key component of the spyware named Pegasus, which was developed by an Israeli company and sold to several states to, for example, eavesdrop on and monitor potential terrorists, but also journalists and politicians. According to the publications of the research network "Pegasus Project", which clarified the connections around the spyware, the software was used, for example, in connection with the murder of journalist Jamal Khashoggi. European states like Hungary also allegedly relied on Pegasus to monitor investigative journalists. The Pegasus Project also evaluated a list of 50,000 phone numbers that were originally leaked to the organizations *Amnesty International* and *Forbidden Stories*. Among them were numerous famous personalities. Among the heads of state and government who were spied on during their respective terms of office were the President of France, Emmanuel Macron, the Prime Minister of Egypt, Mustafa Madbuli, the President of the Republic of South Africa, Cyril Ramaphosa, and the President of the European Council, Charles Michel. Shortly after the security vulnerability in the mobile operating system iOS became officially known, Apple closed it as part of an update. Security vulnerabilities like these are sold for millions, precisely because they can be converted into the most effective digital weapons. The high prices, of course, also indicate how rare they are. Last but not least, however, it also becomes clear that one of the biggest problems of cybersecurity has adopted the logic of capitalism and has become a market. This discussion also includes the fact that manufacturers of software and electronics, unlike, for example, car manufacturers, are not liable for their products and their safety.

Cybersecurity in the Digitally Networked World

With the increasing digitalization of everyday life, the cyber risk and the number of security vulnerabilities also increase. Here too, we must first consider the two levels of software and hardware. At a very basic level, security vulnerabilities are errors in the code, inaccuracies in programming that allow misuse of functions. To get an idea: current estimates suggest that there are about 10 errors in 1000 lines of code. Not every one of these errors necessarily constitutes a security vulnerability. Modern programs like internet browsers easily have 20-30 million lines of program code. An MacOS operating system from Apple comprises far more than 86 million lines of code. These figures should suffice to demonstrate the effort that must be made to find security vulnerabilities. By the way, more lines of code do not necessarily mean better programs. On the contrary: this increases the potential for even more security vulnerabilities to be found. For comparison: The Space Shuttle, which NASA used to bring several astronauts and many tons of material into Earth orbit, needed no more than 400,000 lines of code, and their computers had the performance of today's calculators.

The functioning of the market in the consumer electronics sector also influences cybersecurity. Since the release of the first iPhone, fans have expected a completely new model with a completely new operating system, functions, and speeds at least every year. This rhythm has been adopted by numerous other manufacturers and even surpassed in some cases. With the increasing release rate of new devices and the number of lines of code in mind, it must be clear to everyone: error-free software cannot exist. Now, if we also consider the ever-increasing number of devices that are networked with each other, not only does the complexity increase, but also the number of possible attack points. A frequently cited example is the smart home. In fact, it is enough if the WiFi password is stored unprotected on the networked light bulb to gain access to a network. It should be noted that a smart home alone— apart from the dangers that arise for the individual—does not yet pose a general security risk. However, a city in which a third or half of the households consist of smart homes could become a collective problem, as it is an interesting and lucrative target for attacks.

The vulnerability of states is thus increasing due to the advancing networking of citizens or private households and other devices. From this connection, far-reaching considerations and very concrete measures arise that governments must face. For example, is it in the interest of national security to buy up all zero-day vulnerabilities offered on the black market in the darknet? Or should a law be passed that obliges manufacturers to buy such security vulnerabilities and fix them with a software patch or take responsibility in the event of damage? There has long been an awareness at the state level of the dangers and risks associated with security vulnerabilities. In the USA, there has been a specific review process at the federal level since 2008 ("Vulnerabilities Equities Process", or VEP for short), in which each case is analyzed and evaluated as to how to deal with a zero-day vulnerability. If it is a security vulnerability that can be used for an attack, there are two options at the end of the process: either keep the knowledge about a vulnerability secret in order to possibly use it yourself, or share it with the manufacturer so that they can close it. It was not until 2016, following a request under the Freedom of Information Act, that it became known that numerous US government institutions use the VEP. A year later, the US government officially published the plans around the VEP. Another year later, in the fall of 2018, the German federal government also began to deal with the topic and establish its own VEP process.

While it was a correct step to make cybersecurity part of the political agenda, it expresses another, much more far-reaching problem. Dealing with vulnerabilities such as zero-day security vulnerabilities or other cyber risks is understood as a national task. However, it is a global threat. We all use technologies from the USA, China, or Japan. If now every government in the world tries to deal with these threats in its own, country-specific way, the underlying structural problem will not be solved. Of course, several interests are at odds here, limiting the scope for action: the protection of one's own population, international security considerations, the secrecy of one's own military capabilities, and economic interests. Zero-day vulnerabilities are also used for intelligence activities such as espionage operations or digital surveillance, because for obvious reasons no defense or solution has been created for this yet. This means that intelligence services, the military, or even law enforcement agencies that benefit from the vulnerabilities themselves or want to use them offensively, even have a genuine interest in keeping them open. Therefore, a dangerous game is currently being played in the field of cybersecurity. Both malicious actors such as hacker groups or cyber criminals and governments and their institutions research and collect security vulnerabilities, but keep information about them secret. Because the same gap can be used both for defense and for attack or surveillance of the opponent. As long as there is no rethink here, nothing will change in the overall situation and the level of danger in cyberspace and the information space. On the contrary: With the spread of cheap electronics with lower security standards and increasing networking, the global cybersecurity risk is increasing.

A Race Against Time

Zero-day vulnerabilities have a half-life. Several studies have dealt with finding out their exact lifespan. The data basis and also the results of such investigations are only a rough approximation of reality, given the comparatively opaque overall situation. However, since the security gaps have a high tactical relevance, it is important to deal with this question. Because the tactical value of a vulnerability, which is known to become useless as soon as it is recognized by the other side or the manufacturer, rises and falls with its lifespan. A certain part of the security gaps, about a quarter of them, are discovered and closed relatively quickly. Some of them, about another quarter, can survive and be used for up to ten years.

The factor of time also plays a role in fixing security vulnerabilities. The name "Zero-Day" does indeed say that developers have zero days, but this does not yet say anything about how long they actually need to find a solution and roll it out to all users. The same applies, by the way, to the other side: those who discover the gaps and want to exploit them for their purpose usually need a few weeks to a month before they have programmed, tested, and are ready to deploy an exploit tool. The situation is very similar with patch development. Its completion can also easily take up to two months. The time required naturally depends very much on the type of security vulnerability. In most cases, it goes much faster until a patch is developed, as the majority of vulnerabilities in program codes are rather minor errors. Often, one day is enough to close a gap. With security vulnerabilities in operating systems or other programs, it is also added that all users—from the individual to the corporation with thousands of employees or computer-aided production halls—must carry out an update or the installation of the security patch. This can also lead to a delay that can be exploited by attackers. On average, all these interrelationships and complications mean that a time window of approximately 200 days to a few years is available to exploit a serious security vulnerability.

Can a State Protect Itself Against Cyber Warfare?

Cybersecurity and defense is both a state task and an individual, rather technical matter. An example of the latter is the so-called "Kill Switch". This is a security measure, for example for military-used laptops. To prevent these from falling into the wrong hands, or these causing any damage, they usually have a very specific key combination that must be pressed within a certain predefined period. If this input does not occur once, this leads to the immediate deletion of the entire hard drive. With precautions like these, it should be ensured that certain information can never fall into the wrong hands. An alternative to this is the so-called "Geofencing". Here, a limited space is defined using geographical coordinates, within which a device works or data stored on it can be accessed. If someone tries to steal the device and hack it at a safe place for their own purposes, either all data is deleted or access is denied. By the way, these two techniques are also used in the hacker scene to make it difficult to provide evidence in the event of police or other access.

In view of the scenarios of the cyber war of the future outlined above, states are increasingly thinking about suitable protective measures to defend against large-scale cyber attacks and assaults. Of course, no country is able to completely stop all threats from cyberspace. Today, this works similarly to the defense against planned terrorist attacks. In order to identify potential perpetrators in time, the intelligence services, public prosecutors and special units must, however, proceed with appropriate methods, which repeatedly put them in the situation of having to weigh up between the rights of the individual and the protection of the general public. A cyber attack on a state is a comparable aggressive act, which is usually directed against civilian institutions or people. For governments, it is not easy to protect these without at the same time reaching the limits of data and information protection.

In the discussion about digital defense tools, Isaac Ben-Israel from Tel Aviv University has often brought up the concept of a "Cyber Dome". This is the digital equivalent to the Iron Dome, a mobile ground-based defense system that is supposed to protect cities like Tel Aviv and other inhabited areas in Israel from missile attacks. The system is considered extremely effective and therefore the desire to transfer it to the cyber world is understandable. However, such a concept cannot be translated one-to-one into the digital world. Because the truth about online defense systems also includes: Too much security on the net by the state brings restrictions. A system that would have a comparable impact as the Iron Dome would be so invasive that every single citizen would feel attacked in their privacy. How the equation of cybersecurity and privacy can be solved is not clear to this day and perhaps the struggle for both will accompany us for a very long time.

A look at the literature can be revealing here as to what this means in concrete terms. Let's remember George Orwell's *1984* again. Much of what was conceived as fiction back then is reality today. In cities like Beijing, but also London, surveillance of public space is a reality. There are between 60 and 70 cameras for every resident. However, this form of observation is only a small aspect of what can be used as "security technology". This is supplemented by the evaluation of movement data, credit card and payment data or search engine queries. With the help of biometric analysis tools, a pretty accurate picture can be created, without the knowledge and consent of people, of exactly who is where. Anyone who believes that collecting this data is unproblematic only needs to look at the countries that have already taken a step further. If there is knowledge about people's behavior, this can be used to not only monitor them, but also to control them. For example, good, law-abiding behavior can be rewarded within the framework of a point system. Those who make a special effort receive a high social credit score and associated privileges such as access to certain rooms, the ability to borrow bicycles or cars without depositing a deposit, discounts on public transport or tax relief. Just the awareness that our own communication is recorded and evaluated has a direct influence on how we express ourselves. Here too, we can ask ourselves what history teaches us about how people react to such power relations. The next chapter therefore deals in detail with how, for example, camouflage and deception can also be a way out for the individual.

In conclusion, however, I would like to once again champion the study of the past and learning from history. This is not only a lesson of this book—forensics also relies on this approach and thus also makes a significant contribution to defense. When it comes to uncovering actors and naming the perpetrators of a cyber attack, this is usually done in two steps. The first step is a technical forensic examination, also known as IT forensics. All traces that attackers have left in the affected computers and systems are examined and secured. Here, technical artifacts and indications are collected that could provide clues to the attackers. The second step is characterized by forensic history. Even if attackers imitate the patterns of others in order to divert suspicion to others through deception, it shows that hackers are also people. Every person behaves consciously or unconsciously in a way that is unique to them. The scientific study of past cyber attacks therefore also serves to protect against future attacks.

8

Survival in Cyberspace: Strategies for Every Individual

Considering how things have developed since about 1930, it's hard to believe in the survival of civilization.

George Orwell

Das hier ist eine verdammt harte Galaxis. Wenn man hier überleben will, muss man immer wissen, wo sein Handtuch ist!

Douglas Adams

This book is titled *The Art of Cyberwar*. As we have learned from Sun Tzu, the art of war actually involves very concrete instructions, recommendations for action, and strategic as well as tactical considerations. One could therefore also expect to find some solid advice here on how to ideally behave in cyberwar. On the one hand, this book is not a guide, but on the other hand, history does hold a lot of insights and lessons, which can be understood as a kind of "to-do" for peacetime. So let's face the question: What does one need to survive in cyberspace today?

© The Author(s), under exclusive license to Springer Fachmedien   **243**
Wiesbaden GmbH, part of Springer Nature 2024
P. Kestner, *The Art of Cyber Warfare*,
https://doi.org/10.1007/978-3-658-43879-1_8

Here too, history and literature can provide us with relevant material from which we can learn. Up to this point, a lot has already been said and written about historical wars, famous battles, and other military conflicts. But this book is meant to be more than a book about the military, armies, or wars. Because cyberwar is something that breaks the boundaries of all previous forms of war, redefines laws, and can also have consequences on an individual level. Cyberwar affects all people equally, and that's why we also have to deal with it on a very personal level. If what was said above about the new war and hybrid cyber warfare is actually true, then each individual must also ask what this development means for them. Because in a cyber attack, the population can be thrown into chaos. Critical infrastructures can fail, there can be power outages, supply chains can break down, or the gasoline can run out. Anyone who wants to get a clear picture of what the consequences of such a scenario might look like is recommended to read the novel *Blackout* (2012) by Marc Elsberg, which I will come back to later. Especially dealing with such stories and engaging with the historiographic details can provide enormous assistance.

The "Byzantine Problem", the Human Factor, and a Warning

This is exemplified, for example, by the "Byzantine Problem" or "Byzantine Fault". This is a phenomenon described in information technology. The term describes a specific error pattern in which several points (e.g., processors in a complex system or network) cause errors. Even though it is a fascinating field, I do not want to delve too deeply into the technical details here, because the truly interesting thing is something else. When you hear about the Byzantine Problem in the field of information technology, it is usually quickly pointed out that the term has its origins in history and has something to do with generals—but in the rarest cases is the exact course of events told, but only briefly touched upon to move on to the technical description of why complex information systems can fail. The historical background is the conquest of Constantinople, which almost failed. The year is 1453. Constantinople (today's Istanbul) is the capital of the Eastern Roman Empire (also: Eastern Rome, Byzantine Empire, or simply: Byzantium). At this moment, the Byzantine Empire had existed for almost a thousand years. As is typical for declining empires, Byzantium was already marked by decadence and a sense of decline. In the east of the country, large areas fell to the Turkish Seljuks, and in Western Europe, the Catholic Church was spreading. At the same time, the Ottoman Empire had been rising since the thirteenth century and was expanding into Asia Minor, Europe, and areas controlled by the Turks. Constantinople had already been unsuccessfully besieged several times in this process. The city was important not only because it was the capital of the Byzantine Empire. It also stood for wealth and power. The geographical location of Constantinople made it an enormously wealthy trading city for many centuries. This is due to its optimal location: it is located directly on the Bosporus, the strait that connects the Mediterranean with the Black Sea and thus represents the most important trade route between Europe and Asia. So a lot was at stake, and Emperor Constantine XI tried desperately to defend his city and organize help. In the end, he was so desperate that he was even willing to unite the Orthodox Eastern Roman Church under the leadership of the Catholic Pope as part of the church union.

The moment to attack Constantinople was therefore more than favorable. And so Sultan Mehmet II ordered the deployment of the Ottoman army, which, depending on the source, was between 50,000 and 400,000 men strong. Despite all efforts, however, only 10,000 men were available to defend Constantinople, a fact that Emperor Constantine XI kept secret. He also knew that the city had one of the best defense systems of the time. This included more than 20 km of city walls, which were arranged in several successive rows at critical points and had ditches more than 20 m wide. In addition, there were high defense towers. However, the 10,000 men were not enough to adequately man all the defenses. Initially, the Ottomans tried to besiege the city and attack at individual critical points—for example, from the water, where there was only a single wall for defense. In the first weeks, the Ottomans launched several storm attacks, but were unable to use their numerical superiority. In part, the attackers suffered heavy losses. Therefore, the tactic changed, which now was to attack from all sides at the same time. According to legend, a competition broke out among the Ottoman generals. After such a long siege, everyone wanted to be the first to succeed in taking the city and go down in history as a great general. When it came to the concrete preparation of the final attack, however, the generals also had to coordinate with each other to ensure a coordinated approach. Since everyone was confident of victory, they gradually took the risk of making a small distortion when passing on information to the other, in order to gain an advantage for themselves. Instead of passing on the planned time (around 5 a.m.), the first general withholds a quarter of an hour. Such effects can then add up and lead to completely uncoordinated behavior. When the Byzantine problem is spoken of in computer science, it is usually about this principle of consensus building within complex systems. The human factor, which is also told in this story, i.e., the element of glory that each general wants to secure for himself, is usually omitted. However, this is often a key to understanding complex networks. Because behind the computers and network points there is always also a human being, who needs to be understood just as much as the technical system and its functioning.

Unfortunately, the sources do not describe in detail how the conquest of Constantinople took place. However, one can assume that a considerable amount of myth-making was involved. Stories like this should therefore be enjoyed with caution. Either way, the Byzantine problem continues to demonstrate to this day that even apparent superiority does not eliminate the human factor. Also interesting, regardless of the truth, is the fact that this historical episode has found its way into computer science. This also shows the power of history or stories, because consensus building without the involvement of a third party was long considered an unsolvable problem—just as Constantinople was considered an impregnable city. Today, the Byzantine problem or its solution has become a standard in the finance industry.

Be a Spartan!

At the very beginning of the book, we already dealt with antiquity. In doing so, we already heard about the competing city-states in Asia Minor and also about the notorious Spartans. Anyone who has already seen the movie *300* knows the myths that surround this small tribe. But what is this myth based on? The Spartans were indeed considered superior fighters in antiquity. This military superiority on the battlefield can be traced back to the principle of eternal training for the unforeseen. This strength is rooted in the Spartan education system, which was characterized by its strictness and hardening. From the age of seven to eight, male children were separated from their parents and had to undergo rigorous physical training that prepared them for service in the army. Therefore, their education included both training in combat techniques and reading and writing. In addition, they only received the bare essentials they needed to survive, thus getting used to hunger or learning to procure food for themselves, for example through hunting. Those who persevered were ready at the age of 20 to join the army of Sparta.

The behavior of the Spartans is of interest for the present time for a very specific reason. Because what do we do when we move in cyberspace? We sit at the computer or smartphone and are usually in our own four walls—a safe space where we actually have nothing to fear. Often we are also on the move in public places—there are numerous distractions that prevent us from paying attention to small details or inconspicuous things. Or we encounter cyberspace at work, where we use it to exchange with colleagues or to transmit data and information—in these situations, we then rather focus our concentration on our professional activity and not on other things. All of these are learning situations in which we are trained to deal with cyberspace. Because cyberspace lies like a veil over all other areas of life, whether we consciously perceive it or not. It is also, and one almost has to say "unfortunately", a very comfortable place that is not perceived as something disturbing or even threatening. This is precisely where the danger lies. Because if we do not train our consciousness to be mindful, it slackens like a muscle that has not been used for a long time. Perhaps it would be a good exercise to ask ourselves: How would the Spartans today prepare for deployment in cyberspace?

(Re-)Know Yourself

It is one of the oldest basic maxims of Western philosophy: Know yourself. According to legend, this exact phrase was written above the Oracle of Delphi. It is also no coincidence that this sentence, in its Latin translation, "Temet Nosce", appears in a key scene of the film The Matrix (1999, directed by Lana & Lilly Wachowski). In the scene, Neo (Keanu Reeves) speaks with the Oracle (Gloria Foster) to find out if he is the chosen one. The world depicted in *The Matrix* is in many ways suitable for understanding our real cyber world. The entire world in which the people in the film live consists of the Matrix, a projection, ultimately of data. Further up, we wrote that cyberspace must also be understood as something that permeates everything else and relates to each other. In this respect, the Oracle's sentence from the Matrix film can also be understood as something that helps us in our world. What does it mean to know or recognize oneself? It means understanding oneself and the motivation of one's own actions. Are we driven by power, greed, lust, wealth, or fame? Those who think about the inner drivers in the decisive situation can often prevent the worst. The greatest dangers often lurk when such base instincts are addressed. The promise of quick money, the satisfaction of lust, or the greed for power and fame simply work too well. Another aspect of self-knowledge is: Everyone is vulnerable. In cyberspace, any weakness one has will be exploited. Testing vulnerabilities for future attacks is one of the standard procedures of hackers and other malicious actors planning cyber attacks or cyber operations. Anyone who stores sensitive data (photos, passwords, etc.) unprotected on the computer or publicly discloses personal, private information should not be surprised if such actors ultimately use it to harm them. Developing a healthy trust in other people is part of good social coexistence. However, this should not be misunderstood as blindly trusting all people. But since there is this natural tendency in us to initially suspect the good in others, this is shamelessly exploited on the internet. This is also because we are in an environment where we feel comfortable when we surf the net. Often we are in our own apartment, lying on the couch, or at a place that is not threatening, like the subway, a bus, or public space. We humans trust other people even when we shouldn't. Many know the situation when you already have a strange feeling in your stomach and the suspicion is close that something is just too good to be true. And yet you click on an email attachment, follow a link, or download a file. It is precisely these weak moments that can be avoided if we know ourselves and know how we function personally, but also how we function as humans. Such lessons are particularly necessary where people are active at or in critical infrastructures or private and military interfaces. Because a lot is at stake there and even small mistakes can have big effects. Here too, one can illustrate material from literature or the film sector. Think, for example, of the scenes of mass panic from the thriller series *Blackout* (2021) with Moritz Bleibtreu in the lead role. The series is based on the novel *Blackout—Tomorrow it's too late* by Marc Elsberg, who in it works through what it means to include the reaction of the entire population in the considerations when a cyber attack leads to a widespread power outage in Europe.

The Failure of the Senses

Our brain is certainly one of the most fascinating organs that exist in nature. Not only because it is capable of unfathomable insights, but also because our species history is preserved in it and its physiological structure. This has advantages, but also glaring disadvantages, as we will see shortly. The oldest part of our brain, the brainstem, developed already 500 million years ago. Vital functions such as breathing, regulation of the heartbeat, and food intake are located there. Since it represents our evolutionary past and essentially resembles that which reptiles also have, it is also called the reptilian brain. Simply put, this part of our brain becomes active when it comes to unconsidered actions, purely emotional behavior, or particularly strong affects. The task of the reptilian brain should not be underestimated. In many situations and over many millennia, it ensured our survival. If our ancestors were fleeing from a predator, they knew in fractions of a second whether it made sense to attack, play dead, or better run away. Even though our living environment has fundamentally changed, this brain area is still present and active. But now, virtual dangers are completely different in their appearance and process, so our number one defense organ no longer has a chance to react adequately. We have to prepare for this. The reptilian brain has become obsolete in the digital age. This is because we physically and sensually feel real dangers. However, we do not feel anything at the computer. If something dangerous happens on the screen, it does not trigger a reflex in humans. The laptop does not get hot and there is no loud noise. This means that the only sensory organ that we can train for the new dangers and risks is our brain—more precisely, our frontal lobes and temporal lobes, where functions such as impulse control, social behavior, and memory are located. Another tactic in the digital age could therefore be: Turn on your brain and think about the story. To this end, it can be helpful to think of trigger points for virtual events. These can be mnemonic aids, such as visualizing email attachments always as a small virtual wooden horse, or habits, such as looking around before giving out your private data, even if you are alone in the room. There are no limits to the imagination and the more individual such a memory system is, the more effectively it works.

How do I Hide in the Cyber World?

Digitization has brought numerous aspects that have fundamentally changed life. This also includes the so-called transparent human. As soon as you use a technical device, surf the internet, or even just enter the public space that is monitored by cameras, you leave data traces, whether you want to or not. Where this development can lead is revealed either by looking at countries where this type of technical surveillance is already advanced, such as in China, or by looking at literature such as the work *1984* by George Orwell, which was already discussed in more detail in the introduction. The challenge that arises in such a world is: Is there still a possibility to be invisible? Or asked differently: How can I hide? There are several possibilities that one can consider. One leads back to Sun Tzu and the two techniques of camouflage and deception. For example, if you want to cover your tracks, you can resort to simple tricks. Instead of buying a ticket that clearly shows where the journey is going, you buy 5 tickets that all point in different directions. If you want to make sure not to be tracked via your own mobile phone, you can simply put it in one train, but take another. Admittedly, such actions involve a certain monetary and logistical effort and are more for the professionals—but the good news is that there are still ways to cover your tracks or mislead possible pursuers in the digital age. With these examples, I am not so much trying to give practical tips, but to sharpen thinking about which digital traces we leave behind that are readable for others. Inspirations for further possibilities in this regard can also be found in films like the already mentioned *The Man Who Never Lived*. It depicts several old techniques against which no technology, no matter how advanced, can do anything. A proven approach to leaving no digital traces and communicating securely with each other is to write small notes and pass them unnoticed. All the techniques described in the first chapters from the analog world such as steganography and cryptography or the tricks of the secret services are more relevant than ever in this context. A variation of communication via handwritten notes was actually used for many years in Afghanistan by the Taliban. They wrote small notes and stuck them on trash cans. If you didn't know what it was really about, you had to assume it was trash. The more digital surveillance is expanded, the more important it is to think about ways to escape the cyber world. For this, there is hardly anything more valuable than following proven historical traces, techniques, and procedures.

Ghost in the Shell

The phrase "I have nothing to hide" is often encountered in the debate about anonymity on the internet and individual behavior when it comes to personal data and the protection of privacy. However, statements like these overlook the fact that one's own identity is a valuable asset, the value of which may only truly become apparent to us once it has been taken from us. Because identity theft is a widespread phenomenon. It's all about the old tactic of camouflage and deception: Whoever commits crimes in the name of another can thus deflect suspicion from themselves and shift the blame onto others.

Because criminal prosecution works with the methods of forensics and will initially come across the natural person whose identity they have determined. Of course, technology is also evolving in this area. With the help of semantic networks, a method from the field of artificial intelligence, the assignment of identities can be facilitated by analyzing data traces and metadata—provided there is enough of it. However, this should not lull anyone into a sense of security, but rather show that we are dealing with a stage of future cyber warfare that is becoming increasingly important.

But it's not just us humans who have the ability to camouflage and deceive. Thanks to recent developments in the field of artificial intelligence, we are increasingly encountering the phenomenon of deepfakes, which was already described above. The fear of them is precisely the fear of losing one's own identity. These can not only invent a pseudo-identity, but can also be trained to imitate an existing identity. All the information we leave behind in the digital space can be used to steal an identity. One then becomes nothing more than a nameless person. The famous cyberpunk narrative *Ghost in the Shell*, which dates back to a Japanese manga by Masamune Shirow from 1989, takes this development further. What happens when an identity can lead a life of its own independent of a human body? Literally translated, the original title of "Ghost in the Shell", which consists of three components, means as much as: "Attack", "Shell" and "Mobile Task Force". In Japanese, a very pictorial language, there are many allusions and ambiguities. "Shell" can also mean "veil". In English, on the other hand, "Shell" also means "shell", but in the field of computer science it also means a "user interface". The various comics and film adaptations of *Ghost in the Shell* all tell of a future in which people have synthetic body parts or organs implanted to optimize themselves. Such people, who are made up entirely or partially of implants, are also called cyborgs. In this world, it is also possible to transfer the mind of a human, i.e. his identity, completely into an artificial cyborg. This combination becomes problematic the moment a hacker manages to overcome the security barriers between Ghost and Shell and become the "puppeteer" by taking control of the Ghost in the Shell. From today's perspective, this clearly sounds like a bleak vision of the future and a dystopia. However, it should not be forgotten that there are already numerous developments today that point exactly in this direction. Neuralink, another company by Elon Musk, is working on an electronic interface that can connect the human brain to a computer. With the Brain-Computer Interface (BCI), direct communication between humans and machines should become possible. For this purpose, a corresponding chip is implanted in the brain, which reads out the electromagnetic currents of the nerve cells. In this way, it should be possible in the future to control computers and other technical systems directly with thoughts. Although it is still a long way from this point to the transfer of consciousness from humans to a machine. But the first steps that point in this direction have already been taken.

A Note on Bitcoin and Other Cryptocurrencies

When it comes to hiding, or the ability to escape the cyber world or even flee from a country with a repressive government, one inevitably hears about Bitcoin and other cryptocurrencies. Because these represent a way to move one's own assets unnoticed across national borders. The narrative that keeps coming back in this context is as follows: The more a state seeks access to its citizens and "scans" them, the more popular digital currencies become, because they are supposed to enable the state to withdraw control and take it over themselves. Indeed, it seems tempting to simply remember twelve terms and be able to travel anywhere in the world you want, yet have all your assets with you. The elegant thing about this solution: You can cross borders without any technical devices and yet have the key to the digital currencies with you. The effectiveness of this narrative can even be read from the development of the exchange rates. Every time there are tensions in countries like Taiwan, China, Russia or Afghanistan, the exchange rates rise because people are trying to get their money out of the country in this way.

However, a note is allowed here, as there is no absolute certainty about this fact in the future: At the latest when the reports about the development of quantum computers increase, one should recall the race between the "hare and the hedgehog" or the cryptograms and the code breakers.

Do What No One Expects

But let's return to the dialectic of hiding and being found. An important tool for evaluating digital traces is the analysis of behavioral patterns. As is well known, humans are creatures of habit and that's why behavior can be predicted so well from knowledge of past events. Sun Tzu already relied on tactics of attack and defense through confusion. Malicious actors often rely on this tool. In the digital age, surely nothing causes more confusion than disinformation and alternative facts. But this is just one of many examples. Confusion can also be created through automated bot programs or deepfakes, which can give the impression of being many people or the same person. But the tactics of confusion can also be used for defense purposes. With our data and behavioral patterns, we leave traces on the net that allow others to understand us and exploit possible weaknesses. One way to create confusion is to use many, and if possible, anonymized email addresses for different purposes. Anyone who uses only one email address for everything is easy to identify and an easy target for an attack. Also, the use of pseudonyms makes it difficult for the other side to get a clear picture of a person.

Nothing is for Free!

In the digital age, the rule is: Either you pay or you are the product. This principle is one of the most valuable insights that carries great potential for protection. It applies to all activities online. As is well known, attention on the net is the new currency, which in turn can be worth a lot of money. Countless attacks by Trojan horses were only successful because enough people believed that they might have won something by chance, that there is something for free if they click on a link or that they were lucky in some other way. The real Trojan horse was a poisoned gift, a lesson that too many have unfortunately forgotten.

Many may find such a reference to ancient Greece unhelpful because the time then is not comparable to today. And yes, at first glance, one seemingly has little against the overwhelming power of large corporations, hackers, or malicious actors. Nevertheless, it depends on the individual and his ability to be mindful at the right moment. This mindfulness can be trained when we look back at history and think about the human and all too human. Because often it is base instincts that are addressed: the greed for money, the promise of closeness and security, or lust. Therefore, one should always remind oneself: If something costs nothing, you are the product.

"Back to the Roots"

In many respects, the lessons gathered in this chapter could be titled "Back to the Roots". Because it's about a return to basic, deeply human insights. The specific countermeasures that can be derived from this are of an individual nature and can hardly be generalized. Therefore, guides and fixed rules should always be viewed with some suspicion. They can contain useful things, but those who rely too much on them can fall into a trap.

So one could also say that it's a matter of lifestyle. We need a new awareness of what survival in the cyber world means. Many people would be surprised at how helpless and stranded they are without their smartphone. What would you do if you were suddenly left without any technical aids in a forest area? How do you survive in modern everyday life today without a mobile phone? Here, everyone has to find a new and individual form of survival. Since the digital world is characterized by visibility, data, and information, one could describe its opposite as "Ninja Style". Literally translated from Japanese, Ninja means 'hidden'. The Ninjas, a specially trained group of fighters in ancient Japan, mastered the art of hiding and concealing. They are adept at making themselves invisible and camouflaging themselves. The ability to hide undercover is probably one of the most effective methods of self-protection—then and now, in the digital age, even more so. It puts you in a position to observe the situation or the other person in relative safety or to wait. It thus represents the antithesis to real-time and the associated problem of immediate action. It gives you time to think and reflect.

The Psychology of the Masses, the Individual, and the Primitive Man

When we seek answers in the field of psychology, we find further tactics that promise success. On the one hand, when we take a closer look at the phenomenon of mass psychology. The French philosopher Gustave le Bon first observed and described this phenomenon in detail around 1900. In his study "The Psychology of the Masses" he writes:

> "The main characteristics of the individual in the mass are thus: the fading of conscious personality, the predominance of the unconscious being, the direction of thoughts and feelings by influence and transmission in the same direction, the tendency to immediately realize the instilled ideas. The individual is no longer himself, he has become an automaton, whose operation his will no longer controls. Merely by the fact of being a member of a mass, man thus descends several steps from the ladder of culture. As an individual, he may have been an educated individual, in the mass he is a creature of instinct, thus a barbarian."

The individual can thus understand himself in relation to the mass and more or less unconsciously surrender to it and merge with it. Likewise, he can consciously understand the functioning of the mass and behave accordingly as if he were part of the mass, while actually using the mass for camouflage. Thus, merging with the mass can be used as a method of becoming invisible.

The mass can also be used for camouflage and deception in other respects. A mass does not necessarily have to be a mass of people. Although le Bon primarily thought of large crowds because he encountered them as a modern phenomenon. But today, the phenomenon of being overwhelmed with information and data can also be understood as a mass phenomenon. Anyone who wants to hide can accordingly also use a large number of bots that appear as copies of their own self, but leave traces in always different directions.

Knowledge from the realm of psychology is generally a useful tool for understanding and seeing through the mechanisms of attack and defense in the cyber world. Attackers often appear as "sexy", while defenders come across as "boring". Such a distinction may be simplistic, but in history it is often observed in this simple form. Here is another quote from the *Psychology of the Masses:*

> "History teaches us that the moment the moral forces, the equipment of a society, have lost their dominion, the final dissolution is brought about by those unconscious and crude masses, which can be quite well characterized as barbarians."

A good supplement to Le Bon's explanations is a somewhat lesser-known text by Sigmund Freud, the inventor of psychoanalysis. In the text "Our Relationship to Death", which he published in 1915, shortly after the outbreak of the First World War, he writes in the face of the mass death that shocked him: "War brings the primitive man in us back to the fore." What does he mean by the primitive man? He explains this in his psychological study:

> "The primitive man has adopted a very strange attitude towards death. (â€¦) The death of another was right for him, was considered the annihilation of the hated, and the primitive man had no qualms about bringing it about. He was certainly a very passionate being, more cruel and malicious than other animals. He liked to murder and did so as a matter of course. The instinct that should prevent other

animals from killing and eating beings of the same species, we do not need to attribute to him. The prehistory of mankind is therefore filled with murder."

From Freud's perspective, the fifth commandment "Thou shalt not kill!" only makes sense against this background, because it shows that "we descend from an infinitely long line of murderers." Such sentences are hard for many people to bear, because we would like to have a better image of ourselves as humans and of humanity. The idyllic depictions of primitive men as hunters and gatherers, peacefully roaming the steppes, may be a nice idea, but could be further from reality than we would like.

Cyber warfare will test the psychological side of man and his relationship to death in a completely different way than in Freud's time. Because the modern battlefield is digital. The mass death, as it was then observable on the battlefield, will hardly exist in this form anymore. Rather, we are experiencing a virtualization of killing. Soldiers can sit thousands of kilometers away in a container and stare at screens on which they see live images transmitted by drones. Then they decide about life and death and maybe step outside an hour later and find themselves in a peaceful environment. What does this setting do to the primitive man in us?

9

Propaganda—How it Worked in the Past and What it is Today

The first casualty of any war is the truth

Hiram Johnson (attributed)

Exactly who this quote originates from remains unclear to this day and may also be a punchline that fits the content of the sentence all too well. But even Sun Tzu knew: "All warfare is based on deception." Therefore, there is no need for an exact origin of the truth contained in the sentence attributed to Hiram Johnson. What counts: Today, this insight is more relevant and explosive than ever. Through influence, disinformation, and propaganda, political and military goals can be achieved today that would have required the deployment of legions in "Ancient Rome".

© The Author(s), under exclusive license to Springer Fachmedien Wiesbaden GmbH, part of Springer Nature 2024
P. Kestner, *The Art of Cyber Warfare*,
https://doi.org/10.1007/978-3-658-43879-1_9

Propaganda as Part of Digital Warfare

The fact that we are dealing with such an increased threat situation here is also due to a simple fact. It is extremely cost-effective and so far possible without significant consequences to attack targets in cyberspace. In addition, attacks in this area can be well camouflaged, so they do not appear as such to an untrained eye. No tank rolls here and no soldier fires a single shot. But often it is enough to commission digital mercenaries to move bits and bytes to undermine the law of another state and to undermine the legitimacy of its history and culture. Within the framework of hybrid warfare, these goals can contribute to the overarching strategy just as much as a direct attack—perhaps even more effectively. The means and methods of propaganda are so ideally suited for this purpose because power is at their core. The power to interpret reality. Whoever succeeds in imposing a certain interpretation of reality has changed it without using violence. A narrative that questions the right of a state to exist must therefore be understood as a weapon in the information space. If a war is prepared accordingly, this can weaken the opponent to such an extent that military forces can be used much more easily.

More Than Propaganda

Here it is once again proven true: The battlefield of the future is also digital. Propaganda and disinformation campaigns can be a significant part of the preparation phase in the context of hybrid warfare. This can, but does not have to be followed by a military strike—usually it only becomes clear years later what purpose certain actions served. Numerous other escalation levels can be imagined that can put pressure on a country over years and decades. Starting with media influence, undermining and delegitimizing governments and societies, to disinformation and subversion—the variants of soft warfare are diverse and are much more than "just" propaganda. Nevertheless, they aim at the heart of countries and the people who live in them. They attack moral and value perceptions, try to exploit gaps in the legal system, and increasingly migration is also used as a weapon. The attack on critical infrastructure takes place in winter to force people to flee. Or information is deliberately spread that immigration into a country is possible via a certain route. The manipulation of information and its conversion into a weapon opens up a new attack vector in hybrid warfare.

The War of the Future is an Information War

Every war in the future is inevitably also to some extent an information war. Even in history, this aspect, albeit with rudimentary means, always played a role. In the future, however, it will no longer be a sideshow, but more and more a central place of combat. On the one hand, and above all, because information gathering has long since become a central concern of every state and intelligence service. On the other hand, because media reporting, at least since newspapers became a mass medium, plays a crucial role in terms of information dissemination and thus also morale and propaganda. In the age of social media, this is even more true, as many people no longer receive their information through editorial content or no longer trust the formerly established media. This opens the door to the manipulation of information, the spread of fake news, and propaganda.

We mentioned above in connection with hybrid warfare that it can be advantageous to operate in gray areas. The more trust in neutral information is undermined, the easier it is to unsettle the population of a hostile state, disrupt internal cohesion, and undermine their motivation. Such actions directly and indirectly contribute to possible war goals.

But it's not just about influencing or manipulating the masses. The individual is also the focus of propaganda attacks. Whether in democracies or autocracies—power always concentrates on individual people or a manageable circle of individuals. The same applies to companies or other organizations. And when it comes to power—this will not surprise the readers of this book at this point—the potential for conflict is not far away. The means and methods of propaganda are like no other in discrediting personalities from the government, public administration, or consular service, or undermining their trustworthiness with smear campaigns. In this context, it is often forgotten that influencing on an individual level does not always have to have something to do with negative reporting. Positive influence through praise, flattery, or seduction can also lead to the goal. It requires a comprehensive knowledge of human nature, interpersonal communication, and the abilities for psychological analysis of a character to play the entire keyboard of influence possibilities. To avoid any misunderstandings: This is the playground of the "absolute professionals" and it takes years to achieve mastery here.

From the Cold War to the Iron Curtain 2.0

In hardly any other war is the power of media and the manipulation of information more evident than in the Cold War. The impression that the world gained of the Russian army and its capabilities since the Iron Curtain 1.0 resulted in incredible fear. The Russian armed forces were considered unbeatable. The fact that this appearance did not always hold up to reality is also part of history. One does not even have to refer to the current war between Russia and Ukraine. From 1979–1989, Russia waged an unsuccessful war in Afghanistan. On 25.12.1979, 40,000 Soviet soldiers marched across the country's borders. The day of the invasion was deliberately chosen: the Western world famously celebrates Christmas on this date, and so it happened that hardly anyone took notice at the beginning. The invasion was justified by the need to support the communist government under the leadership of Babrak Karmal. He officially took over the country as head of government on 27.12.1979. With the support of Soviet soldiers, the plan was to proceed against religious tribal communities. Even though initial war objectives were quickly achieved, it was not possible to bring the country under control. The more Soviet troops were deployed to Afghanistan, the more resistance from religious groups grew. Soon the "holy war" was declared, and alongside regional warlords, the Mujahideen, who are most comparable to guerrilla groups, defended themselves in an increasingly confusing war situation against the occupiers. The Mujahideen were primarily financially supported by the USA. Therefore, the war in Afghanistan is also referred to as a proxy war. It was one of the conflicts in which two nuclear powers were directly or indirectly involved, which were "hotly" fought during the time of the Cold War. The exact course of events during the war is very difficult to reconstruct. One reason for this is the geography of the country. Reporters had a hard time gaining access. Difficult terrain and a raging guerrilla war made neutral reporting almost impossible. In addition, a propaganda war was raging, which continues to some extent to this day. Because who has the interpretive authority over who fought against whom, why the war started at all, which information from the time is correct and which was falsified or distorted, is still disputed by the experts and historians of the involved countries— only this much is certain: We do not yet know the complete truth about the war that the Soviet Union waged in Afghanistan at that time. It is therefore one of the most recent wars that still needs more time to be fully analyzed. A large part of the reporting that was disseminated in the West came about through contacts with the Mujahideen, who were supported by the CIA from the USA. It can be assumed that it was very carefully selected which information was released to the outside world. But also on the other side, war reporting was hardly distinguishable from propaganda. The military operation in Afghanistan, which was carried out to "stabilize" the government, was subject to secrecy. Due to the large number of conscripts who were sent there and lost their lives, the war could not be kept secret. Similar to the Vietnam War in the USA, the Afghanistan War was extremely unpopular among the Soviet population. The battle of narratives shows that the Iron Curtain at that time not only separated two parts of the world in political and economic terms. The competition for interpretive authority and the correct interpretation of reality extends the battle of systems for supremacy into the history books. After recent events, we are already talking about the "Iron Curtain 2.0" by no coincidence.

The time of the Cold War was a high phase of espionage and other intelligence activities. Infiltrating the opposing security apparatus and identifying subjects who could be made useful through blackmail, corruption, or bribery was one of the main goals of both sides.

All these activities also characterize our time and can be observed today in the cyber and information space. On the one hand, proxy wars between hostile nations can be observed. On the other hand, digital weapons such as hacking tools, satellite information, data obtained through hacks, or jammers are exchanged between friendly countries, for example, to test their effectiveness. This shows that such tactics can be used not only for attack but also for defense. Through confusion, disinformation, and the spreading of alternative facts, the impression of a state's superiority can be conveyed, which does not necessarily have to correspond to reality. Just think of the numerous fires that Sun Tzu advises to light at night to give the impression of a large army. Such (straw) fires are lit online today—preventively and for deterrence.

The high utility and effectiveness with which it is possible to manipulate large masses of people today make it unlikely that these means will not be used—especially since they are much "cheaper" today. Online information is already almost reaching the goal of "realtime" and costs very little. However, one does not necessarily have to look for current examples. In the past, Russia in particular successfully relied on a comprehensive propaganda apparatus. The manipulation of media and the spread of fake news has a long tradition there, stretching from the USSR to Putin's Russia. There is also increasing evidence in recent history that the country is still masterful at using misinformation in such a way that it damages the political and social structure of another country and changes public opinion in Moscow's favor. The patterns that can also be observed in current conflicts are therefore well known, and some of them are as old as the history of mankind itself. Often, only the medium through which such messages are disseminated changes. The invention of email was not even necessary to spread fake news en masse. In fact, examples can be found since the invention of the printing press, which enabled the mechanical and thus simple copying of written products. The so-called leaflet was the first mass communication medium in media history. However, it was not initially used for political purposes—at least not in the sense that we understand the term leaflet today and how, for example, the Scholl siblings and the White Rose used it. Since the churches and monasteries had a monopoly on written products at the time, it is not surprising that religious content dominated at the beginning. However, some of the early leaflets also contain information on military or political developments. It was only when the leaflets evolved into multi-page pamphlets, the precursor to the daily newspaper, that the potential of mass-produced publications was discovered. From the time of the Reformation and during the Thirty Years' War, the leaflet became more political and the leaflet is indispensable from the war propaganda of the twentieth century. Not only resistance groups like the aforementioned White Rose relied on this medium. The war leaflets, which were distributed in the form of leaflet bombs, were also a central part of psychological warfare. Both in the First World War and in the Second World War, the warring parties spread leaflet newspapers and other propaganda material in the enemy territories. The Wehrmacht used a specially converted rocket launcher for this purpose, which was modified so that about 100 leaflets could be shot more than 3.5 km into enemy territory in the projectiles. Today, it is the troll farms, such as those in Russia or China, that feed Telegram channels and state-affiliated influencers on social media with disinformation to destabilize societies thousands of kilometers away. Leaflets become Twitter messages, loudspeaker systems, like those South Korea has set up on the border with North Korea to blast the neighbor with propaganda broadcasts, become YouTube videos. There are numerous examples that show: The medium can change, but the functionality remains the same.

Propaganda as the Opposite of Diplomacy

Propaganda also includes its opposite: diplomacy. While propaganda uses language as a weapon, with information as its ammunition, diplomacy attempts to smooth the waves with language, establish connections, and reconcile differences and opponents. If diplomatic negotiations fail, the use of military means, sanctions, or other coercive measures is often the result. A lot depends on the success of diplomatic relations. For this to be effective in the age of cyber warfare, diplomacy must also keep up with the times. In other words, the use of data analysis, artificial intelligence, and all other means provided by the digital age must become the "state of the art" of diplomacy. The use of the most modern and secure communication technology is already standard—just think of the famous red telephone, which became a symbol for a direct connection. Any misunderstandings in communication via third parties should be eliminated via this connection. The encryption method used was the one-time pad method described above, one of the safest and most complex encryption methods ever.

A prerequisite for diplomatic talks is the availability of relevant information. Obtaining this and filtering it out from the vast amounts of data that are generated and transmitted every day is becoming increasingly difficult. Without the methods from the field of artificial intelligence, diplomacy can hardly operate on an equal footing. But this must be its claim, because its importance is growing in the face of cyber warfare. Diplomacy, whose goal is to maintain or establish peace, must immunize itself against foreign influence, manipulation, and disinformation. On the other hand, diplomats think in similar terms to the military. They have strategies and tactics with which they try to achieve their goals, and are of course also masters in verbal camouflage, deception, and manipulation.

The use of AI methods knows hardly any limits. As already mentioned, big data methods can help to sift through large amounts of data for relevant information. AI systems are also suitable for designing and checking various scenarios for negotiations. Another category of algorithms can be trained to develop predictive capabilities. One area of application for this is the voting behavior of different countries in the UN General Assembly. Especially when it comes to resolutions such as the Cybercrime Resolution or cyber sanctions, preparations can be made in advance according to the probable scenarios. Given that we live in a complex world where multilateral negotiations are conducted and relationships are built and maintained, scenario design can help manage this complexity. Even without any technical aids, diplomatic negotiations often take place in a mode of approximation and slow probing, but can quickly and unpredictably gain momentum. In addition to the firmly established communication channels and institutions, there is increasingly the occasion to communicate ad hoc at the international level. Efficient knowledge acquisition can provide a decisive tactical advantage at the negotiating table. Because usually there are a multitude of different actors with different goals and information sitting there. The faster and more efficiently reliable knowledge is available, the more solid and sustainable are the decisions that can be made in the end.

The diplomatic world is also one mediated by the media. Because what is reported in newspapers still has a direct and indirect influence on world events. The press of a country is always also a source of information about the activity of governments. Therefore, a free press is such an important value for the Western world on the one hand. At the same time, the media have such a great influence on diplomacy on the other hand. The latter must therefore keep a close eye on and analyze publication activity. Since a lot is at stake in the field of international relations, the fight is fierce. Sometimes the boundaries between diplomatic efforts and propaganda blur. Because influencing public opinion is certainly one of the tools that governments around the world use to gain an advantage. Social media have long been part of the arsenal of possible channels. At this point, it is almost superfluous to mention that it is a Herculean task to manually monitor all content and forms of publication activity. Monitoring is therefore another area in which AI methods can help to successfully conduct diplomatic relations.

For diplomacy, it is therefore essential to familiarize oneself with the latest methods and, if possible, to understand and master them better than the other side. Especially since the methods from this relatively young research area are not yet one hundred percent reliable, it should be a claim of the relevant bodies to gain experience with them early on in order to get used to dealing with them. It is also important to learn what is possible with these methods and what is not. Because above all, the use of AI offers an advantage in efficiency and accuracy. And this is also important: tradition and modern technology do not mutually exclude each other. The nature of diplomatic work itself is not changed by this—its level, its accuracy and quality are, in the best case, significantly improved and its security ensured. In hardly any other political area do tradition and history count as much as in the field of diplomacy. But since strategic skill in negotiations is also central, the added value that can result from the use of modern technologies should not be ignored. Because one thing is clear today: these new technologies will not disappear. In addition, the information space is already fiercely contested and will become the dominant theater of cyber warfare in the future. It is therefore important to master the entire spectrum of information warfare—from propaganda to diplomacy.

At the Border of Propaganda: Technology for Influencing Language and Human Behavior

The effect that is to be achieved with propaganda as well as with diplomatic negotiations is the change in human behavior. The fact that artificial intelligence is repeatedly mentioned in this context has nothing to do with the idea that we are dealing—now or in the future—with a machine that has a kind of consciousness or takes over the tasks of humans. Rather, we already have technical methods today that enable us to analyze data and especially language in such a way that we gain an information advantage. Specifically, this works by having a certain amount of data, such as texts or audio files, combed through by an algorithm for recurring patterns. This is also referred to as machine learning, as these classes of algorithms independently evolve and learn. In a certain sense, these are indeed learning machines. Since the computing power and storage capacity of computers have developed so rapidly in recent years, such systems are now capable of analyzing unimaginable amounts of data in a short time. Depending on the question, the focus can be on semantics, i.e., specific content, or on sentiment, i.e., the emotional state. Especially with spoken language, the tone, volume, or speed of what is said can be included in the analysis. For machines, which have neither consciousness nor real intelligence, to provide meaningful results about categories like these, they need to be trained. This initially requires time. The intelligent systems must first learn to understand what a word is, that there are words that are names for people and places, that certain words refer to larger thematic complexes and belong together, and that certain sentences and phrases appear in a close context and can, for example, refer to emotional states. Gradually, a database is created in this way, which in turn serves as the basis for further analyses. Once such a system is available, it can analyze large amounts of data for semantic patterns, which can then bring a tremendous time advantage. Because even an entire ministry would not be able to read the daily influx of all tweets—about 500 million per day or 6000 per second—let alone systematically evaluate them. Therefore, the knowledge that can be gained in this way means power. And this is the power to communicate precisely. Because whoever has identified a group of people through the analysis of social media data, who have shown themselves to be particularly emotional in their previous statements, finds it correspondingly easier to formulate messages in such a way that they are well received by them. Voting behavior can be influenced as well as purchasing decisions. How quickly we get into areas with such technologies that are not as harmless as advertising becomes clear when we look at so-called "predictive policing". Here, too, data is examined using ML algorithms to identify places in a city or a neighborhood where there is a higher probability of law violations. Police officers are then sent to these places—usually social hotspots—in advance to possibly prevent crimes through their presence. Predictive policing is no longer a vision of the future, but already a practiced reality in Germany. Such software solutions are mainly used in the field of prevention work. Security companies that are used at events and large-scale events also work with such programs. Films like *Minority Report* (2002, directed by Steven Spielberg) and the eponymous story by Philip K. Dick from 1956 also show the limits and risks associated with such technologies. *Minority Report* depicts a dystopian world where people live in a surveillance state and are persecuted for crimes they have not yet committed. With examples like this, we are increasingly leaving the information space and moving closer and closer to the world of 2084, which will be the subject of the final chapter.

Part IV

Outlook: The Future of Cyber Warfare

After having dealt with the development of cyber warfare up to this point, we will finally venture a brief outlook into the future. How will this development continue? What awaits us in ten or a hundred years? Is everything already lost or is there still some hope in the end that everything will turn out for the best?

10

The World in 2084

> *I cannot teach anyone anything.*
> *I can only make them think.*
> *Socrates*

> *In peace, prepare for war.*
> *In war, prepare for peace.*
> *The art of war is of vital importance to the state.*

> *It is a matter of life and death, a road either to safety or to ruin.*
> *Hence it is a subject of inquiry which can on no account be neglected.*

It is time to summarize the results of this book and provide an outlook on what they mean for the future of humans on this planet. When it comes to the topic of cyberwar, nothing is closer than looking into the future. Because we have certainly not yet experienced *the* cyberwar in its pure form and its full extent, although we can already clearly see its beginnings.

© The Author(s), under exclusive license to Springer Fachmedien Wiesbaden GmbH, part of Springer Nature 2024
P. Kestner, *The Art of Cyber Warfare*,
https://doi.org/10.1007/978-3-658-43879-1_10

On the Relevance of this Book

This book was written with the awareness that many elements presented here can already be observed in the present. At the same time, everything written here is based on the claim to capture something that extends far beyond our time and helps to understand the future of cyberwar. Of course, recent conflicts also show that many old strategies and tactics are still being used. Unfortunately, lessons from the past are often forgotten and old mistakes are repeated. The drivers that lead to conflicts are still the same and are certainly not changing quickly. At the same time, the attentive reader will not miss that numerous elements of Sun Tzu and Clausewitz have not lost their relevance. It may be questioned whether all those who are familiar with these authors and their works have drawn the appropriate lessons from their reading.

Of course, new developments can already be seen today: Hybrid warfare is becoming more and more standard and there is more technology in use than ever before. Moreover, the latter plays an increasingly decisive role on the battlefield, which extends beyond borders through cyber. The areas of information gathering and espionage are also taking place at a completely new (technical) level, although the basic principles remain the same. Disinformation and propaganda exist today on all digital channels, because the aim here is to win the war of narratives. The victor decides whether it was a special operation or a war of aggression in the end.

Nevertheless: We have not yet seen the real "cyberwar" or "digital war", although one can already see in which direction it will go. It is already apparent today that all levels of previous military considerations, namely air, land, sea, and space, will from now on be accompanied by a new dimension, cyberspace. Cyberspace thus becomes a fifth dimension that simultaneously spans all four and cannot be separated from the individual dimensions. For this reason alone, cyberspace and the considerations associated with it will become increasingly important in the future. Cyberspace and the digital dimension are already an integral part of current conflicts. The "war in space" is also slowly taking shape. Starting with military reconnaissance satellites to Elon Musk's satellite armada, which can also be used for tactical or military purposes. The Chinese government is already openly considering which technology needs to be developed to shoot down such satellites.

Some Thoughts on the Current War in Ukraine and Israel

More than once while writing this book, I had to think about the current war in Ukraine and Israel and many times I surely had current examples in mind, even though I referred to older ones. There is a good reason for this. In these current wars, many elements seem familiar to us. We believe we have identified some actions as mistakes and others as "classic methods". But here too, history teaches us to exercise a certain caution. Rarely is it the case that a clear view of reality is possible in the heat of battle. Many very educated and highly intelligent contemporaries have commented on wars they could observe. In the rarest of cases, however, they managed to get a clear and comprehensive impression of the big picture. And so it is today: At present, it is not possible to make really reliable statements about which actors are driving which actions with which motives. I even fear that it will take decades before this conflict can be processed, evaluated and classified by independent bodies. We are currently in the middle of the action, few will be able to take a neutral stance. Since we are all hit by the full force of waves of disinformation, propaganda and deliberate confusion, it is all the more difficult to distinguish right from wrong. To form a judgment now would be premature and most likely not correct. In the "hot phase", everyone is blinded or seduced by propaganda. Only after many years of clean processing, with a sober view and after the "first history writing of the victors" can the real picture of this conflict be drawn. As hard as it may be, but no matter what we think right now, we could be fundamentally wrong. Time not only heals all wounds, but it also gives a new perspective on things that we did not understand or saw differently before.

At this point, it is important for me to emphasize that we should not presume to believe we know a solution, or pretend to have the right view of things. With regard to the current conflict in Ukraine, Israel or Iran, some time must pass before everything that is happening there can be processed. In a few years, the war in Ukraine or Israel will fit into the series of past wars and can be evaluated. Hopefully, the coming generations can learn something from it. Because one thing is certain: The next war is sure to come. Quite freely after the quote: "Peace is just a pause between two wars."

The Winners Write History

As the saying goes, history is written by the victors. This insight is very old and can be observed again and again over the centuries and millennia. It is no coincidence that Gaius Julius Caesar wrote a book about the *Gallic War*, which he himself led. Writing history is never an objective act, where the only goal is to put what happened on paper.

It is always also about the interpretation of facts, the deliberate demonstration of connections, and the reconstruction of a very specific sequence of events. I think, the more time passes, the more "neutral" and accurate the analysis becomes. Because it starts with the selection of events that are included in the books and which are not.

But the past also teaches us something else: Even if there is an attempt to hide what has happened or to twist the facts too much, the truth eventually comes out. Therefore, it is worth making a precise distinction at this point. History is the image of the past that a society agrees on. The past is the sum of all past events that have led to a certain point. And truth is a concept that comes into play whenever reality is distorted by lies, twisting of facts, or other forms of deformation. Because especially in the twentieth century, it could be observed again and again that the truth—often with years or decades of delay—eventually comes to light. This is also due to the fact that a media revolution has taken place in modern times. Before that, books were the main sources of historiography. From the First World War onwards, new media come into play: film footage, radio messages, audio recordings of eyewitness statements, etc. But this not only changes the source situation and the type of documents. They are available in larger quantities, making it more difficult to falsify information. And the speed at which the events are processed also increases—to the point where real-time processing becomes a problem again.

Since history in this book often served as a key witness and as material from which lessons for the present are to be derived, this approach itself should be questioned and critically examined at the end. Because, as just explained, history itself can be deceptive. Not only because it is first written by the victors. But also because it is not the same for everyone. What I mean by this becomes clear when we ask ourselves, for example, what the history of Europe is. On the one hand, we can answer this question mythologically. According to Homer and the Greek historian Herodotus, Europe was the beautiful daughter of the king of the Phoenicians, Agenor. Zeus, the father of the gods, fell in love with Europe and abducted her in the form of a bull, which was so beautiful and gentle that Europe sat on its back. He kidnapped her to Crete and fathered several children with her, whose descendants then spread throughout the Mediterranean. Europe, quasi the mother of the European peoples, stands for their diversity and the connection of different nations. In contrast, if we look in the history books, we can read about how—also on the island of Crete—around 2000 BC, the first high culture in Europe was established with the Minoans. The influences of the Minoans can be found in numerous cultures that spread from Greece to the European mainland. With a little imagination, one could say that the myth and historiography tell the same story with different means or in a different form. How far the writing of such origin myths and narratives of the same past can diverge is also demonstrated by a look at the different textbooks used in European countries today. Even though Poland, Germany, Belgium, France, Austria, or Hungary are part of the same European Union—in the subject of history, a different version of the common European past is told in each country. Depending on the perspective, certain events do not occur at all, are presented completely differently in their causes, or individual people appear in a completely different light. Who tells the story can indeed be decisive when it comes to the individual view of events.

Nevertheless, I would like to advocate approaching the reading of historiographical texts with a certain serenity. If one accepts that there is no absolute truth here and cannot be, then the view becomes free for certain timeless truths and insights that cannot be eradicated even by a different perspective on what happened. I am speaking here primarily of the five drivers of power, greed, fame, wealth, and desire, which have repeatedly led to conflicts and wars in the course of human history and will certainly continue to do so in the future.

The World in 2084

In the introduction, we began by reading George Orwell's novel *1984* as an example of how it is possible to better understand the present and derive crucial knowledge from a story. Therefore, I would like to attempt here to design a vision of the world of 2084.

In a city that has grown so high and so far beyond its borders that it almost covers a continent, lives one of the great-great-grandchildren of Winston Smith. The city functions smoothly despite its unimaginable size, for the world of 2084 is fully digitized and automated. Ultra-fast maglev trains transport residents around the clock in the shortest possible time from one point in the city to another. Winston Smith 2.0 can only smile tiredly at the mobility problems of the early twentieth century. They seem as far removed to him as the dinosaur bones in the museum. In this future, the digital world has become second nature to humans. Via eye implant, virtual reality becomes part of the body. Web 6.0 and reality completely merge with each other. The major protagonists of early digitization such as Google, Apple, Microsoft, and Meta were destroyed shortly after their heyday by the trend of decentralizing software and services. The foundation for this technology was laid by the mythological figure Satoshi Nakamoto, whose existence is still speculated, researched, and debated in 2084 in special Nakamoto temples—a mix of museum, club, and hobby basement for technology enthusiasts. Nakamoto's invention of Bitcoin in 2009 provided the philosophy and ideal for a life in the digitized world. Decentralization, anonymity, and the protection of privacy are the highest goods. However, these are still fiercely contested. Again and again, there are power-hungry individuals or companies who are a thorn in the side of these basic values of a free cybersociety. They want to use the technology for surveillance and control purposes. The political struggle has shifted and is now fought at the software level. Changes to the code require majorities and consensuses that need to be won. For this, there are powerful lobbying associations on the one hand, and targeted cyber operations on the other, aimed at finding people's vulnerabilities. Personal data has become the most coveted commodity with incalculable value. Countless people have already fallen victim to identity theft or extortion. A digital identity loss is equivalent to a societal death, as one is ultimately robbed of all ability to act. One can no longer vote, identify oneself, or authenticate. Access to the most important facilities and the internet is thus denied. In addition, corruption has also taken on alarming dimensions.

Although there are no longer any national borders and humanity is expanding ever deeper into space, where new colonies are being established on foreign planets. Yet new conflicts over territorial claims and the distribution of resources are flaring up there. Of course, the "old patterns" play a role here again, which is why the memory of the past must be protected and preserved from the highest level, in order not to repeat the mistakes of the past. For even though the new borders have been shifted into space, one thing has not changed among the rulers who are waging new wars over territorial claims on other moons and planets: they are still driven by their old urges for power, fame, greed, lust, and wealth.

A Glimmer of Hope

Even though much of what I have compiled in this book sounds as if the cyber war could only lead to a dark world of confusion, deception, and manipulation, where everyone fights against everyone and people's actions are shaped by base instincts, my message is quite different. Because the future is in our hands. Whether we will evolve in one direction or another is not clear from today's perspective. It depends much more on whether we manage to learn from history, or whether we let ourselves be deceived again and again. But perhaps nothing brings my hopeful attitude to the point as much as an old Native American proverb that says: "Every person carries a good and an evil wolf within them. Which one comes to the fore depends on which one we feed."

References

Afheldt, Horst: *Verteidigung und Frieden. Politik mit militärischen Mitteln*, Hanser Verlag, 1976.

Albrecht, Ulrich/Lock, Peter/Wulf, Herbert: *Arbeitsplätze durch Rüstung?: Warnung vor falschen Hoffnungen*, Hamburg, Rowohlt Taschenbuch, 1978.

Arbeitskreis atomwaffenfreies Europa (Eds.): *Alternativen Europäischer Friedenspolitik*, Berlin, Selbstverlag, 1982.

Bengtson, Hermann (Eds.): *Fischer Weltgeschichte, Bd. 5, Griechen und Perser. Die Mittelmeerwelt im Altertum I*, Frankfurt a. M., Fischer Taschenbuchverlag, 2001.

Benz, Wolfgang: *Rechtsextremismus in Deutschland: Voraussetzungen, Zusammenhänge, Wirkungen*, Fischer Taschenbuch, 1994.

Bölsche, Jochen: *Der Weg in den Überwachungsstaat*, Hamburg, Rowohlt Verlag, 1979.

Bon, Gustave le: Psychologie der Massen (1895), Stuttgart, Alfred Kröner Verlag, 2021.

Boserup, Anders/Mack, Andrew: *Krieg ohne Waffen?*, Hamburg, Rowohlt Taschenbuchverlag, 1980.

© The Editor(s) (if applicable) and The Author(s), under exclusive license to Springer Fachmedien Wiesbaden GmbH, part of Springer Nature 2024
P. Kestner, *The Art of Cyber Warfare*,
https://doi.org/10.1007/978-3-658-43879-1

Broszart, Martin/Heiber, Helmut: *Die Republik von Weimar*, München, dtv Verlagsgesellschaft, 1966.

Büssem, Eberhard/Neher, Michael: *Arbeitsbuch Geschichte – Mittelalter Repertorium: 3. – 16. Jahrhundert*, Stuttgart, UTB, 2003.

Caesar, Gaius Julius: *Der Gallische Krieg*, München, Goldmann Verlag, 1981.

Der Deutsche Bundestag (Eds.): *Fragen an die deutsche Geschichte. Ideen, Kräfte, Entscheidungen – von 1800 bis zur Gegenwart*, Berlin, Kohlhammer Verlag, 1984.

Deutsch, Karl W.: *Politische Kybernetik – Modelle und Perspektiven*, Freiburg, Rombach Verlag, 1970.

Die Bundesregierung: *Weißbuch 2016. Zur Sicherheitspolitik und zur Zukunft der Bundeswehr*, Berlin, 2016, online veröffentlicht: https://www.bmvg.de/resource/blob/13708/015be272f8c0098f1537a491676bfc31/weiss-buch2016-barrierefrei-data.pdf

Drewitz, Ingeborg (Eds.): *Strauß ohne Kreide. Ein Kandidat mit historischer Bedeutung*, Reinbek bei Hamburg, Rowohlt, 1980.

Eichhorn, Peter: *Gewalt und Friedenssicherung. Grundtypen politischer Gewalt*, München, Claudius-Verlag, 1973.

Faber, Richard/Funke, Hajo: *Rechtsextremismus, Ideologie und Gewalt*, Berlin/Leipzig, Edition Hentrich, 1995.

Frank, Anne: *Tagebuch*, Frankfurt a. M., Fischer Taschenbuchverlag, 2001.

Gordon, Thomas: *Gideon's Spies: The Secret History of the Mossad*, St. Martin's Griffin, 2000.

Haffner, Sebastian: *Anmerkungen zu Hitler*, Frankfurt a. M., Fischer Taschenbuchverlag, 1981.

Haffner, Sebastian: *1918/19 – Eine deutsche Revolution*, Hamburg, Rowohlt Verlag, 1979.

Haftendorn, Helga: „Theorie der Internationalen Politik", In: Woyke, W. (Eds.) *Handwörterbuch Internationale Politik. Uni-Taschenbücher, vol 702,* Wiesbaden, VS Verlag für Sozialwissenschaften, 1986.

Heine, Peter: *Terror in Allahs Namen: Hintergründe der globalen islamistischen Gewalt*, Freiburg im Breisgau, Verlag Herder, 2015.

Hofer, Walther: *Der Nationalsozialismus. Dokumente 1933–1945*, Frankfurt a. M., Fischer Bücherei, 1960.

Jakobeit, Cord: *Kriegsdefinition und Kriegstypologie*, 2016 online veröffentlicht unter: https://www.wiso.uni-hamburg.de/fachbereich-sowi/professuren/jakobeit/forschung/akuf/kriegsdefinition.html

Jürgs, Michael: *BKA: Die Jäger des Bösen*, München, C. Bertelsmann Verlag, 2011.

Kihn, Martin: *Asshole: Wie ich lernte ein Schwein zu sein und dabei reich und glücklich wurde*, Ullstein Verlag, 2009.

Kogon, Eugen: *Der SS-Staat – das System der deutschen Konzentrationslager*, München, Heyne Verlag, 1988.

Krieger, Wolfgang: *Geheimdienste in der Weltgeschichte: Spionage und verdeckte Aktionen von der Antike bis zur Gegenwart*, München, C.H.Beck, 2003.

Langer, Ralph: *Stuxnet und die Folgen. Was die Schöpfer von Stuxnet erreichen wollten, was sie erreicht haben, und was das für uns alle bedeutet*, Langer Communications, 2017, online veröffentlicht unter: https://www.langner.com/wp-content/uploads/2017/08/Stuxnet-und-die-Folgen.pdf

Linn, Susanne/Sobolewski, Frank: *So arbeitet der deutsche Bundestag – 18. Wahlperiode*, Berlin, NDV, 2016.

Moestl, Bernhard: *Shaolin – Du musst nicht kämpfen, um zu siegen!: Mit der Kraft des Denkens zu Ruhe, Klarheit und innerer Stärke*, Knaur Taschenbuchverlag, 2010.

Ohne Autor: *Handbuch der Militärattachés in Deutschland*, Berlin, ProPress Verlag, 2006.

Peters, Buts: *RAF. Terrorismus in Deutschland*, München, DVA, 1991.

Pfeffer, Jeffrey: *Macht – Warum manche sie haben, und andere nicht*, Börsenmedien-Verlag, 2011.

Reißmann, Ole/Stöcker, Christian/Lischka, Konrad: *We are anonymous. Die Maske des Protests – Wer sie sind, was sie antreibt, was sie wollen*, München, Goldmann Verlag, 2012.

Simson, Werner von: *Die Verteidigung des Friedens: Beiträge zu einer Theorie der Staatengemeinschaft*, München, Beck Verlag, 1975.

Singh, Simon: *Geheime Botschaften. Die Kunst der Verschlüsselung von der Antike bis in die Zeiten des Internet*, dtv Verlagsgesellschaft, 2001.

Ström, Pär: *Die Überwachungsmafia: Das lukrative Geschäft mit unseren Daten*, München, Carl Hanser Verlag, 2005.

Taschner, Rudolf: *Die Mathematik des Daseins: Eine kurze Geschichte der Spieltheorie*, München, Carl Hanser Verlag, 2015.

Unterseher, Lutz: *Frieden mit anderen Waffen*, Berlin, Springer Verlag, 2011.

Vilmar, Fritz: *Rüstung und Abrüstung im Spätkapitalismus: eine sozio-ökonomische Analyse d. Militarismus*, Reinbek (bei Hamburg) : Rowohlt-Taschenbuch-Verlag, 1973.

Woyke, Wichard (Eds.): *Handwörterbuch Internationale Politik*, VS Verlag für Sozialwissenschaften, 2005.

Wulf, Christoph (Eds.): *Friedenserziehung in der Diskussion*, München, Piper Verlag, 1973.

Zolfagharieh, Mehran: *Carl von Clausewitz und Hybride Kriege im 21. Jahrhundert*, Marburg, Tectum Verlag, 2015. Studie „Stuxnet und die Folgen" von Ralph Langer

Printed in the United States
by Baker & Taylor Publisher Services

Printed in the United States
by Baker & Taylor Publisher Services